ACTS

ACTS

◆

H. A. IRONSIDE

Revised Edition

Introductory Notes by
Arno C. Gaebelein

LOIZEAUX
Baltimore, Maryland

First Edition, 1943
Revised Edition, 1998

ACTS
© 1998 by Loizeaux Brothers, Inc.

A Publication of Loizeaux Brothers, Inc.
*A Nonprofit Organization Devoted to the Lord's Work
and to the Spread of His Truth*

Unless otherwise indicated, Scripture quotations are taken from
the King James version of the Bible.

Introductory Notes are taken from
Gaebelein's Concise Commentary on the Whole Bible.
© 1970, 1985 by Loizeaux Brothers, Inc.

Library of Congress Cataloging-in-Publication Data

Ironside, H. A. (Henry Allan), 1876-1951.
Acts / H. A. Ironside: introductory notes by Arno C. Gaebelein.
p.   cm.
Rev. ed. of: Lectures on the book of Acts. 1943.
ISBN 0-87213-429-6 (pbk.)
1. Bible. N.T. Acts—Commentaries.
I. Ironside, H. A. (Henry Allan), 1876-1951.
Lectures on the book of Acts. II. Title.
BS2625.3.I76   1998
226.6'07—dc21   98–10838

Printed in the United States of America
10 9 8 7 6 5 4 3 2

CONTENTS

Introductory Notes   7

Author's Introduction   13

1. The Waiting Period   17

2. Pentecost   29

3. Healing the Lame Man   51

4. The Rejected Stone   59

5. The Exalted Prince and Savior   73

6. Checking Dissension in the Church   87

7. Stephen's Defense and Martyrdom   95

8. The Gospel's Entry into Samaria   103

9. The Conversion of Saul of Tarsus   115

10. The Conversion of Cornelius   137

11. Peter's Defense   145

12. Through the Iron Door   157

13. The Beginning of World Evangelism   163

14. Paul and Barnabas in Galatia   179

15. The First Church Council   185

16. How the Gospel Entered Europe   195

17. Paul at Thessalonica, Berea, and Athens   209

18. Paul Continues His Second Journey   217

19. Magnifying the Name of Jesus   233

20. Paul Begins His Farewells   247

21. Paul's Final Visit to Jerusalem   265

22. Paul's Personal Testimony   275

23. Paul before the Sanhedrin   285

24. Paul's Defense before Felix   297

25. Paul and Festus   313

26. Paul before Agrippa   317

27. God's Sovereignty and Man's Responsibility   327

28. Paul In Rome   337

   Author Biography   345

INTRODUCTORY NOTES

BY ARNO C. GAEBELEIN

The Writer of Acts

T The book of Acts, the great historical document of the New Testament, records the beginning of the church on earth. There is no doubt that the writer of the third Gospel is also the one whom the Holy Spirit selected to write this account of the establishment of the church and the events connected with it. This becomes clear if we compare the beginning of Luke with the beginning of Acts.

The writer of Luke said, "It seemed good to me also, having had perfect understanding of all things from the very first, to write unto thee in order, most excellent Theophilus, That thou mightest know the certainty of those things, wherein thou hast been instructed" (1:3-4), and the writer of Acts began, "The former treatise have I made, O Theophilus, of all that Jesus began both to do and teach." The "former treatise" is the Gospel of Luke and therefore the writer of Luke must be the penman of the book of Acts. Though we do not find Luke's name in either the Gospel or the second book, there is no doubt that he wrote them both.

Luke's name is mentioned a number of times in the Epistles, and these references give us the only reliable information we have about him. Colossians 4:14 refers to him as "the beloved physician." Philemon 24 mentions him as one of Paul's "fellowlabourers." The last Epistle Paul wrote indicates that Luke was in Rome with the apostle and was faithful to him when others had forsaken that

7

prisoner of the Lord (2 Timothy 4:11). From Colossians 4 we can gather that Luke was a Gentile, for after mentioning his fellow workers who were "of the circumcision" (4:11), Paul listed Epaphras, who was one of the Colossians and a Gentile, then Luke and Demas.

The reason that the Holy Spirit selected a Gentile to write first the Gospel that pictures our Lord as man and Savior, then the book of Acts, is as obvious as it is interesting. Israel had rejected God's gift, and the glad news of salvation was now to be spread to the Gentiles. The Gospel of Luke, addressed by a Gentile to a Gentile (Theophilus), is the Gospel for the Gentiles; and Luke the Gentile was also chosen to give the history of the Gospel going forth from Jerusalem to the Gentiles.

There are numerous internal evidences that the writer of the third Gospel was the instrument through whom the book of Acts was given. For instance, in both books there are about fifty peculiar phrases and words that are rarely found elsewhere.

Luke was an eyewitness of some of the events recorded by him in the book of Acts. Proof of this is the little word "we" in the narrative. He joined the apostle Paul during his second missionary journey (Acts 16:10), went with Paul to Macedonia, and remained some time in Philippi. He was the apostle's fellow traveler to Asia and Jerusalem (Acts 21:17), and was with him during his imprisonments in Caesarea and Rome. By the end of the two years mentioned in Acts 28:30 Luke no doubt had completed the book of Acts.

The Contents and Scope of the Book

Acts 1:1 gives us an important hint: We read that "the former treatise" (the Gospel of Luke) concerned "all that Jesus *began* both to do and teach" (italics added). The book of Acts therefore contains the *continuation* of the Lord's actions, now from the glory.

The activity of the risen and glorified Christ can easily be traced through the entire book. Here are a few illustrations: (1) In the first chapter He acted in the selection of an apostle to take the place of Judas. (2) In the second chapter He poured forth the Holy Spirit. Peter declared, "This Jesus hath God raised up, whereof we all are witnesses. Therefore being by the right hand of God exalted, and having received of the Father the promise of the Holy Ghost, he hath shed forth this, which ye now see and hear" (Acts 2:32-33). (3) At the end of the second chapter Christ "added to the church daily such as should be saved" (Acts 2:47). (4) In the third chapter He displayed His power in the healing of the lame man. Throughout the book of Acts we behold Him acting from the glory—guiding, directing, comforting, and encouraging His servants.

The book also contains the historical account of the coming of the Holy Spirit on the day of Pentecost. His coming marks the birthday of the church. After that event the Comforter is present with His people as well as in them. In Acts we see Him filling the Lord's servants, guiding them, fitting them, and sustaining them in trials and persecutions; and we behold Him as the great administrator in the affairs of the church. Over fifty times He is mentioned, but no doctrines of the Holy Spirit are given. What we find in Acts are practical illustrations of the doctrines that are found elsewhere in the New Testament.

The contents of Acts also include the activity of Satan—the enemy, the hinderer, and the accuser of the brethren. We behold him acting through his different instruments, as the roaring lion or the cunning deceiver with his wiles. Wherever he can, he attempts to interfere with the progress of the gospel. So in this book we see three supernatural beings in action: the risen and glorified Christ, the Holy Spirit, and Satan.

The human characters prominent in Acts are Peter and Paul. The apostle Peter is in the foreground in the first part, but after the twelfth chapter he is mentioned only once more. Then Paul comes on the scene with his great testimony about the gospel of Christ.

A hint concerning the scope of the book is found in Luke 24:47, where the risen Christ says "that repentance and remission of sins should be preached in his name among all nations, beginning at Jerusalem." In Acts 1:8 the Spirit of God reports this commission of the Lord in full; there we read that when Christ is about to ascend, He says, "Ye shall be witnesses unto me both in Jerusalem, and in all Judaea, and in Samaria, and unto the uttermost part of the earth." The book of Acts shows how this mission is carried out.

The witness begins in the city where our Lord was crucified. Then the gospel goes forth from Jerusalem and all Judea to Samaria, and after that to the Gentiles; through the apostle Paul it is heralded in the different countries of the Roman empire. Jerusalem is in the foreground in Acts, for the witness was to be "to the Jew first" (Romans 1:16), but the end of the book takes us to Rome, where Paul is a prisoner, a most significant and prophetic circumstance.

A careful study of the contents of this great book will take us back to the beginning and show us the path that the Lord has marked out for His church on earth. In the light of Acts we will see the dark picture of the present-day confusion and departure from God and His Word; but as the faithful remnant we will also find comfort and direction, along with much earnest exhortation to greater faithfulness and more holy boldness in preaching the gospel and standing up for the faith.

OUTLINE

OF THE BOOK OF ACTS

I. THE MINISTRY OF THE APOSTLE PETER (1:1—12:25)

A. The Gospel Is Confined to the Jews (1:1—7:60)

B. The Gospel Is Taken to the Gentiles (8:1—12:25)

    1. The Samaritans and the Ethiopian Hear the Word (8:1-40)

    2. Paul, the Apostle to the Gentiles, Is Converted (9:1-31)

    3. Peter Performs Miracles in Lydda and Joppa (9:32-43)

    4. Cornelius, a Roman centurion, Becomes a Believer (10:1—11:18)

    5. Christ Is Preached in Syrian Antioch (11:19-30)

    6. Herod Imprisons Peter (12:1-25)

II. THE MINISTRY OF THE APOSTLE PAUL (13:1—28:31)

A. His Three Great Missionary Journeys (13:1—21:40)

B. His Testimony from Jerusalem to Rome (22:1—28:31)

AUTHOR'S INTRODUCTION

The book of Acts is the story of early Christianity. This book gives us a great many principles that should guide us in Christian effort at the present time. One is reminded of the Lord's word to Moses when He commanded him to build the tabernacle: "Look that thou make them after their pattern which was showed thee in the mount" (Exodus 25:40). God has given us in the book of Acts a pattern of Christian testimony, missionary effort, world evangelism, and building of Christian churches—a pattern which we would do well to follow. Certainly we can be assured of this: the closer we come to following this holy pattern, the greater blessing will attend our efforts.

The title of this book as given in our English Bibles is of course not inspired. These titles have been added to the books by editors. Sometimes they seem to have been given with great exactness; in other cases we may question their appropriateness. Actually this book does not contain the acts of the apostles as a whole. The fact of the matter is, very few of the apostles are even mentioned in it. The book is largely limited to the ministry of two of them—Peter, who was one of the twelve, and Paul, who was an apostle of a different order altogether and not one of the twelve. He did not know our Lord on earth, but received his commission directly from Heaven. Actually the book might be called, as others have suggested, The Acts of the Holy Spirit; or, if you will, The Acts of the Risen Christ

13

through the Holy Spirit Working in the Church on Earth. In this book we have brought before us in a wonderful way the work of that promised Comforter who came to earth to witness to the glory of our Lord Jesus Christ and to convince men of sin, and of righteousness, and of judgment.

It is always well, in beginning the study of any book, to have an outline of it in mind. The Acts divides readily into two main parts. In chapters 1–12 we have the activity of the apostle Peter; in chapters 13–28 the activity of the apostle Paul. The first division is readily subdivided. In chapters 1–7 we have the transitional period in which God was still largely occupied with His earthly people Israel before the Word began to go out to the Gentiles. When I use the term *transitional period* I always like to explain what I mean. There was no transitional period in the mind of God. At the moment the work of Christ was accomplished, salvation was ready to be offered to all men everywhere. On the cross the heart of God was seen as going out to the whole world. In this portion we see our Lord, before His ascension, instructing His disciples to go to the uttermost part of the earth with the gospel. When the Holy Spirit came on Pentecost He empowered the twelve to speak many tongues that the miracle of Babel (which divided the original tongue into many different languages) might be undone and the gospel go out to all the world. But God is very gracious. He takes into account how slowly we apprehend things and so He bore patiently with His disciples and the early Christians for years while they confined their ministry exclusively to the lost sheep of the house of Israel and Samaria.

The second subdivision includes Acts 9–12, in which we have the ministry going out to the Gentiles. Chapter 9 records the conversion of Saul of Tarsus and his commission as the apostle to the Gentiles. In chapters 10 and 11 we have the apostle Peter going to the house of Cornelius and thus bringing the gospel to the first Gentile family. We also read of the mighty work of grace that began in Syrian Antioch. It was not at Jerusalem that the vision of world conquest was manifested, but in Antioch of Syria, a Gentile city north of Palestine, where certain traveling Jewish Christians ventured to preach the gospel to the Greek-speaking population of that idolatrous city. As a result, many of these heathen Gentiles were brought to a saving knowledge of the Lord Jesus Christ, and the first Gentile church was established. The church was further nurtured by the teaching of Saul and Barnabas.

Later, when a famine broke out in Judea, Saul and Barnabas went up to Jerusalem, to bring alms to the Christians there. This act of kindness showed the bond that now had been forged between the believing Jews and the believing Antiochians.

The twelfth chapter of the book of Acts concludes the first division of the story of the early days of Christianity. In the records of these first twelve chapters the work was centered in Jerusalem and Judea, and the ministry was largely to the Jewish people, the people of Israel.

Chapter 13 begins the second division of the book of Acts, which deals with the great work of world evangelization. In this chapter we find ourselves in an altogether different atmosphere. Antioch in Syria is the center, and the work spreads in large measure among the Gentiles, though the Jews are not neglected. The river of grace was overflowing the artificial boundary that even good men were seeking to throw about it. Some of the godliest men could not understand that the middle wall of partition between Jew and Gentile was broken down in the cross and they were still confining their message to God's ancient people (Ephesians 2:14). Finally the crisis came in regard to world missions, and we read in the earlier verses of Acts 13 how God placed on His servants' hearts the responsibility of sending out the gospel to the whole world. In chapters 13 through 21 we read of Paul's three missionary journeys.

In Chapters 22–28 we follow Paul step by step as he answers the charge of sedition, first on the temple stairs in Jerusalem, then before the chief captain himself, and later before Felix, Festus, and King Agrippa. As the book of Acts closes Paul is in prison in Rome still sharing the gospel message with the unsaved. Wherever Paul went he preached to unregenerate men the kingdom of God. He lifted up the Lord Jesus Christ as the One who died and rose again and has been exalted to God's right hand, there to be a Prince and Savior. This is the gospel, and we are to carry it to the world today.

CHAPTER ONE

THE WAITING PERIOD

Notice the way Luke introduced the book: "The former treatise have I made, O Theophilus, of all that Jesus began both to do and teach." This tells us at once that the book of the Acts is, if we may so say, volume two. This author has written an earlier volume and the story begun in that volume is continued in this one. What is that earlier volume? We have no difficulty in determining that, for we see that the Gopel of Luke was also addressed to this man Theophilus. In reading Luke 1:1-4 we observe that the Gospel of Luke is "the former treatise" to which the author of Acts refers. In the Gospel of Luke we have the things that Jesus began to do and teach, and in the Acts we read of the work He continued to do, after His ascension to Heaven, through the work of the Holy Spirit here on earth.

Salutation (Acts 1:1-2)

Who was this man Theophilus? We might wish we had fuller information regarding him. We merely have his name; it is mentioned twice, but in such a way as to give us some suggestions at least regarding his station in life. He is called in the introduction to Luke, "most excellent Theophilus." The words translated "most excellent" were used only in addressing a Roman official, generally one set over a country. So Theophilus was evidently an official of the Roman empire, probably a governor of a province, who had an interest in the story of our Lord Jesus Christ. Luke addressed his Gospel to him and gave him his full title, "most excellent

Theophilus." When he wrote his book of Acts he addressed the same person, but you will notice he omitted the "most excellent." That may be more significant than we think. I like to think it means that this Roman official, as a result of reading the Gospel of Luke, had come to such definite knowledge of the Lord Jesus Christ that he had openly proclaimed himself a Christian. And perhaps because of that he had either resigned or was dismissed from his office and so was no longer addressed as "most excellent" but simply as a brother in Christ. His name itself is significant. *Theophilus* means "a lover of God."

Notice the order of the verbs in verse 1. "Of all that Jesus began both to do and teach." *Doing* should always come before *teaching*. If there is anything that we as servants of Christ need to keep in mind it is this: there will be no more power in our messages than there is power in our lives. It is as we live for God that we are fitted to speak for God. We are called on to *do* before we *teach*. In the Old Testament we read of Ezra, "For Ezra had prepared his heart to seek the law of the Lord, and to do it, and to teach in Israel statutes and judgments" (Ezra 7:10).

Do you know why there is so much powerless preaching today? Because there is so little walking in obedience to the Word of God. If you and I would be witnesses for Christ we must be careful to see to it that we do before we teach; in other words, that we obey the Word of God ourselves before trying to instruct others. If the Word of God has no power over our own lives, we cannot expect to have power over other lives. If we are selfish, proud, haughty, egotistical, carnal, worldly, or unfaithful to the truth we know, we cannot expect others to be blessed by the message we proclaim. A holy minister is a tremendous weapon in the hand of God. An unholy minister is a disgrace to the Lord Jesus Christ.

Our blessed Savior has set us the perfect example. He came to do and then to teach. For thirty years His ministry consisted largely in doing. He lived before the Father for thirty years and during all those years there was not a flaw in His life. Then at the appointed time He went forth to teach. Now that He has ascended on high He is still doing and still teaching through the power of the Holy Spirit in men of God sent to carry His message to a lost world.

Luke spoke in verse 2 of the period between the Lord's resurrection and His ascension, during which He instructed His disciples. The expression, "He was taken up," occurs four times in this chapter (verses 2, 9, 11, 22). What does it imply? Our Lord Jesus came forth from the grave, the resurrected man with the same body that was crucified on Calvary. The body that was laid in Joseph's new tomb was raised from the dead in resurrection power, and in that body He appeared to His disciples. During the period of forty days He instructed them as to His program for the months and years to follow. Then when the forty days were ended, He was taken up in His physical body. He sits in Heaven today on the right hand of the Majesty on high in the very body that once hung on Calvary's cross.

That is the teaching of the Word of God. This is the Christ—not some spirit-being altogether different from us, but a real man in Glory at God's right hand. "There is one God, and one mediator between God and men, the man Christ Jesus; Who gave himself a ransom for all" (1 Timothy 2:5-6). And, oh, the blessedness of knowing that His tender, loving heart is concerned about us and the trials we are going through. "We have not an high priest which cannot be touched with the feeling of our infirmities; but was in all points tempted like as we are [apart from] sin" and "he is able to succour those that are tempted" (Hebrews 4:15; 2:18).

The Kingdom of God (Acts 1:3-11)

Our blessed, adorable Lord Jesus, was taken up; but before He was taken up He gave commandments to the apostles He had chosen. There was nothing haphazard about what their Master expected. "To whom also he showed himself alive after his passion by many infallible proofs." When Luke wrote this, many of the people who had known the Lord Jesus on earth were still living. They could back up his testimony and say, "Yes, we saw Him and handled Him; we know He was in the same body and was the same blessed Savior who died for us on Calvary."

"Being seen of them forty days, and speaking of the things pertaining to the kingdom of God." He was the rejected King. His own people said, "We will not have this man to reign over us." When

Pilate said, "Shall I crucify your King? The chief priests answered, We have no king but Caesar." But God acknowledged His kingly title and He has taken Him up to Glory and He is seated there on His father's throne, waiting till His enemies be made His footstool (Hebrews 10:13). God calls on a world of rebellious sinners to concede His authority and thus recognize even now the claims of the kingdom of God. That kingdom will not be set up in full display until Christ returns to earth, but at the present, during His absence, all who believe on Him have been brought out from the authority of Satan into the kingdom of the Son. Wherever the message of His love goes and men recognize Him as Lord and King, we have the expression of the kingdom of God in its present mystical sense. It is called in Matthew's Gospel the kingdom of Heaven. When the Lord comes back, He "shall send forth his angels, and they shall gather out of his kingdom all things that offend" (Matthew 13:41). Though rejected by the world, He is the absent King and the one we gladly own as our Savior and our Lord.

But now as they went forth to witness, it was not to be in their own power. "The promise of the Father" (Acts 1:4) was the promise that the Holy Spirit would come to earth to endow redeemed men and women with divine power, that they might go and proclaim the gospel. Our Lord Jesus Christ had told His disciples of the coming of the Comforter. He told them not to hurry, not to run before they were sent, but to abide in Jerusalem until that blessed One, the third person of the Godhead, would come to earth. He was to fill them, baptize them, and then thrust them out to carry the gospel to all men everywhere.

There is no other way of explaining the marvelous results of the apostles' preaching than this—they were empowered by the Holy Spirit of God. Just as there was a definite time when God the Son came to dwell on earth for a limited period, so there was a time when God the Holy Spirit came to earth to indwell believers in the Lord Jesus Christ and to strengthen and preserve them. Christ was born in Bethlehem exactly in accordance with Old Testament prophecy; the Holy Spirit came to earth on the day of Pentecost exactly as foretold in type in Leviticus 23 and in accordance with the promise of the Lord Jesus.

He said, "For John truly baptized with water; but ye shall be baptized with the Holy Ghost not many days hence." Those to whom our Lord spoke had already been baptized with John's baptism, but they needed this baptism of the Holy Spirit to fit them for their service and, as we shall see later, to unite them into one body.

Christ had previously spoken to them of the things pertaining to the kingdom of God. As Jews they of course knew from the Old Testament prophets that the day would come when their people would be restored to their land and, as a regenerated nation, be the means of blessing to the whole earth. "Israel shall blossom and bud, and fill the face of the world with fruit" (Isaiah 27:6). They were looking for the coming of the kingdom and the restoration of Israel, and so they asked, "Lord, wilt thou at this time restore again the kingdom to Israel?" This was a most sensible question to them, though we may not think so. We do not have the background they had. Did the Lord say, "No, you have lost your chance; these Old Testament prophecies are canceled and never will be fulfilled." No, indeed. He simply said, "It is not for you to know the times or the seasons, which the Father hath put in his own power." I wish we could always remember that. The kingdom of God has not yet come, but some day it will be set up on this earth, and men are still trying to figure out the exact time when that will take place. Men persist in endeavoring to ferret out that which is the Father's own secret, and so they attempt by various ways to find out when the King will come. But to all such our Lord says: "It is not for you to know the times or the seasons, which the Father hath put in his own power." Some day He will make everything plain. When God's time comes prophecy will be fulfilled to the letter. Jesus Himself said, "Of that day and hour knoweth no man, no, not the angels of heaven, but my Father only" (Matthew 24:36).

But while it was not for them to know the time when the kingdom will be set up, there was something they might know: "Ye shall receive power, after that the Holy Ghost is come upon you: and ye shall be witnesses unto me both in Jerusalem, and in all Judea, and in Samaria, and unto the uttermost part of the earth." That was the divine program for the evangelization of the world. There was no cutting it up into separate little dispensations, as some imagine, but the Lord laid out the whole program from the beginning.

Notice the order in which they were to evangelize. They were to start at Jerusalem, in God's eyes the guiltiest city on earth. In Jerusalem the people had cried, "Away with him, away with him, crucify him" in spite of Christ's testimony and His mighty works, even the raising of Lazarus from the dead. The Lord Jesus commanded them to begin at Jerusalem and tell them of God's grace, even for the guiltiest and the worst. Then when they had told the gospel story there, they were to go to the surrounding country of Judea, and then move on to Samaria (to that mixed people who were hated by the Jews and hated the Jews in return). They were to tell them that the Lord Jesus was the Savior for them, that He had died and risen and was waiting to forgive all who would put their trust in Him. Then nothing was to hold the messengers back, but they were to go on to the uttermost part of the earth. That was the commission. They were slow in carrying out this commandment of the Lord, but as the years have gone on Christian hearts have taken courage, and the work of world evangelization has progressed in the order given.

> When he had spoken these things, while they beheld, he was taken up; and a cloud received him out of their sight. And while they looked stedfastly toward heaven as he went up, behold, two men stood by them in white apparel [two glorious beings from Heaven itself]; which also said, Ye men of Galilee, why stand ye gazing up into heaven? this same Jesus, which is taken up from you into heaven, shall so come in like manner as ye have seen him go into heaven (Acts 1:9-11).

"This same Jesus." Oh, I love those three words. Don't you? No change in Him. And nineteen hundred years in Glory haven't changed Him in the least.

Preparation for the Coming of the Holy Spirit (Acts 1:12-14)

And so the heavens were closed and there was committed to the church the commandment to carry the message into all the world.

First Jesus had said, "Tarry ye in the city of Jerusalem, until ye be endued with power from on high" (Luke 24:49). The new dispensation was to be ushered in by the coming of the Holy Ghost, ten days later.

Notice how the disciples occupied those intervening ten days. First, in verses 12-14 we find them given to prayer and supplication. We read that they returned to Jerusalem "a sabbath day's journey." That is, a short distance over the brook Kedron.

"And when they were come in, they went up into an upper room." Possibly this was the same upper room in which they had observed the Passover, though we cannot be absolutely certain. There the eleven disciples continued in prayer and supplication. Nor were they alone—"With the women [the godly women], and Mary the mother of Jesus, and with his brethren."

Notice that Mary the mother of Jesus, was among them, but you will observe they were not praying to Mary, nor were they burning candles to her. They were not addressing themselves to her, nor asking her for any blessing; but Mary, the mother of Jesus, was kneeling with the eleven and the women, and all together they prayed to the Father. The church of God wandered far from that in the centuries that followed when it exalted Mary almost to the place of a female divinity. Over the portals of a church in South America there is an inscription in Spanish, which translated into English reads, "Come unto Mary, all ye burdened and distressed with your sins, and she will give you relief." Our blessed Lord used those words of Himself when He said, "Come unto me, all ye that labour and are heavy laden, and I will give you rest." They have put the mother in the place of her incarnate Son.

It is an interesting fact that this is the last time in the Bible we read of Mary the mother of Jesus. From this time on she passes out of sight; she takes her place with the rest of God's people who were waiting for Pentecost and for the evangelization of the world to begin. She passes quietly off the scene in her womanly place, probably to find a home with the apostle John in accordance with the words of the Lord Jesus, for you will remember the Lord committed her to him (John 19:26-27).

Then, notice the brethren of Jesus were in this prayer meeting.

You will remember when He was here on earth we read, "neither did his brethren believe in him" (John 7:5). The members of His own household, brought up side by side with Him, did not believe that their brother Jesus could be the Anointed of Jehovah and the One of whom the psalmist had sung and the prophets had prophesied. But now that Christ was risen from the dead, His brethren believed in Him, and a little later on we see His brother James as one of the most prominent disciples in the city of Jerusalem.

"These all continued with one accord in prayer and supplication." What a beautiful picture! This was the preparation for the coming of the Holy Spirit. But do not misunderstand. The coming of the Spirit did not depend on their prayer. It had been predicted that He must come on the day of Pentecost. But that being settled in the mind of God, He moved on the hearts of His people that they might be in a prayerful attitude. They were to be endued with power. You see, when God is going to do some great thing He moves the hearts of people to pray. He stirs them up to pray in view of that which He is about to do so that they might be prepared for it. The disciples needed the self-examination that comes through prayer and supplication, that they might be ready for the tremendous event which was about to take place—the coming to the earth of God the Holy Spirit to dwell in believers and empower them to witness for Him.

Mathias Chosen (Acts 1:15-26)

In these verses we have the last official act of the old dispensation. The apostles were mourning the loss of one of their number. There were now only eleven and God had chosen twelve. Twelve in Scripture is the number of perfect administration, and Jesus had said, "Ye which have followed me, in the regeneration when the Son of man shall sit in the throne of his glory, ye also shall sit upon twelve thrones, judging the twelve tribes of Israel" (Matthew 19:28). But one apostle was missing. Would there be an empty throne then? Would there be one less? No; God had provided for that.

I know some people think the apostles made a mistake in electing a successor to Judas, and that God meant the apostle Paul to be the twelfth. But Paul is never linked with the twelve; in fact there are twelve apart from him. The twelve are to have a special place in the coming kingdom in connection with administering the affairs of Israel. Seated on twelve thrones they will judge the twelve tribes. Paul had a unique ministry and will have a special place in the coming kingdom.

How then were they to fill the vacancy? Peter evidently acted as the Lord instructed before His ascension. He had told them many things pertaining to the kingdom of God. He explained to them what He wanted them to do, so they were not left to guess at the mind of the Lord. Peter acted in full accord with the instruction received when he stood before the disciples, about 120 of them, and said, "Men and brethren, this scripture must needs have been fulfilled, which the Holy Ghost by the mouth of David spake before concerning Judas, which was guide to them that took Jesus. For he was numbered with us, and had obtained part of this ministry" (Acts 1:16-17).

What a pitiful thing that was! For three and a half years Judas had belonged to that apostolic company. He walked with Jesus, heard the teaching of Jesus, saw the same marvelous miracles, yet all the time this man was out of harmony with the rest. Jesus, who knew the hearts of men, said as He looked at them, "Have not I chosen you twelve, and one of you is a devil?" (John 6:70) He did not say, "One of you is in danger of becoming a devil." He knew one of them did not believe, had all the time treasured traitorous thoughts, was corrupt and utterly untrustworthy. Yet this same one had walked with the rest of them, was numbered with them and obtained part of their ministry. How that ought to speak to us!

It is not enough to take the Christian name, become members of the Christian churches, submit to the ordinance of baptism, participate with believers in the Lord's supper or give of our money to further the affairs of Christ. We need to be sure we have definitely opened our hearts to the Lord Jesus, that we have received Him as our own personal Savior. Judas failed here. I believe Judas thought of Christ as the promised Messiah; I believe Judas thought Jesus would declare Himself King and reveal Himself in the overthrowing of the Roman government. It is one thing to think of Him as

Messiah; another to trust Him as one's own Savior and receive Him as one's own Lord. Judas failed there.

Let us be warned therefore and make sure ours is not just an intellectual recognition that Jesus is God's Son, the rightful King and Savior of sinners, but that He is *our* Savior and *our* Lord. "If thou shalt confess with thy mouth the Lord Jesus, and shalt believe in thine heart [truly believe] that God hath raised him from the dead, thou shalt be saved" (Romans 10:9). But He says, "Many will say to me in that day, Lord, Lord, have we not prophesied in thy name? and in thy name have cast out devils? and in thy name done many wonderful works?" And Jesus will say to them, "I never knew you: depart from me, ye that work iniquity" (Matthew 7:22-23). Of His own He says, "My sheep hear my voice, and I know them, and they follow me: And I give unto them eternal life; and they shall never perish" (John 10:27-28). Notice that He will say of His own sheep, "I know them." He will say of those who are lost, "I never knew you." He will never say to any in that day, "I used to know you," for they will be manifested then as never having been born of God.

In Acts 1:18 we have the sad end of Judas, so far as this life is concerned. In the Gospels we are told Judas was overtaken with remorse. Matthew wrote, "Then Judas, which had betrayed him, when he saw that he was condemned, repented himself" (Matthew 27:3). Ordinarily, the word for repentance implies a true change of mind, but the word used here simply means Judas was filled with remorse. When he realized what he had done, he was stricken with horror and brought the money to the chief priests and elders and threw it down, crying, "I have betrayed the innocent blood." And they, being cold, calculating, and religiously hardened, answered with indifference: "What is that to us? see thou to that" (Matthew 27:4). Judas fled from them and we are told he hanged himself. They were so religious and punctilious they said in effect, "We can't put this money into the treasury, because it is the price of blood." Therefore they used it to purchase a plot of ground in which to bury strangers, those who did not have relatives to claim them.

Some think we have a contradiction here. The Gospel says Judas went out and hanged himself (Matthew 27:5). The book of Acts says, "Now this man purchased a field with the reward of iniquity;

and falling headlong, he burst asunder in the midst, and all his bowels gushed out." There is no contradiction. Peter simply supplied further information. I think even as I read the words I can see the horrid picture. Judas, distracted by the awful sense of his guilt, driven by remorse for what he had done, rushes out. He sees a tree perhaps on the edge of a cliff, nooses himself to it and leaps into space. His body is torn asunder and the horribly sickening spectacle lies there for all to see—the end, so far as earth is concerned, of the man who sold the Savior for thirty pieces of silver!

I know people who are selling Him for less than that! I know people who are selling their hope of Heaven for a little worldly pleasure. I know some who are selling the Lord for the satisfaction of fleshly lusts and carnal indulgences! Judas sold Christ for money. What are you selling Him for, unsaved friend? At whatever price, it is a bad bargain. You are bound to lose out in the end. Judas lost out in this life. What about the life to come? you ask. Can we follow him out into eternity? Yes, with the aid of the words of the Lord Jesus Christ we can follow Judas beyond the tree where he hung, where his body burst asunder. Jesus said, "It had been good for that man if he had not been born" (Matthew 26:24). What does that mean? It means unending judgment to the utmost limits of eternity awaited Judas. If a time ever came when Judas repented, terrible though his crime, then it would have been a mercy that he had been born. But for him there was only an absolutely hopeless eternity, as there is for all who reject the Lord Jesus Christ. "He that believeth on the Son hath everlasting life: and he that believeth not the Son shall not see life; but the wrath of God abideth on him" (John 3:36).

Peter, divinely guided, remembered two passages of Scripture and quoted from the Septuagint version. The first was from Psalm 69:25, referring to the betrayal of Christ, "Let his habitation be desolate, and let no man dwell there." Peter said that is fulfilled. And in Psalm 109:8 is another passage, "Let another take his office," or, as translated in the King James version, "his bishoprick."

So Judas, lost, forfeited everything. Now somebody else must take his place. The number of the twelve must be complete, so they set forth two—Joseph and Matthias—and prayed and said, "Thou, Lord, which knowest the hearts of all men, show whether of these two thou hast chosen, That he may take part of this ministry and apostleship, from which Judas by transgression fell, that he might go to his own place." The place of the utterly lost and ruined! So they cast their lots and the lot fell on Matthias; he was numbered with the eleven apostles, thus making the twelve.

Does somebody object to the manner of his election! It was the Old Testament method. In the book of Proverbs we read, "The lot is cast into the lap, but the whole disposing thereof is of the Lord" (Proverbs 16:33). This was the last of the Old Testament economy: the new economy began on Pentecost.

And so we read in Acts 2:14, "Peter, standing up with the eleven." That includes Matthias, to make twelve. And in chapter 6:2 we read "the twelve called the multitude"—so God Himself applied the term *twelve* to the eleven and Matthias. These are the twelve who are to sit by and by on the twelve thrones, judging the twelve tribes of Israel.

CHAPTER TWO
PENTECOST

We are to consider now the next great event following the marvelous things recorded for us in the Gospels. First, there was the incarnation of our Lord Jesus—the coming to this earth of God the Son to unite man with deity. Then Calvary, when Christ gave Himself a ransom for all to put away our sins. Next, the physical resurrection of the Savior. In Acts 2 we have Pentecost, the coming of another person of the Godhead, the Holy Spirit, to dwell in the church on earth and to empower believers to carry the message of grace everywhere.

The Meaning of Pentecost (Acts 2:1-21)

Notice the opening words, "And when the day of Pentecost was fully come, they were all with one accord in one place." At that time the believers in Jerusalem numbered about 120 and they could all be together, and—more important—they were all of one accord. But do not make a mistake. Pentecost did not come because they were all in agreement and in one place; they were there expecting Pentecost, in obedience to the words of the Lord Jesus Christ. Pentecost was a predetermined epoch in the mind of God and the Word of God. It had been settled from all past ages just when the Holy Spirit was to descend and take up His abode with the people of God on earth. The Lord Jesus had said that the Father would send the Comforter and "He shall take of mine, and shall show it unto you" (John 16:15). He also said, "Tarry ye in the city of Jerusalem, until ye be endued with power from on high" (Luke 24:49).

The Holy Spirit was to introduce a new dispensation and God had definitely settled the time when that dispensation would begin—the day of Pentecost. In Leviticus 23 we read of Israel's ecclesiastical or sacred year with the great festivals that belonged to it. Among them was the Passover in the spring (on the fourteenth day of the month Nisan), foretelling the death of our Lord Jesus Christ. When Passover came He died; that was, the appointed Passover. He observed Passover on the evening before His death. The Jewish day began with the evening of one day, as we would count, and went on to the evening of the following day; so on the first evening Jesus ate Passover with His disciples, and before the next evening He died, the spotless Lamb on Calvary. "Christ our Passover is sacrificed for us: Therefore let us keep the feast, not with old leaven, neither with the leaven of malice and wickedness; but with the unleavened bread of sincerity and truth" (1 Corinthians 5:7-8).

If you continue in Leviticus 23 you will see that on the morrow after the sabbath they were to bring a sheaf of the firstfruits. We are told Christ has been raised from the dead and "become the firstfruits of them that slept" (1 Corinthians 15:20). So just as Passover typified the death of Christ, the firstfruits typified His glorious resurrection, the firstborn from the dead.

Returning to Leviticus 23, we read in verses 15 and 16:

> Ye shall count unto you from the morrow after the sabbath, from the day that ye brought the sheaf of the wave offering [that is, the firstfruits]; seven sabbaths shall be complete: Even unto the morrow after the seventh sabbath shall ye number fifty days; and ye shall offer a new meat offering unto the Lord.

Fifty days had to elapse from the offering of the firstfruits until the feast of Pentecost. *Pentecost* really means the "fiftieth day," so God had ordained that this feast should be observed in Israel as the type of the beginning of a new dispensation when a new meal offering would be offered to the Lord: "Ye shall bring out of your habitations two wave loaves...baken with leaven." These could not typify our Lord because they had leaven in them: leaven is a type of sin and He was the sinless one. But the loaves do typify those who through the death of the Lord Jesus Christ are presented to God a new creation, Jew and Gentile, sinners in themselves but their sins judged in the light of the cross of Christ. Therefore Pentecost was the beginning of a new age, that of the church, the body of Christ.

When the day of Pentecost came, the apostles, in response to the command of the Lord Jesus, were together in one place. Just where was that one place? It is not as easy to decide as one might think. A good many take it for granted it was in the upper room where the 120 gathered for prayer, but when we turn back to Luke we read, "And they worshipped him, and returned to Jerusalem with great joy: And were continually in the temple, praising and blessing God" (Luke 24:52-53). They abode in an upper room, but day after day they went to the temple. In the temple courts there was a great deal of liberty and there they gathered together to praise and bless the Lord. Different groups met among themselves; there a group of Sadducees with their teacher, and here a group of Pharisees with their instructor. The disciples came there to praise God and it may very well have been there that the Holy Spirit descended. That may also account for others being present and hearing all that was going on. On the other hand, the upper room may have been in a public place and the sound as of a rushing mighty wind may have commanded the attention of the people and caused them to flock to that upper room. Personally, I feel the likelihood that it was in the courts of the temple that they were gathered when the Holy Spirit came.

We are told there was the sound "as of a rushing mighty wind." The Lord Jesus had used wind as a symbol of the Holy Spirit in speaking of the new birth: "The wind bloweth where it listeth, and thou hearest the sound thereof, but canst not tell whence it cometh, and whither it goeth: so is every one that is born of the Spirit" (John 3:8). The Holy Spirit could not be seen, but His presence could be felt and heard. "And it filled all the house where they were sitting."

"And there appeared unto them cloven tongues like as of fire, and it sat upon each of them." The people looked on in amazement. What looked like fire however was not fire; it was the visible manifestation of the descent of the Holy Spirit. Just as when the Lord Jesus Christ came up from His baptism in the Jordan the Holy Spirit was seen descending like a dove and lighting on Him, so now tongues

like as of fire were seen resting on the heads of the disciples. Doubtless these tongues had special meaning. The hour had come when
God was to lift from men the curse of Babel. At Babel God so confused and divided the spoken language that they found themselves
speaking in many languages. Now the Holy Ghost had come with
power to enable His messengers to witness in many tongues to the
finished work of the Lord Jesus Christ.

"And they were all filled with the Holy Spirit, and began to speak
with other tongues, as the Spirit gave them utterance." Immediately
they were all filled. The Holy Spirit came on Pentecost for two purposes. He came to usher in the new dispensation, to baptize into one
body all believers. Were they not the children of God? Yes, but
they were just so many separate units. However when the Spirit of
God came they were all baptized into one Spirit, one body. More
than that, they were empowered for testimony. The Spirit had come
to take of the things of Christ and reveal to believers the things of
God and to anoint them as they went out to proclaim the gospel to
others. This was for all nations. There is not a hint here that this is
to be confined just to Israel. God gave these Jewish disciples power
to present the Word in the languages of all the people who had
come to Jerusalem to keep the feast of the Lord.

The question has been raised whether the miracle was in the disciples speaking different languages, or in the ears of the hearers.
That is, did the apostles speak in their native Galilean tongue but
the people heard them in their own languages? Verse 4 answers this
plainly: "They...began to speak with other tongues, as the Spirit
gave them utterance." These Galileans who may never have learned
any other language than their own now suddenly found themselves
so possessed by the Holy Spirit that their tongues were loosed and
they began to speak and preach intelligently in the languages of the
people gathered there to listen. These people, amazed, murmured
to one another, saying, "Behold, are not all these which speak
Galilaeans? And how hear we every man in our own tongue, wherein
we were born?" Then there follows a long list of the different people
represented there; most of them were Jews, many were proselytes,
and others not listed among either group. The last to be mentioned
are Cretes and Arabians. These were probably Gentiles and yet as

they listened they said, "We do hear them speak in our tongues the wonderful works of God." No wonder they marveled.

But still others there listening to the apostles couldn't understand; they heard what seemed gibberish to them. They said, "These men are full of new wine." It seemed as if they were drunk, uttering nonsensical sounds that meant nothing. This situation was illustrated very clearly to me some years ago in San Francisco when a group of us were in the habit of going down to the worst part of the city every Saturday night where hundreds of sailors from the ships in the harbor would pass. We held a street meeting from eight o'clock until midnight, speaking to all classes of men. One speaker, now a missionary in Argentine Republic, was a Spaniard by birth, yet spoke fluently French, Italian, Portuguese and other languages. When he would see a group of French seamen passing (the name of their ship on their caps), he would suddenly call out to them in their own language and speak to them for perhaps twenty minutes. Then, as he sighted a group of Portuguese sailors (easily distinguished by their uniforms) he would swing over and talk to them in Portuguese and they would gather in close. Later he might speak to a group of Spaniards or Mexicans and then perhaps to some Italians. There was rarely a Saturday night when he did not speak in all of these different languages. More than once I have seen persons come up and say, "What is the use of listening? He is drunk. You can't understand a word he says!" They did not know the language, and that is the way it was on Pentecost. Peter and his companions were not acting strangely, but as they spoke in different languages those who couldn't comprehend came at once to the conclusion that they were drunk.

"But Peter, standing up with the eleven, lifted up his voice, and said unto them, Ye men of Judaea, and all ye that dwell at Jerusalem, be this known unto you, and hearken to my words; For these are not drunken, as ye suppose, seeing it is but the third hour of the day" (that is, just nine o'clock in the morning, and ordinarily folks did not get drunk so early). "But this [power, this manifestation, this Spirit that is working] is that which was spoken by the prophet Joel," and he then quoted most accurately from the Old Testament prophecy that refers to the beginning of the millennium. It has reference to the time when God will pour out His judgment on the nations and when the Lord Jesus will come the second time to establish His kingdom here on earth and the Holy Spirit will be poured out on all flesh. But Peter quoted that part referring to setting up the kingdom in power and glory, and he said to those finding fault and objecting, "*This* is *that* which was spoken of by the prophet Joel."

There is a great deal in the prophecy which yet remains to be fulfilled, but Peter was saying that that same Spirit which was working on Pentecost that day is the Spirit which by and by will be poured out on all flesh. Joel said, "It shall come to pass in the last days...I will pour out of my Spirit upon all flesh," Notice the universality of this. This is something for the whole world in that glorious millennial day, and this coming of the Holy Ghost, this Pentecostal blessing, is also for the whole world today. I wonder sometimes at those who tell us that God endued only Israel with such power. He was contemplating the untold millions of Gentiles—those already born and those to be born down through the centuries—when the Spirit of God came with the message for all of them. "I will pour out of my Spirit upon all flesh: and your sons and your daughters shall prophesy, and your young men shall see visions, and your old men shall dream dreams." The coming of the Spirit of God takes hold of a man or woman and gives them an illumination they would not ordinarily have. He opens up to them the Old Testament, reveals the things to come, and gives them an understanding of the work of our Lord Jesus Christ and its effects on human sin and needs.

"And on my servants and on my handmaidens I will pour out in those days of my Spirit; and they shall prophesy." To prophesy is to proclaim the truth of God, but notice the prophecy from Joel has not all been fulfilled. "Blood, and fire, and vapour of smoke: The sun shall be turned into darkness, and the moon into blood, before that great and notable day of the Lord come." Joel's prophecy carries us on to the coming of the Lord, when He will establish His kingdom and put down all iniquity. But the same Spirit who will work then is the One who came on Pentecost and has been working in power the last nineteen hundred years. It is He who enables servants of God to go into all the world and preach the gospel to every creature, for we read, "It shall come to pass, that whosoever shall call on the name of the Lord shall be saved." Do not try to limit that "whosoever." It is the same "whosoever" that is in John 3:16: "For God so loved the world, that he gave his only begotten Son, that whosoever believeth in him should not perish, but have everlasting life." Here the message is stated in a different way but the meaning is the same.

"Whosoever shall call upon the name of the Lord shall be saved" (Acts 2:21). And so the Spirit of God has come. The Comforter is here and the saints of God have received the Spirit and have thus been baptized into one body and in the power of the Spirit are called to go forth and proclaim the gospel message to the ends of the earth. Have you called on the name of the Lord? Have you trusted Christ as your own Savior? Then doubt not, but accept the words of the Holy Ghost Himself, "Whosoever shall call on the name of the Lord shall be saved."

Peter's Sermon on Pentecost (Acts 2:22-36)

I suppose the sermon preached by the apostle Peter in Jerusalem on the day of Pentecost is the most widely used sermon ever preached. We know from Scripture that the results were three thousand souls turned to the Lord.

What was the character of this sermon and what was there in it that so appealed to the people? Of course in trying to answer this we need to remember that the circumstances were most remarkable. The Lord Jesus Christ had fulfilled three and a half years of His wonderful ministry in the land of Israel. By His many miracles He had manifested His messianic power, and His character showed that He was the Son of God. A number believed on Him and a great many rejected Him, and those who had rejected Him crucified Him. Three days later He rose from the tomb, appeared to certain selected persons repeatedly for a period of forty days, and then ascended into Heaven. After this the Spirit Himself came on the day of Pentecost as predicted and in fulfillment of Old Testament prophecy. There were gathered at Jerusalem a vast throng of people from all the different countries to which the Jews had been dispersed during the centuries. They had come to keep the feasts at Jerusalem, first the Passover and then Pentecost; and as they listened to Peter's message it came home to their consciences with peculiar power.

Never again will there be such circumstances, and that is one reason we can never expect to see a duplicate of that power or even to see a single sermon used as effectively as that one was used. But as we consider the content of it, it will at least suggest to us the type of sermon that God can use to convert sinners. The first thing is simplicity. Not a word was uttered that day that a child of adolescent age could not have understood. Peter did not need someone to explain his words. His hearers did not need to go away to consult a dictionary. He had clothed his message in such a manner that the simplest, the most illiterate could understand.

In the second place, Peter's sermon was centered on the Lord Jesus Christ. He held up Christ, crucified and risen, and that is the message God has promised to bless. He has sent His servants into the world to preach the gospel, the good news about His Son. Peter did not argue; he did not go into abstruse theological problems; he told them about the death and resurrection of the Lord Jesus Christ. As he told of that, the Spirit touched the hearts of his hearers with tremendously convicting power. I am afraid we forget it is the plain, simple story that reaches the people and brings them to the knowledge of salvation.

We sometimes sing,

> I love to tell the story
> Of unseen things above;
> Of Jesus and His glory
> Of Jesus and His love.
> (A. Catherine Hankey)

Yet we spend so much time speaking of other things and so little time on that wondrous story. I wouldn't be surprised if our hearers didn't feel like reminding us of that other hymn,

> Tell me the story often,
> For I forget so soon,
> The early dew of morning
> Has passed away at noon.
> (A. Catherine Hankey)

That is what the world needs! That is what men and women are crying for.

"Ye men of Israel, hear these words." You see, Christ came in the beginning not to the Gentiles but to the lost sheep of the house of Israel. While the disciples were to go to the uttermost part of the earth, He distinctly said they must begin at Jerusalem. Jerusalem had had the greatest privileges and yet it had crucified the Son of God. So this message was to the very people who had rejected Christ—the nation of Israel.

"Jesus of Nazareth, a man approved of God among you by miracles and wonders and signs, which God did by him in the midst of you, as ye yourselves also know." The term "Jesus of Nazareth" speaks of His humanity; it speaks of the lowliness of His character. He, who is over all, God blessed forever, stooped to become a carpenter of Nazareth.

The great Japanese evangelist, Kagawa, in speaking of the many blessings the gospel brought to the Japanese said that it had taught the people of Japan, even those who had rejected its saving message, the dignity of the laboring man. Before the gospel came, the laboring man was looked down upon with absolute contempt, but when Christian missionaries arrived to tell the story of the Son of God who became a carpenter, who shed His blood on the cross for our sins, it changed the whole conception of people toward the laboring class. That has been true all over the world. The laboring people were hardly more than slaves when Jesus came, and now there is little actual slavery in civilized nations. Some are enslaved by cruel and ruthless laws, but the arrival of the gospel message changes completely the attitude toward those who toil and labor. Jesus of Nazareth labored. God anointed Jesus of Nazareth who "went about doing good, and healing all that were oppressed of the devil" (Acts 10:38).

Peter in the beginning does not rise any higher than that. He does not dwell on the deity of Christ at first. He tells them, "[Here was] a man approved of God among you by miracles and wonders and signs." In other words, Peter is telling them this man is the Messiah. God had put His seal upon Him. This was the One whom the prophets had proclaimed and of whom the psalmists had sung, and what have they done with Him? Let me ask you the question, What have you done with Him? You know why He came, why He died. What have you done with Him? Have you opened your heart to receive Him? Have you trusted Him as Savior? If not, you are as guilty and in some respects even more guilty than they in those days. What did they do? "Him, being delivered by the determinate counsel and foreknowledge of God, ye have taken, and by wicked hands have crucified and slain."

Notice how two things come together here that often trouble thinkers among men: God's predetermined purpose and wicked man's free will. God had predetermined that His blessed Son was to come into the world and give His life a ransom for sinners. Jesus came "not to be ministered unto, but to minister, and to give his life a ransom for many" (Matthew 20:28). But God had not predetermined that men should curse Him, spit on Him, and heap every kind of indignity upon Him. These things were of men's godlessness led on by Satan. Peter said in effect, "God sent Him; God knew all that would take place; but you are responsible for your sins in that you laid hold of Him and with your wicked hands crucified and slew Him."

When man would do his worst, God gives His best. Man showed the malevolence and iniquity of his heart; he cried, "Away with Him, away with Him, crucify Him," and then the ruthless soldiers nailed Him to that cross of shame. But when man had done all that, God said, "This, My beloved Son, is the great sin offering for the guilty. Even for the men rejecting Him now, for the men who crucified Him and put Him upon the cross, His soul was made the offering for sin." By His death redemption was procured, which God offers freely to all men everywhere. In answer to what man did, we see God acting in power.

"Whom God hath raised up, having loosed the pains of death: because it was not possible that he should be holden of it." When sin had been atoned for and the sin question settled, it was righteousness on the part of God that demanded that His Son be brought back again from the dead. In the resurrection of our Lord Jesus Christ we have the evidence of God's satisfaction with the work done. So the risen, crucified One is now set forth as the Savior of all who put their trust in Him.

The apostle Peter continued his sermon by quoting from three Psalms showing how the Old Testament Scripture had opened up to him. Before His ascension Jesus said of the Holy Spirit, "He shall take of mine, and shall show it unto you" (John 16:15). And so now, guided by the illumination of the Holy Spirit, Peter turned to passage after passage in the book of Psalms and showed how all were being fulfilled in Christ. First he referred to Psalm 16.

> For David speaketh concerning him, I foresaw the Lord always before my face, for he is on my right hand, that I should not be moved: Therefore did my heart rejoice, and my tongue was glad; moreover also my flesh shall rest in hope: Because thou wilt not leave my soul in hell, neither wilt thou suffer thine Holy One to see corruption. Thou hast made known to me the ways of life; thou shalt make me full of joy with thy countenance (Acts 2:25-28).

You may say these words are expressed by David in the first person. When he wrote Psalm 16 one might have imagined perhaps those experiences were to be his own, but Peter showed it was the Spirit of Christ speaking through David, leading him to write as he did.

These things are not all true of David. David could not say, "Thou wilt not leave my soul in hell, neither wilt thou suffer [me] to see corruption." David's soul was left in Hades (the state between death and resurrection) and his body did see corruption. But Peter said, "Men and brethren, let me freely speak unto you of the patriarch David, that he is both dead and buried, and his sepulcher is with us unto this day" (Acts 2:29). But David was a prophet, and as a prophet was looking forward to Messiah's coming. Therefore knowing that God had sworn with an oath to David that his son was to sit forever on his throne Peter declared that it was of Jesus God spake. "He seeing this before spake of the resurrection of Christ, that his soul was not left in hell, neither his flesh did see corruption."

It is very interesting to note how these Old Testament prophecies meet in the Lord Jesus Christ. Prophecies that never could have been fulfilled in anyone else were all fulfilled in Him. He walked in accordance with these beautiful words in Psalm 16.

As the apostle Peter traced the life of Jesus through the grave and up to the throne of God, he was moving on to the resurrection. He continued,

> This Jesus hath God raised up, whereof we all are witnesses. Therefore [He, the risen One] being by the right hand of God exalted, and having received of the Father the promise of the Holy Ghost, he hath shed forth this, which ye now see and hear (Acts 2:32-33).

Understand what Peter is saying. The man Christ Jesus in His human body has gone up to Heaven and has taken His seat at the right hand of the Majesty on high. He is now the Mediator. God has given to Him the Holy Ghost without measure that He might shed forth the Holy Spirit upon men here on earth. Would you need evidence stronger to show you that Peter truly understood the deity of our Lord Jesus Christ? Can you imagine a mere man pouring out the Holy Spirit in this way? The Holy Spirit in Himself is a person of the Godhead. Jesus, God the Son, was commissioned by God the Father to give God the Holy Spirit to those who believe on Him.

"For David is not ascended into the heavens." Oh, somebody says, then David's soul is sleeping in the grave. No, that is not what is meant. David's body lies in the grave, David is not yet ascended into Heaven in his physical body, but Christ Jesus has gone up into the heavens in His glorified body. David, looking on by faith, wrote in Psalm 110, "The Lord said unto my Lord, Sit thou on my right hand, Until I make thy foes thy footstool." Peter said, as it were, "My brethren, the man who died on the cross was foreseen by David sitting at the right hand of God the Father, waiting for the moment when all creation will be subject to Him, when all His foes will be made His footstool." This is his climax and on this he bases his exhortation—an exhortation that I bring you today, those of you who may be out of Christ.

"Therefore let all the house of Israel know assuredly, that God hath made that same Jesus, whom ye have crucified, both Lord and Christ." Consider the goodness of God. The house of Israel had rejected Christ. Jew and Gentile had united in the evil act of His crucifixion, yet so great is the love of God that He sent Israel this special message. They had been set aside as a nation. Jesus said some time before, "Your house is left unto you desolate" (Matthew 23:38). They were set aside as a nation then, but God was yearning after them still.

We need to remember that the word *Christ* means "the Anointed" and is the equivalent of the Hebrew term *Mashiach* or *Messiah.* Our Lord Jesus is God's anointed King. Men said, even His own people said, "We will not have this man to reign over us" (Luke 19:14). But God has raised up from the dead the One whom the nation rejected and He has confirmed His Messiahship to Him in resurrection. He has declared Him to be Lord and Messiah.

You will notice there is no pleading, no begging, no urging to make a decision in Peter's sermon. But the moment Peter comes to the conclusion, at once there is a move among the people and a great response.

The Pentecostal Response (Acts 2:37-47)

This brief portion of the book of Acts is one that requires very careful and thoughtful examination. A great deal of controversy has raged around it, and very many serious misconceptions have been drawn from it.

The apostle Peter had just preached his wonderful sermon setting forth the life, the death, and the resurrection of the Lord Jesus Christ. He had particularly emphasized the fact that the Lord Jesus came to the nation of Israel in accordance with Old Testament prophecy as their Messiah. He was the One they had been looking for down through the centuries, but they failed to recognize Him when He came. They rejected Him and delivered Him over to the Gentiles to be crucified; but Peter concluded with this triumphant word, "Therefore let all the house of Israel know assuredly, that God hath made that same Jesus, whom ye have crucified, both Lord and Christ."

The effect of Peter's message was tremendous. We are told in Acts 2:5, "there were dwelling at Jerusalem Jews, devout men." He was addressing himself not to the ribald crowd that had been in front of Pilate's judgment hall who cried, "Crucify Him, crucify Him." Rather he was addressing primarily devout Jews who were awaiting the coming of the Messiah, also a number of proselytes from the nations who had the same sincere expectations. When these honest men heard Peter's proclamation, we read, "They were pricked in their heart." This was the work of the Holy Ghost. He so carried the message home to their hearts that they were deeply stirred.

They did not attempt to deny what Peter said. On the contrary, they accepted the message. Having accepted the message we can be very sure of this—they were already born of God. The apostle Peter wrote in the first chapter of his first Epistle, "Being born again, not of corruptible seed, but of incorruptible, by the word of God, which liveth and abideth for ever...And this is the word which by the gospel is preached unto you." These people had heard the gospel and believed the message, and that implies necessarily they had received divine light and were regenerated. They turned to Peter and the rest of the apostles and cried out in deep distress, "Men and brethren, what shall we do?"

Now, I want you to notice this. Their cry was not the same as the question of the Philippian jailer of which we read in Acts 16. These brethren did not say to Peter and the rest of the apostles, "Men and brethren, what must we do to be saved?" That was not in their mind at all; but they said, "Men and brethren" (and you will see from the very term of address used that they recognized their brotherhood with the men who had been preaching) " what shall we do?"

What is involved in that question? I think it is very easy to understand. These, as I said, were devout men. They had been waiting earnestly, believingly, for the Messiah. Peter had just shown them that the Messiah had come. The nation had rejected God's anointed King. They had refused Him whom God sent to deliver them. When Pilate asked, "Shall I crucify your King?" they answered, "We have no king but Caesar." These men were troubled. They had expected Christ to set up His kingdom here on earth. But He had gone away to Heaven where God had seated Him on His own throne; but what about this nation He was to reign over? What were they to *do*? They really meant to ask, "Men and brethren, in view of the fact that our King has already come and our people did not realize it and He has been rejected and crucified, what then are we going to do?" They were not simply questioning their individual salvation. They were questioning the fate of the nation to which they belonged. What was to happen? What shall we do now? Is there any way this dreadful thing can be undone? Is there any way the Christ who had been rejected can appear again and the people be given another opportunity? Is there any way by which the sentence can be revoked? What shall we do?

Peter said, "One thing you can do is repent." Repent! What does that mean? *Repent* means literally a change of mind—a change of mind that involves not only looking at things differently from an intellectual standpoint, but involves complete moral reformation, complete change of attitude. And so Peter said, "Repent, change your attitude." They showed what their attitude was when Christ was presented to them and they spurned Him. Now he says in effect, "Change your attitude. Instead of spurning Him, instead of rejecting Him—receive Him! It is true He has gone away from earth, that He is not here to establish His kingdom, but He still lives and is exalted at God's right hand. Repent. Rightabout-face! Instead of going on as a part of the nation that rejected Him, change your mind, and separate from the apostate group by taking your stand for Christ."

That is the message we would give today to every one of our dear Jewish brethren everywhere. People do not understand sometimes why we should have Christian missions to the Jews. Do not the Jews have a good religion of their own? Then why should we bother with them? Well, you see, we believe the testimony of Moses and the prophets and we grieve to think that the Jewish people, just as the Gentiles, have rejected the Lord Jesus Christ. So in obedience to the word of Jesus Christ we go to them, as to the Gentiles. Peter said to all men everywhere and particularly to Israel who rejected and spurned Him, "Change your attitude toward the Lord Jesus Christ. Instead of trampling on His grace, open your heart to Him." Thank God, there have been tens of thousands of Jews who have changed their attitude toward the Lord Jesus Christ and have crowned Him Lord of their lives whom the nation has rejected.

Next he called on them to do something that would separate them visibly from this nation that is under condemnation: "Be baptized, every one of you, in the name of Jesus Christ, for the remission of sins." As part of the nation they were responsible for the rejection of Christ. Now Peter said, "In accord with your changed attitude toward Jesus Christ give this outward witness—be baptized in the name of the One you have rejected, and God will look at you standing there and you will no longer be under condemnation as are those who rejected Christ. Rather you will be under His grace because your sins are forgiven." It was not baptism, but change of attitude toward Christ, that gave them forgiveness. The baptism was the outward manifestation of their hearts' new attitude.

Some people have supposed that because Peter said, "Be baptized in the name of Jesus Christ," he was suggesting a different baptismal formula from that the Lord Jesus gave in the Gospel of Matthew. They fail to recognize that in Matthew 28 the Lord was telling them in what name they were to baptize believers. He said, "Go ye therefore, and teach all nations, baptizing them in the name of the Father, and of the Son, and of the Holy Ghost." He used the preposition meaning "baptizing them *unto* the name of the Father, and of the Son, and of the Holy Ghost." That is the revelation of God in Christianity. The Jew knew God in the sense of the triune God, for the word *Elohim* implies God-triune. But the Lord Jesus Christ gave the full revelation and in essence He said, "You go and baptize converts in the name that implies the fullness of deity." They proceeded to do as He told them, and as they undertook to baptize they did it in the name of Jesus. They preached in the name of Jesus; they healed in the name of Jesus; they wrought signs and wonders in the name of Jesus; they baptized in the name of Jesus. Being baptized in the name of Jesus implies baptizing as instructed by Him—in the name of the Father, and of the Son, and of the Holy Spirit.

So there is no confusion here. This is not a different kind of baptism. It is not a different name from that given in Matthew's Gospel. This comes out very clearly in Acts 19. There Paul, in coming to Ephesus and talking to certain disciples, said:

Have ye received the Holy Ghost since ye believed? And they said unto him, We have not so much as heard whether there be any Holy Ghost. And he said unto them, Unto what then were ye baptized? And they said, Unto John's baptism. Then said Paul, John verily baptized with the baptism of repentance, saying unto the people, that they should believe on him which should come after him, that is, on Christ Jesus. When they heard this, they were baptized in the name of the Lord Jesus. And when Paul had laid his hands upon them, the Holy Ghost came on them (Acts 19:2-6).

If they had been baptized as Christians before, they would have known of the Holy Spirit, for He is spoken of in the baptismal formula.

So that passage definitely proves the formula of baptism given in Matthew 28 is the one by the authority of, and in the name of, the Lord Jesus Christ. In other words the apostles said, "Be baptized by the authority of the Lord Jesus Christ for the forgiveness of your sins, and the past will no longer be held against you. You will no longer be looked on as part of the nation that rejected the Christ, and in token of this God will give you the gift of the Holy Spirit as He has given it to us." The coming of the Holy Spirit had ushered in the new dispensation, and they were to be brought into all the blessings of the new covenant. Notice the breadth of this: "For the promise is unto you, and to your children, and to all that are afar off, even as many as the Lord our God shall call" (Acts 2:39).

When he used the term "afar off" he did not mean those in distant lands; but his meaning is essentially moral, spiritual, covenantal. In Ephesians 2 we see that Paul used that term to refer to Gentiles, those not in covenant relation with God:

Wherefore remember, that ye being in time past Gentiles in the flesh, who are called Uncircumcision by that which is called the Circumcision in the flesh made by hands;...being aliens from the commonwealth of Israel, and strangers from the covenants of promise, having no hope, and without God in the world: but now in Christ Jesus ye who sometimes were far off are made nigh by the blood of Christ.... [He] came and preached peace to you which were afar off, and to them that were nigh (Ephesians 2:11-13, 17).

You see, the Jew is nigh in the point of covenant privilege, the Gentile is a stranger to the covenant—he is afar off. Peter on the day of Pentecost proclaimed salvation not only to the Jews, as some have ignorantly said, but to the Jews and their children and then "to all that are afar off, even as many as the Lord our God shall call."

Let us never lose sight of the universal character of the gospel message. Christians have a message for the whole world, and now as God looks at men there is neither Jew nor Greek, neither bond nor free, neither barbarian nor cultured, but all are sinners and all need a Savior. There is no difference, for "all have sinned and come short of the glory of God"; and again, "There is no difference between the Jew and the Greek: for the same Lord over all is rich unto all that call upon him."

Peter proclaimed this universal message, applying it first particularly to those at Jerusalem. Also we are told, "with many other words did he testify and exhort, saying, Save yourselves from this untoward generation." Someone may ask, "what did Peter mean by that? I thought one of the first principles is that men cannot save themselves; men are absolutely helpless, dead in trespasses and sins, and yet Peter said, 'Save yourselves.'"

He did not say, "Save yourselves from Hell and save yourselves from the wrath of God," but, "Save yourselves from this [perverse] generation." In other words, separate yourselves by baptism from this untoward generation that is rejecting the Lord Jesus Christ. You see, the wrath of God was hanging over that generation. The Lord Jesus had predicted that shortly after His ascension the temple would be destroyed; not one stone would be left upon another (Luke 21:5-6). That nation, as a nation, was subject to judgment. Now, Peter says, if you want to escape that judgment, save yourselves by being baptized in the name of the Lord Jesus. What was the response to Peter's admonition?

"Then they having received his word were baptized." You will notice the King James version reads: "They that gladly received his word were baptized." Some Greek texts include the word *gladly*, but since the King James version was translated many older texts have been discovered and they omit that word. I am always rather suspicious of persons who receive the Word with gladness and joy. One wonders if the Spirit of God has really done His probing work in the conscience. We would rather see men facing their sins before God—demonstrating a changed attitude toward self, a changed attitude toward sin. That makes people serious, thoughtful, sober; it makes people sad. Thank God when sinners have been made serious and faced their sins honestly before God. When they look up to the Lord Jesus Christ and honestly receive Him, then they are made glad.

So on the day of Pentecost thousands of people received the Word and immediately acted in accordance with their faith. They were baptized and their baptism cut them off from the Christ-rejecting nation of Israel and at the same time brought them into a new fellowship altogether. It brought them into the Christian company.

"The same day there were added unto them about three thousand souls." Added to whom? To the 120 company of believers mentioned in Acts 1:15. Now the body had grown.

We see four things affirmed in the lives of these new believers. "They continued steadfastly." They were not the kind that come forward, bow down and confess their sins, professing to accept the Lord Jesus Christ. Then taking a little copy of the Gospel of John, they leave their names with the one dealing with them, walk out of the church and never appear again. The early believers, having become united with the Christian company, entered into fellowship with them. "They continued steadfastly in the apostles' doctrine." They had no written New Testament yet. They depended wholly on the Old Testament and on oral ministry. Since the apostles were divinely-taught teachers, the believers continued where they could get the instruction they needed.

If you profess to accept Christ as Savior, see that you are often found where the Word of God is opened up. We have the whole New Testament today and now God would have His people gather together, "not forsaking the assembling of ourselves together, as the manner of some is" (Hebrews 10:25). Some people say, "Oh, I do not need to go to hear the Word. I do not need to go to the gatherings of the people of God. I can go out and worship God in nature." But as you speed through the country enjoying the passing vista, I am afraid you are not giving many thoughts to God and His testimony. I am afraid it is getting to be the manner of some to lie idly in bed until about 11:30 Sunday morning, and then lazily roll over and turn on the radio or television.

The Christians of the first century continued steadfastly in the apostles' teachings and in fellowship. That is important. We need one another; and because we do, the Spirit of God has come down to knit us together into one body. Think of one of the most frequently quoted verses in the Bible: "The grace of the Lord Jesus Christ, and the love of God, and the communion of the Holy Ghost, be with you all" (2 Corinthians 13:14). Have you ever stopped to think what is meant by the communion of the Holy Ghost? It is God working in our hearts, helping us to enjoy the things of God together in the power of the Holy Spirit.

They also continued steadfastly in the breaking of bread. Breaking of bread is the sweet and sacred ordinance of the Lord's supper. Jesus had said, "This do in remembrance of me." The early Christians did not neglect this. They continued steadfastly in observance of this sacred ordinance.

The fourth thing is they continued steadfastly in prayer. Don't think that means they continued in prayer and fellowship in their own houses. Prayer is an expression of dependence, and when the people of God really feel their need you will find them flocking together to pray. A neglected prayer meeting indicates very little recognition of one's true need. I wonder how many of us continue steadfastly in prayer? Do you ever attend a prayer meeting? You say, "Prayer meetings are too dry for me." How do you know? Wouldn't it be well to try it and see? Wouldn't it be well to come and see what draws people together to pray? You will find you are missing a great deal. The early believers continued steadfastly in prayer. And the outsiders noticed it.

"Fear came upon every soul: and many wonders and signs were done by the apostles" (Acts 2:43). Notice that there is no indication that all the believers performed miracles and wonders. Only the twelve apostles were said to have spoken in other tongues, and only they performed miracles. These were the signs God gave in order to convince the gainsayers.

All believers were together in those early days. There was no sectarianism, no strife, no denominationalism. "And all that believed were together, and had all things common." For a little while they had what some people call a world ideal—a kind of Christian communism. It was founded on love for one another—very different from modern worldly communism. The believers were as brethren in Christ. Tolstoi said, "You cannot have a brotherhood without brothers."

There were special circumstances that led them to sell all their possessions. The Lord Jesus had predicted judgment on Jerusalem, so what was the use of keeping property? The term "all men" (verse 45) does not mean the unsaved, but the Christian company sharing with one another.

Then look at their habit of life. "They, continuing daily with one accord in the temple, and breaking bread [at home], did eat their meat with gladness and singleness of heart, Praising God, and having favour with all the people." Note that the Christians still met in the temple for worship.

Others saw that something wonderful had taken place. They could not help but see it. "And the Lord added to the church [or, to them] daily such as should be saved." Oh, if God's dear people could be found walking in joy and peace before Him, with one accord, continuing steadfast in such sacred fellowship, what an effect it would have on the world outside!

CHAPTER THREE
HEALING THE LAME MAN

In the third chapter of the book of the Acts we have Peter's second recorded sermon. These apostolic sermons are of tremendous interest, or should be, to us today because they show just how God chose to present the message of His grace through the early apostles. Their one theme was Jesus Christ Himself—Christ incarnate, Christ crucified, Christ risen, Christ glorified. They did not seek to occupy the people with abstruse doctrines, nor did they reason about profound theological problems. Instead they presented the person and work of the Lord Jesus Christ in "words easy to be understood." In this they are models for preachers all through the dispensation.

Notice here how the miracle and the message coincided. Miracles were never performed either by Jesus or His apostles simply to amaze the people. These signs were done to reveal the grace of God to needy men and women. This truth comes out here most beautifully.

As the chapter opens we find Peter and John wending their way to the temple to pray. The temple was still standing in Jerusalem. It was to remain there another forty years, though the curtain was torn and the old dispensation had come to an end. But it was still the place where the people gathered together to worship God at the regular hours for prayer. The ninth hour was the time when the evening sacrifice was offered. These sacrifices at the temple had no value now for those who knew the Lord Jesus as the One who had fulfilled all the types and shadows of the law.

As the apostles approached the temple their attention was directed to a poor man who lay at one of the entrances. He was lame and could not walk; he had to be carried daily to the gate Beautiful. We can see him there, holding out his hand, beseeching the more fortunate passersby to contribute to his support. As Peter and John came along, something about them, perhaps their kindly faces, stirred his heart and made him feel that here were two men who would help him, so he asked them for alms. "And Peter," we are told, "fastening his eyes upon him with John, said, Look on us." He was definitely calling the lame man's attention, and the beggar looked up, thinking surely now he was about to receive a coin that would supply his temporal needs. But Peter said, "Silver and gold have I none; but such as I have give I thee: in the name of Jesus Christ of Nazareth rise up and walk."

I am sure that to the very end of his days Peter could have said: "Silver and gold have I none." These early followers of the Lord Jesus Christ did not look upon the gospel ministry as a means of enriching themselves. They had taken the place of poverty and were willing to follow Jesus, no matter what it meant. We remember that when Christ was here He said, "Foxes have holes, and the birds of the air have nests; but the Son of man hath not where to lay his head" (Matthew 9:20). And as the apostles followed Him there was a power in their message that is sadly lacking when men use the gospel merely as a means of personal enrichment.

In connection with this I am reminded of an interesting story of the medieval church. That great scholar, Thomas Aquinas, came to the city of Rome to pay his respects to the one who was then pope. In the course of his visit, the pope proudly showed him all the wonders of the papal palace and took him to his treasury and showed him chests of silver and gold received from every part of the world. With something of a smile on his face, he said, "You see, Brother Thomas, we cannot say, as did the first pope, 'Silver and gold have I none.'" (The Catholic church claims Peter was the first pope.) Thomas Aquinas looked the pope in the eye and fearlessly replied, "No, and neither can you say, 'In the name of Jesus Christ of Nazareth rise up and walk.'" Riches had come, but power had gone. With Peter and the apostles there were poverty and power. They were men who walked with God, esteeming it greater riches than all this world could give to be used of Him in a mighty way. There was identification with Christ in His earthly poverty.

As he uttered the words, "Rise up and walk," Peter reached out and "took him by the right hand, and lifted him up." Immediately the lame man felt new life come into that crippled body of his; new strength came into those legs. We are given a graphic picture indeed. "Immediately his feet and ankle bones received strength. And he leaping up stood, and walked, and entered with them into the temple, walking and leaping, and praising God." You can just see the man fairly dancing with delight, using his newfound strength, like a child skipping along the way. So overcome with joy was he over the miracle that had been done that he was not at all concerned with what people might think of him, or of the strange appearance he made as he ran ahead of the apostles. The people who saw him were filled with amazement too, and were glad for him as they came running, eager to learn more of what had taken place.

Peter said, "Ye men of Israel, why marvel ye at this? or why look ye so earnestly on us, as though by our own power or holiness we had made this man to walk?" Then Peter used the miracle as an occasion to preach the gospel message. He disavowed any power in himself. He would not have people occupied with him or his devoted companion, the apostle John. He turned their eyes away from the servant to the Master of the servant, the Lord Jesus Christ, who had healed the poor cripple.

He began his message with, "The God of Abraham, and of Isaac, and of Jacob, the God of our fathers." He spoke as a pious Jew, and I wish that our Jewish friends everywhere could realize that in Christianity we have the fulfillment of that which all the types in Judaism were but the pictures. We too reverence the God of Abraham, Isaac, and Jacob, for He is the God and Father of our Lord Jesus Christ. He is not another god; not some strange god, but the God who of old appeared to the patriarchs. The Lord Jesus is the promised seed through whom all blessing comes for both Jews and Gentiles.

"The God of our fathers, hath glorified his Son Jesus." Some manuscripts read, "His Servant Jesus." It is not exactly easy to decide which term the apostle Peter used, but it would seem a little more in keeping with his general message to have used the word *servant*; for the Lord Jesus Christ is that anointed Servant spoken of in the book of the prophet Isaiah, "Behold my servant" (Isaiah 42:1). So Peter presented the blessed Lord as the One who came into this world to serve the Father by making atonement for our sins.

Then he drove home to these people the sin they had recently committed in rejecting Him. "Whom ye delivered up, and denied him in the presence of Pilate, when he was determined to let him go." One might feel Peter could have dealt with them more gently, and not have stressed the point that they had denied Christ. But let us remember it is ever the work of a good doctor or surgeon to be faithful to his task. So it is never a kindness on the part of a servant of God to gloss over the sins of the people to whom he preaches. God would have men's hearts probed to the very depths. He would have men realize the corruption of their nature and their sinful acts that placed them in condemnation before God. After all, it is my sin that gives me the right to the blood of Jesus, and it is the blood of Jesus that secures my claim to Heaven.

And so Peter stressed the sin of which they were recently guilty. "Ye denied the Holy One and the Just, and desired a murderer to be granted unto you." When given the choice of either Barabbas or Jesus, they asked that Barabbas be freed and Jesus condemned to die.

Then Peter added, "And killed the Prince of life." One might say, "But they didn't kill Him. It was not the Jews who nailed Jesus Christ to the cross—it was the Gentiles." Yes, but it was Jew and Gentile who together rejected Him and together gave Him up to die. It was in the heart of His own people Israel to destroy Him, so God spoke of His having been slain by them. Actually, no one could kill Jesus. He said Himself, "No man taketh it [my life] from me, but I lay it down of myself. I have power to lay it down, and I have power to take it again. This commandment have I received of my Father" (John 10:18).

It would have been utterly impossible for either Jew or Gentile to put an end to the earthly life of Jesus if He had not voluntarily placed Himself in their hands and gone to the cross. Even when nailed on the tree He did not die of the physical suffering He endured. We are told that when He cried, "It is finished," He then said, "Father, into thy hands I commend my spirit" (Luke 23:46). And when he had said that, the King James version says, "He gave up the ghost." Actually it is, "He dismissed his spirit." The work was done.

His death was voluntary. But we are told in another portion of Scripture, "Whosoever hateth his brother is a murderer: and ye know that no murderer hath eternal life abiding in him" (1 John 3:15). So because they had hatred in their hearts they are said to have killed the Prince of life, whom God raised from the dead.

I would like to pause here and put a question to my readers. What is your attitude toward the Lord Jesus Christ? Have you ever turned to God as a repentant sinner and trusted the Lord Jesus for yourself? If not, you still belong to that world which God judges guilty of murdering His beloved Son. Until you come to the place where you repent of the sin for which the world stands condemned—the death of God's Son—and you take Him as your own Savior, judgment hangs over you because of man's attitude toward Christ—He who "was delivered for our offences, and was raised again for our justification" (Romans 4:25).

Peter said, "God hath raised [Him] from the dead; whereof we are witnesses." That was a very bold statement. This was only a few days after Pentecost. The apostle Peter had nothing to cover up. He could have given witness after witness of people who had talked with Christ and walked with Him. God made the resurrection of His Son abundantly evident so that no one who wanted to know the truth need be misled.

So Peter declared it was through this risen One that the lame man was miraculously healed. "And his name through faith in his name hath made this man strong, whom ye see and know: yea, the faith which is by him hath given him this perfect soundness in the presence of you all."

Then, having driven home to the hearts of the people their own sinfulness and their accountability before God for the murder of His Son, Peter opened for them a door, as it were, into the city of refuge. You will remember in the Old Testament God made special provision for any guilty of putting another man to death unintentionally or through ignorance. Scripture illustrates it like this: If a man, for instance, is chopping wood and his neighbor is near and the ax head flies off and hits the neighbor and the man falls dead, the one who slew him is not to be treated as a murderer. He is guilty of manslaughter, but is not a murderer (Deuteronomy 19:4-6). God commanded that there be six cities located at different points, with good roads to them. The man who unintentionally slays his neighbor is immediately to flee to the nearest city and abide there until the death of the high priest. "And ye shall take no satisfaction for him that is fled to the city of his refuge." (Numbers 35:6-32). The revenger of blood is not to seek him out nor treat him as a murderer.

Peter continued, "And now, brethren, I wot that through ignorance ye did it [killed the Son], as did also your rulers." In other words, "You did not understand: you did not know Jesus was really the Messiah and Servant of God. You thought you were fulfilling God's purpose perhaps in putting Jesus to death. You did it through ignorance." Peter was opening a door to a city of refuge. He was saying in effect, "God is ready to treat you not as a murderer, but as one guilty of manslaughter, and as long as the high priest lives you are safe if you enter the place of refuge." Our High Priest is the Lord Jesus and He lives forever. Those who accept the salvation God has provided are forever secure from the avenger, for God will not permit a charge to be brought against any who are saved by the blood of Jesus Christ. The apostle Paul said, "Which none of the princes of this world knew: for had they known it, they would not have crucified the Lord of glory" (1 Corinthians 2:8). So again you see they did not know. Pilate did not know; the Roman soldiers did not know, neither Jews nor Gentiles understood. That is what Jesus meant when He said on the cross, "Father, forgive them; for they know not what they do" (Luke 23:34).

One thinks of those excited Jews in Pilate's judgment hall demanding the death of Jesus. Pilate asked, "Shall I crucify your King?" And the Jews cried out, "His blood be on us, and on our children" (Matthew 27:25). What a dangerous malediction they were calling down on themselves and their children! I have heard some thoughtless people say that is why the Jews are suffering today and they should suffer. They say Hitler was right, the Fascists were right, and the anti-Semites are right in causing the Jewish people to suffer. Those who speak like that forget this prayer of the Lord Jesus Christ on Calvary. Jesus prayed, "Father, forgive them; for they know not what they do." So instead of charging His blood to either Jew or Gentile, He is declaring that His very death has opened a city of refuge, a way of deliverance from judgment for all who flee to Him for mercy.

Peter explained that even in the very rejection of Christ, God's own Word was being fulfilled. We see this most clearly when we turn to the wonderful fifty-third chapter of the book of the prophet Isaiah. In light of that, Peter urged their instantly turning to God: "Repent ye therefore, and be converted." That is, change your attitude and turn to God. Judge yourselves as sinners before Him. Confess your guilt. Be turned around. That is what conversion implies. When men confess Christ they are turned from the power of Satan to God, from sin to righteousness.

"That your sins may be blotted out." Again we think of the prophet Isaiah, through whom we hear God speaking to Israel. "I have blotted out, as a thick cloud, thy transgressions, and, as a cloud, thy sins: return unto me; for I have redeemed thee" (Isaiah 44:22).

It is necessary to draw attention to a slight change of translation from the King James version, which makes for a clearer understanding of the passage that follows. "Repent ye therefore, and be converted, that your sins may be blotted out, *so that* [not *when*] the times of refreshing [may] come from the presence of the Lord." That is, if Israel will turn to the Lord it will hasten the time when the Lord Jesus will come back again and bring with Him refreshing for all the world. That is still true. The final blessing of this poor world is wrapped up in Israel's repentance. When the people of Israel repent and turn to God they will become the means of blessing to the whole earth.

"And he shall send Jesus Christ, which before was preached unto you: Whom the heaven must receive until the times of restitution of all things,..."Shall we stop there? If we did it would put us on the ground of universal restitutionalism; it would put us in the company with those who say all men eventually are going to be saved.

But that is not what Peter declared. We cannot stop with the comma but must complete the sentence: "...which God hath spoken by the mouth of all his holy prophets since the world began." You see, the sentence as a whole means restitution of all that God has spoken by His prophets. Everything the prophets have spoken will eventually be fulfilled through Christ for He is the Prophet of whom Moses spoke in Deuteronomy 18:15: "The Lord thy God will raise up unto thee a Prophet from the midst of thee, of thy brethren, like unto me: unto him ye shall hearken." That Prophet is our Lord Jesus. God calls on all men to receive Him and put their trust in Him.

"And it shall come to pass, that every soul, which will not hear that Prophet, shall be destroyed from among the people. Yea, and all the prophets from Samuel and those that follow after, as many as have spoken, have likewise foretold of these days" (Acts 3:23-24). Peter reminded his hearers that the prophets had foretold of the days to come when Jew and Gentile would be saved through the death of the appointed Savior that God was to provide.

Then Peter added, "Ye are the children of the prophets, and of the covenant which God made with our fathers, saying unto Abraham, And in thy seed shall all the kindreds of the earth be blessed." How the heart of God goes out to His earthly people Israel. "Unto you first." If any Jewish friend reads these pages, I hope he will listen to these wonderful words, "Unto you first." Unto you, God's chosen people Israel! Unto you first! God has set the nation aside, but His heart goes out in yearning love to every individual Jew.

"God, having raised up his Son [or literally, His Servant] Jesus, sent him to bless you, in turning away every one of you from his iniquities." Salvation, full and free and complete, is offered to Jew and Gentile—to everyone who will turn in repentance to our Lord Jesus Christ.

CHAPTER FOUR

THE REJECTED STONE

A s we pursue our study in the book of Acts we now find the early church coming up against decided opposition by leaders of the old religious system. This was a system that had originally been established by God but had become so greatly corrupted by human additions that it was scarcely recognizable as the Judaism of the days of Moses and the prophets. Our Lord Jesus, you remember, said the Pharisees had corrupted the Word of God by their traditions, "teaching for doctrines the commandments of men" (Matthew 15:9).

The Apostolic Message (Acts 4:1-22)

At this time the Sadducee party was in power in Jerusalem. The Pharisees and the Sadducees constituted the two leading sects among the Jewish people. There were several lesser ones. The Sadducees, we are told later on in the book of Acts, denied that man has a personal spirit, or that angels are personalities, or that there is any resurrection after death, whereas the Pharisees assented to all these things.

It was the Sadducees then who were incensed with the teaching of the apostles in the beginning, for their entire message had to do with the resurrection of the Lord Jesus Christ. Some people speak of the spiritual resurrection of Christ. The spirit of Christ never died. He committed His spirit to the Father as His body was about to die. The body of the Lord Jesus lay for three days and nights in Joseph's new tomb, and it was the body of Jesus that was missing when the tomb was empty. In His body the Lord Jesus appeared to His disciples during the forty days before He ascended to Heaven. Then He was taken up in that very body, and in that body He sits as the exalted man on the throne of God "There is one mediator between God and men, the man Christ Jesus" (1 Timothy 2:5).

The apostolic gospel was the gospel of the risen Christ. There are some who think that they can discern a disagreement between the preaching of the gospel by the twelve and the message proclaimed by the apostle Paul. These bewildered people insist that there are two different gospels, and that Peter preached one gospel, and when Paul was converted he preached another gospel altogether.

It seems to me that anyone who knows the gospel message ought to see at once that there was absolutely no difference between the gospel preached by Peter and the rest of the twelve and that preached by the apostle Paul. Paul explained the gospel he preached:

> Moreover, brethren, I declare unto you the gospel which I preached unto you, which also ye have received, and wherein ye stand; By which also ye are saved, if ye keep in memory what I preached unto you, unless ye have believed in vain. For I delivered unto you first of all that which I also received, how that Christ died for our sins according to the scripture; And that he was buried, and that he rose again the third day according to the scriptures (1 Corinthians 15:1-4).

This—and nothing else—is the gospel! Nothing can be added to that. The apostles preached a great many other things that were not included in that, but they were not the gospel. The gospel is that Christ died for our sins, that He was buried and that He rose again the third day. That was exactly the gospel which was preached by Peter on the day of Pentecost, and after the healing of the lame man as recorded in Acts 3. Nothing else is the gospel. There is no other gospel.

The apostle Paul wrote in Galatians, "Though we, or an angel from heaven, preach any other gospel unto you than that which we have preached unto you, let him be accursed" (1:8). Did Peter preach another gospel? Was Paul pronouncing a curse on Peter? Surely not, because Peter's gospel was exactly the same as Paul's gospel. Then Paul goes further, "As we said before, so say I now again, If any man preach any other gospel unto you than that ye have received, let him be accursed" (Galatians 1:9). So you see it would have put Peter in a very bad light indeed if he had been preaching any other gospel than that preached by the apostle Paul, but he preached Christ crucified, buried, and risen. Paul preached Christ crucified, buried, and risen. Their messages as to this were identical.

The confusion arises when other things that accompany the gospel are spoken of as the gospel itself. Peter told Jewish believers on the day of Pentecost certain things that Paul never told Gentile believers, but these things were not the gospel. And other things Paul told the Gentile believers, in addition to the gospel, constituted a further revelation that God had given him. If we can get this clear, there will be no further trouble.

When a person believes the message that Christ was crucified and died then rose from the dead, that person is born of God. But after he is born of God there may be a great many other things he needs to know.

Let us continue with the story of the presentation of the gospel to the people of Jerusalem. After the healing of the lame man, Peter found an opportunity to preach the gospel. The leaders of the people were drawn together and indignantly protested against this, "being grieved that [the apostles] taught the people and preached through Jesus the resurrection from the dead" (Acts 4:2).

Notice, not the resurrection of the dead simply, but the resurrection *from* the dead. Scripture teaches both. Scripture teaches the resurrection of the dead. It tells us some day all men will be resurrected. The doctrine of the resurrection of the dead runs all through the Bible. In Christianity we have something new—the resurrection from among the dead. First in the case of our Lord Jesus Christ, and then all believers who will have died up to the time our Lord returns in the air. They will be raised from among the dead. The unsaved dead will be left in their sins.

It was this doctrine—resurrection from among the dead—that stirred these Sadducees and stung them to bitter opposition. They seized Peter and John as they spoke in the temple and put them in jail overnight, "for it was now eventide." While they were locked up the Word was still bringing forth fruit, "and the number of the men [who believed] was about five thousand." This does not mean five thousand more were converted; but that added to the three thousand converted on the day of Pentecost, there were now some two thousand more. Notice how clear that is. They believed, and because they believed were added to the company. Men are saved when they believe in the Lord Jesus Christ.

The next day all the dignitaries, including the high priest and his family, were gathered together at Jerusalem. They brought Peter and John before them and inquired by what authority or in what name they had acted, demanding in effect, "Who gave you two men authority to usurp the functions of the ministry? We did not give you authority and we are the chief priests in Israel. In what name and by what power was this lame man healed?" They thought perhaps to overawe these two plain, unlearned fishermen. Little did they know about the Holy Spirit who had baptized them into Christ and anointed them for service. "Peter, filled with the Holy Ghost." You will notice that as long as the apostles acted in obedience to what the Lord had told them to do they were filled with the Holy Ghost.

Some people have an idea that being filled with the Holy Ghost is a unique experience that comes from praying a long time until suddenly an overwhelming sensation overcomes them. That is just an emotional experience. When people walk in obedience to the Word of God, when they do the thing the Lord tells them to do, He fills them with His Spirit and gives them power to carry on in accordance with His commandment.

So Peter, filled with the Holy Spirit said,

> Ye rulers of the people, and elders of Israel, If we this day be examined of the good deed done to the impotent man, by what means he is made whole; Be it known unto you all, and to all the people of Israel, that by the name of Jesus Christ of Nazareth, whom ye crucified, whom God raised from the dead, even by him doth this man stand here before you whole (Acts 4:8-10).

There you have the gospel! Is there any difference between that
and Paul's gospel? No, it is the same glorious message. Christ was
put to death, He was crucified, but God raised Him from the dead.
All our salvation depends on that fact. "If Christ be not raised,
your faith is vain; ye are yet in your sins" (1 Corinthians 15:17).
The minister of the gospel today proclaims the living Christ, declaring that the same One who trod the hills and valleys of Palestine
so long ago now sits exalted on the throne of God. He is a Prince
and a Savior, now offering redemption and remission of sins to all
who put their trust in Him. God's raising of His Son from the dead
was the token of His perfect satisfaction in the work Jesus accomplished on the cross. No one but the risen Savior could have saved
sinners like you and me. We need a power outside of ourselves; He
lives to exercise that power on our behalf. Peter said, through Christ
"doth this man stand here before you whole."

Then he directed their attention to a passage in Psalm 118, the
Psalm to which our Lord Jesus Christ had referred them before He
was crucified. Peter said, speaking of the risen Christ, "This is the
stone which was set at nought of you builders, which is become the
head of the corner."

The Jews had their own explanation of this verse. It is only a
legend, but it is very illuminative. The story goes that when the
temple of Solomon was in the course of construction all the stones
sent up from the quarry below were practically of the same size and
shape. One day a stone was found different from all the rest, and the
builders said, "There is no place for this stone. There must be a
mistake." So they rolled it to the edge of the cliff and tumbled it
down into the valley of Kedron below the temple area. As the years
went on (Solomon's temple was seven years in building) they were
finally ready for the chief cornerstone; so they sent down the order
for it. They were told "You must have it there; we sent it to you
long ago." Their search proved fruitless, until an old workman said,
"I remember now. There was a stone different from the rest and we
thought there was no place for it and tumbled it down to the valley
below."

So, the builders went down to the valley of Kedron and there
they found the stone, now covered by lichens and debris—the very

stone they had rejected. So they had to hoist it to the top of the cliff, then back to the platform and put it into place. It fit perfectly. The stone the builders rejected had become the headstone of the corner.

Every Jew knew that story and knew what Peter meant when he said, "This is the stone which was set at nought of you builders, which is become the head of the corner." In other words Peter was saying, "Jesus was God's Anointed and you rejected Him, crucified Him, but God has raised Him from the dead and in resurrection has made Him the chief cornerstone of the new temple He is building." That new temple is the church spoken of in Matthew's Gospel, "Upon this rock I will build my church; and the gates of [Hades] shall not prevail against it."

Then Peter drove home to them that it was Christ or nothing, Christ or judgment, Christ or Hell; no other way to be saved except through Christ. "Neither is there salvation in any other: for there is none other name under heaven given among men, whereby we must be saved." Oh, I wish I could shout that loudly enough to be heard from one end of the earth to the other! None but Christ; God's only Savior! His precious atoning blood is the only remedy for sin. Have you trusted Him?

A troubled young man went one night to a gospel meeting. His conscience convicting him, he felt he ought to come to Christ, but he thought, *Some other time—not tonight.* Just as the meeting was closing he observed a placard reading. "Remember, it must be Christ or Hell, and to neglect the one is to choose the other." The young man, startled, thereupon decided, "I can't neglect Him. I must choose Him." Have you made the choice and taken Him as your Savior?

We read that the Jewish leaders perceived that Peter and John were unlearned and ignorant men. That is, they did not have any college degrees or diplomas. "They marvelled; and they took knowledge of them, that they had been with Jesus." They could see the evidence of their association with Christ in the firmness of their faces, in their boldness and bravery in standing against the people who crucified the Savior. The more you and I associate with Christ, and the more we spend time with Him in prayer and in reading His Word, the more people will take notice that we have been with Jesus.

Why did they want to say anything against the obvious holy power of the Lord Jesus Christ? Their attitude revealed the bitter hatred of wicked man's heart toward the Savior whom God has provided. They desired to explain the miracle away because they did not want to repent. They did not wish to face their sins or to get right with God. They said to the disciples, "Go outside a little while, we want to talk this thing over." Can you not see these crafty religionists talking among themselves? "What are we going to do? It is manifest to all in Jerusalem that a miracle has been done and we cannot deny it. We wish we could, but we can't." That is what they meant. There was the living evidence in the man leaping and dancing and praising the Lord. He had a new pair of legs! "Let us threaten them not to speak at all or preach in the name of Jesus." And that is the attitude the powers that be in many lands have taken throughout the centuries but, thank God, they have not been able to stifle the message or the messengers. Peter spoke up, "Whether it be right in the sight of God to hearken unto you more than unto God, judge ye. For we cannot but speak the things which we have seen and heard." We were commissioned by God to do this. You see, Peter recognized Jesus, who commissioned them, as God revealed in flesh.

"So when they had further threatened them, they let them go, finding nothing how they might punish them, because of the people: for all men glorified God for that which was done." The common people were stirred; they realized a mighty miracle had been performed among them and knew that Peter and John were God's servants. "The man was above forty years old, on whom this miracle of healing was showed." He was there to speak for himself and to bear witness to the power of the name of Jesus.

We have listened to Peter preaching on the day of Pentecost. We have heard him preaching after the healing of the lame man. Now we have heard him again as he stood before the Sanhedrin. And in every instance he preached the same gospel as the apostle Paul preached later on—how Christ died, was buried, and rose again from the dead. Somebody may assert that the Epistle to the Galatians says that Peter is to preach the gospel of the circumcision and Paul of the uncircumcision. It does; but it means that to Peter it was given to preach the gospel to the Jews, and to Paul it was given to preach the gospel to the Gentiles. But both of them were to preach the gospel! That is the point; there is only one gospel and only one Savior—and that Savior is our blessed, risen, glorified Lord.

The Second Psalm (Acts 4:23-31)

In the rest of Acts 4, as well as in many other parts of the book of Acts, we find that the early saints were no longer acting simply as individuals, but as members one of another. We read that after being threatened by the religious leaders and being released, "they went to their own company." This Christian company might have looked like another sect. They worshiped in the temple just as the Sadducees and the Pharisees and other Jewish groups did, although they held different views. Now God was using persecution in order to draw a line of demarcation between those of the new creation and those who belonged to the old dispensation.

"Being let go, they went to their own company." They sought out those who like themselves, washed in the blood of Jesus Christ, had been baptized by the Holy Spirit. There they told all that the chief priests and elders had said to them, and the whole company joined in praise and prayer to God.

"They lifted up their voice to God with one accord, and said, Lord, thou art God, which hast made heaven, and earth, and the sea, and all that in them is." Then the Spirit of God brought to their minds the marvelous prophecy of the second Psalm. They exclaimed, "Who by the mouth of thy servant David hast said, Why did the heathen rage, and the people imagine vain things? The kings of the earth stood up, and the rulers were gathered together against the Lord, and against his Christ."

One of the very first results of the reception of the Holy Spirit by these early believers was that the Old Testament Scriptures, which had been largely sealed to them before, were now opened up in a very wonderful way. They were given a spiritual understanding that was lacking even when they walked with Christ here on earth. Think back a little, when the Lord tried to make clear to them that He must go to Jerusalem to be crucified and that in three days he would rise from the dead. They reasoned among themselves, "Rise from the dead? What could that mean?" They had no understanding of the

Old Testament Scriptures. You remember on the resurrection day when those two disciples walked on the road to Emmaus, regretting the loss of their Master and Leader, how Jesus came to them and said,

> O fools, and slow of heart to believe all that the prophets have spoken: Ought not Christ to have suffered these things, and to enter his glory? And beginning at Moses and all the prophets, he expounded unto them in all the Scriptures the things concerning himself (Luke 24:25-27).

Their eyes had been closed before. They had not realized the implication of these Old Testament prophecies. But after the Holy Spirit came these believers were no longer left to their own understanding. He revealed Christ to them. He made the things of Christ clear and plain. He explained to them the second Psalm. It had been in their Bible all those years but they did not know it referred to Jesus.

You will notice Psalm 2 is made up of twelve verses divided into four sections of three verses each. If you look carefully you will perceive there is a different speaker in every one of those four sections.

In the first section you hear the voice of the world—the religious world, the political world; all classes of men united against the Lord Jesus Christ.

> Why do the heathen rage, and the people imagine a vain thing? The kings of the earth set themselves, and the rulers take counsel together, against the Lord, and against his anointed, saying, Let us break their bands asunder, and cast away their cords from us.

That is just another way of saying, as they did in Pilate's judgment hall, "We have no king but Caesar."

The apostles added, "For of a truth against thy holy child Jesus, whom thou hast anointed, both Herod, and Pontius Pilate, with the Gentiles, and the people of Israel, were gathered together." Do not try to put the blame on any one particular company. Do not say the

Jews were the Christ-killers. The Gentiles were just as guilty. All joined together. They all said, "Let us break their bands asunder." They all agreed in saying, "We will not have this man to reign over us."

In the second section you hear God the Father speaking. "He that sitteth in the heavens shall laugh: the Lord shall have them in derision." His voice is heard ringing down from Heaven. "Yet have I set my king upon my holy hill of Zion" (Psalm 2:4-6). That is to say, men may rebel and refuse to bow to the name of Jesus or acknowledge the authority of Christ, but God says, "I will have My way; you shall not spoil My plans for a moment. My King will reign from Mount Zion." Men imagine they can outwit God, thwart His plans; but God is overruling in all things and works everything according to the counsel of His will.

"For to do whatsoever thy hand and thy counsel determined before to be done" (Acts 4:28). The world could not go one step beyond the divine mandate. God had settled it. Jesus came into the world; they would not have Him—but they could not change God's plans.

His purpose will be carried out in spite of man's evil heart. Isn't that a comforting thought as you look out on the world today? Never before has it been in such a condition, and men's hearts indeed are "failing them for fear, and for looking after those things which are coming on the earth." But He sits over the waterfloods and nothing can transpire in the affairs of men and of nations but in accordance with the permissive will of God. He causes the wrath of man to praise Him (Psalm 76:10) and the remainder (that which would not praise Him) He restrains. Men rejected Jesus, but God said, "My Son is going to reign. I have set Him on My holy hill of Zion."

So in the third section of Psalm 2 beginning with verse 7 we hear another voice, the voice of the Son Himself. What does He say?

> I will declare the decree: the Lord hath said unto me, Thou art my Son; this day have I begotten thee. Ask of me, and I shall give thee the heathen for thine inheritance, and the uttermost parts of the earth for thy possession. Thou shalt break them with

a rod of iron; thou shalt dash them in pieces like a potter's vessel
(Psalm 2:7-9).

Here is the Lord Jesus Christ speaking. He says, "The Father has
confirmed it, the Father has declared that the day is coming when I
will hold the scepter of righteousness, I will rule the nations in accordance with the mind of God." He is not doing that yet, since He
is still the rejected One. But He is sitting on the throne of God now
and is receiving in grace all who come to Him. By and by He is
coming again and will judge the world in righteousness and set up
His glorious kingdom over all the earth.

In the interval, while waiting for Him, another voice is heard—
the voice of the Holy Spirit. We have heard the voice of the world
in arrogant defiance of God; the voice of the Father declaring His
plans will be carried out; and then the voice of the Son assuring us
that all this creation will be subject to Him. Now the Holy Spirit
pleads with men to get right with God before the Son returns from
Heaven.

> Be wise now therefore, O ye kings: be instructed, ye judges of
> the earth. Serve the Lord with fear, and rejoice with trembling.
> Kiss the Son [that is, bow at His feet and kiss His pierced hands,
> yield obedience to Him] lest he be angry, and ye perish from the
> way, when his wrath is kindled but a little (Psalm 2:10-12).

Then you have the precious promise, "Blessed are all they that
put their trust in him." How much this Psalm has meant to God's
people through the dispensations! But it was never understood until
the Holy Spirit explained it. Then the disciples could look back and
see that part of it was already fulfilled in the Lord Jesus Christ's
death and resurrection, and could afford to commit all to Him, and
trust Him for the rest.

They prayed, "Lord, behold their threatenings: and grant unto
thy servants that with all boldness they may speak thy word" (Acts
4:29). The opposition of the world is not to stop the servant of Christ.
The more the world opposes us, the more we are to proclaim God's

remedy for sin, the Lord Jesus Christ. "Neither is there salvation in any other: for there is none other name under heaven given among men, whereby we must be saved."

God gave miraculous signs to authenticate the message in the beginning. He does it sometimes now. He still answers prayer. Do not get the idea that the day of miracles is over. I have seen wonderful miracles in the fifty years I have known Christ. Many missionaries, especially in foreign lands, have told marvelous things of God's miracle-working power. But ordinarily speaking, He is not working in this miraculous way today. He worked in His miraculous power in the beginning so men might know that a new dispensation and age had come.

"Grant unto thy servants that with all boldness they may speak thy word, By stretching forth thine hand to heal; and that signs and wonders may be done by the name of thy holy [servant] Jesus." I have drawn your attention before to the fact that in these early chapters the word translated "child" or "son" here is really *servant*. It was not until after the apostle Paul's ministry began that we are given the full revelation that the Servant is the Son. This is the suffering Servant in accordance with the prophecy in Isaiah 53 and other passages.

The Holy Spirit who had come upon them at Pentecost as a mighty rushing wind now actually shook the place where they were gathered together and they were all filled with the Holy Spirit—that is, filled immediately. You see, we are only baptized once, but we may be filled on many occasions; a special filling for all new forms of ministry. "And they spake the word of God with boldness."

The New Age (Acts 4:32-37)

Then we see how the Spirit of God worked in their hearts and how wonderfully the Lord's prayer was answered. You will remember how Jesus prayed, "That they all may be one, as thou Father, art in me, and I in thee, that they also may be one in us" (John 17:21). Here is the answer to that prayer. For we read, "Neither said any of them that ought of the things which he possessed was his own; but they had all things common." That is altogether different from what is called communism today. It was not forcing the people to give up their possessions; but it was love working in their hearts that made these Christians say, I will gladly share my possessions with those who are more needy.

"Neither was there any among them that lacked: for as many as were possessors of lands or houses sold them and brought the prices of the things that were sold, And laid them down at the apostles' feet" (Acts 4:34-35). They were not forced to do this. No one said, You must sell your property and use your money in this way. But they were moved by the Spirit of God to share with one another.

The chapter closes with an outstanding example of Christian love and charity. We read of "Joses, who by the apostles was surnamed Barnabas." He was given that name because of his character. It means "the son of consolation." I would like to have a name like that. I would like to be the means of consolation to God's people. Barnabas "Having land, sold it, and brought the money, and laid it at the apostles' feet." Here you see love at work. When we are concerned about our own welfare rather than that of other people, it is because we know so little of the controlling love of Christ. Would that God would give us a new baptism of divine love that will move our hearts in gracious consideration for all God's people and for all men everywhere.

CHAPTER FIVE

THE EXALTED PRINCE AND SAVIOR

W e often hear the names of Ananias and Sapphira mentioned rather glibly, suggesting that perhaps they were two of the greatest liars that the world has ever known. One of our former presidents, a man who led a strenuous life and was very straightforward and hated hypocrisy, was in the habit of consigning political associates who made untrue statements to the "Ananias club." And yet, in what did the sin of this couple really consist? And to what degree are we in danger of sinning similarly against God and against His Holy Spirit?

Ananias and Sapphira (Acts 5:1-11)

As we read the record I am sure nobody is struck with the horror of their sin on the surface. Nobody feels that Ananias and Sapphira were very much worse than many of the people we meet every day. And some of us, if our consciences are active, would admit they were not much worse than we are.

What was the offense of Ananias and Sapphira? They pretended to a greater degree of Christian devotedness than they really possessed. That was all; but it was a tremendously evil thing in the sight of God.

We are told Ananias "sold a possession, And kept back part of the price." That may not mean anything to us until we remember the attitude of the first believers as described in Acts 4. Love was working among those early Christians and they were so concerned

73

about their brothers that all selfishness seemed to be banished for the time. We read, "Neither was there any among them that lacked: for as many as were possessors of lands or houses sold them, and brought the prices of the things that were sold, And laid them down at the apostle's feet: and distribution was made unto every man according as he had need" (Acts 4:34-35).

No one told them they had to do this. It was not a rule of the early church that they were to establish a communistic association of some kind. No instructions were given that if men had property they were to dispose of it. The point is this: the Spirit of God, who is the Spirit of unselfishness, was working in such power in the hearts of the early believers they simply could not consider anything as their own. They considered their possessions as a trust from God to be used as a blessing to other people. What a wonderful testimony the church would have today if Christians everywhere regarded that which God put in their keeping as a stewardship from Him, to be used in alleviating the distress of others and assisting Christians in getting out the gospel message. But sadly, we Christians are so concerned about our own comfort, nice clothing, a home for ourselves and the little luxuries of life, that we often forget the deep needs of those about us.

We are reminded by the apostle Paul that we do not find the greatest happiness in using God's gifts for ourselves. In impressing the Ephesian elders with the importance of unselfishness in the Christian life he said, "Remember the words of the Lord Jesus, how he said, It is more blessed to give than to receive" (Acts 20:35). This quote is not found literally in any of the Gospels. How did Paul know that Jesus said that? Evidently those words had been uttered so frequently by the Lord Jesus that they had been carried throughout the world. Indeed those words give us the spirit of the Lord Himself who "came not to be ministered unto, but to minister, and to give his life a ransom for many" (Matthew 20:28).

You know, many Christians are not even tithers. They take all God gives them and use practically everything for themselves and do not think of the needs of others. When it comes to the Lord, an occasional dime or quarter is the extent of their benevolence. Actually they live for themselves; but when God controls the heart, it is different. I might argue, "But is it not my own money? Did I not work hard for it? Have I not earned it?" Yes, but I must remember it was God who gave me the ability to earn it. Of course I have the responsibility of supporting my family, and I need a certain amount to live. But if I am to be a follower of the Lord Jesus Christ, I am to use a large measure for the blessing of others.

At the time of the first Christian believers the curse of God was hanging over Jerusalem. In a little while the city was to be destroyed, not one stone was to be left on another; so these early Christians said, "We will sell what we have to further the work of the Lord and help the needy." They sold their possessions and distribution was made out of a common fund to every man as he had need. And we are given one outstanding example—Barnabas, who had property over in Cyprus. Now judgment was not hanging over Cyprus, so there was no real reason for him to sell his property. But he did sell it and brought the money and laid it at the apostles' feet (4:36-37). Those standing by could not help giving him a certain amount of credit. They probably said, "What a remarkable thing to do! Isn't he a generous man?" He did it out of love for Christ and His people.

Ananias and Sapphira, who were no doubt among those present at the time, may have thought, *We had better get in on this, too.* Then they put their heads together and said, "After all, it is not necessary to bring in all the money." It wasn't! If they had been honest and straightforward and come to the apostles and said, "We have kept some; here is the balance to be used," it would have been all right. But they said, "We do not need to say anything about it. Others are giving their all, but we will keep a little for a rainy day, for a nest egg. Nobody will know the difference. They will take it for granted that this is all, and we will get credit for devotedness." That was what was in their hearts.

And so they came and laid down their money. No doubt the people looked on approvingly and commented, "Isn't that nice of Brother Ananias and Sister Sapphira? Are they not generous?" And doubtless Ananias turned away with a bright, happy countenance, pleased to get the others' approbation. But Peter called him back. He did not say, "We certainly do appreciate this. What a wonderful thing you have done." There was no idle flattery with Peter. "A man that flattereth his neighbor spreadeth a net for his feet" (Proverbs 29:5).

He said, "Ananias, why hath Satan filled thine heart to lie to the Holy Ghost?" Notice that again and again in this part of the book of Acts you read of men being filled with the Holy Spirit. Well, just as it is possible to be filled with the Holy Spirit of God so is it possible to be filled with the spirit of Satan. When the Holy Spirit dominates and controls your entire life, selfishness and everything incongruous with the Christian life disappear. But when you are under the control of Satan you are dominated by that which is selfish and evil.

Ananias was a man who wanted people to think he was thoroughly devoted to the will of God, but Peter said, "Satan filled thine heart to lie to the Holy Ghost." How had he lied to the Holy Ghost? He had not said anything. You do not need to say anything to lie to the Holy Ghost. Lying to the Holy Ghost is a sin that has often been repeated down through the centuries. He is present in the church and people have come into the church and acted hypocritically. They have pretended to devotedness that was not sincere, to a surrender of life they have never actually made. They have pretended to be totally committed to Christ when ulterior motives lay behind their actions. And the Holy Ghost said, "You have lied to Me." It is a serious thing to be untrue in the congregation of God. God desires truth in the inward part. He wants people to be genuine, absolutely honest before Him.

Peter continued, "Whiles it [the land] remained, was it not thine own? and after it was sold, was it not in thine own power? why hast thou conceived this thing in thine heart? thou hast not lied unto men, but unto God." Notice the Holy Ghost is God. Just as the Father is God and the Son is God, so the Holy Ghost is God. Peter explained that in lying to the Holy Ghost, Ananias had lied to God. Don't forget it. God exists eternally in three Persons—Father, Son, and Holy Spirit.

Notice Peter's reasoning. He said in effect, "That was your own land, Ananias. God gave it to you and you were entitled to it. After you sold it you could have kept the money, but you came and put it down as though it were all you received. You gave these people the impression that you were doing what others had done, making full surrender of what God had entrusted to you."

We talk about being surrendered, wholly yielded to God, and yet after all, how much self-seeking comes out in so many different ways! I am a preacher of the Word—a glorious privilege—and if I have prayed once I have prayed a thousand times and said, "Don't let me be able to preach unless in the power of the Holy Ghost." I would rather be struck dumb than pretend it is in the power of the Spirit. Yet it is so easy to pretend. It is so easy to come before men and take the place of an ambassador for God, and still want people to praise the preacher instead of the Lord Jesus. What if He had gifted me with the ability to sing His praises. I have a voice that would thrill thousands and I say, "Lord, I give Thee my voice." Then I sing and as people praise and applaud I take the praise all to myself. I become guilty of the sin of Ananias and Sapphira. Perhaps God has caused somebody else to do the singing and I, who am supposed to be yielded to Him, find envy and jealousy rising up in my heart. I feel that others are appreciated where I am not—and yet I talk about full surrender to the Lord! You see, then I am pretending to devotedness I do not possess.

Perhaps God has entrusted me with money. When opportunity comes I would like to do a little for the Lord and I think I could, maybe, and so after fighting with myself, I decide to part with a dollar or two. God knows I can give much more than that trifling amount. It is true that my Lord appreciates to the full the small coin that comes from the needy purse. How He appreciated the two mites the widow gave! But He would not appreciate two mites from one with fifty thousand dollars in the bank. The way the Lord estimates our gifts is not by the amount we give, but by what we have left. He is not interested in the impression we are making on others at the time. I am sure if the Spirit of God applies this truth to many of our hearts we will realize that Ananias and Sapphira were not sinners above all others. Others have sinned as much, and perhaps we are among them. We need to go before God and cry, "Purge me with hyssop, and I shall be clean; wash me, and I shall be whiter than snow" (Psalm 51:7).

Ananias had no answers for Peter. Even as Peter spoke, Ananias fell down and gave up the ghost. Those standing by carried out his dead body to prepare it for burial. Three hours later Sapphira, evidently missing her husband and wondering about him, came. I suppose she expected everybody to greet her with: "My sister, that was a wonderful gift you gave, you and your dear husband. You are doing a lot for the Lord, and you will get a great reward at the judgment seat of Christ!" But the people were nervous and troubled. They avoided her gaze as she came up to Peter. Peter said, "I want to ask you a question. 'Tell me whether you sold the land for so much ?'" And she, taken by surprise but without a moment's hesitation, answered, "Yes, for so much." That is what some people call a white lie. My dear friends, there is no such thing as a white lie. A lie is as black as its father, and the devil is the father of lies. What Sapphira said was true in one sense. They sold it for so much—and so much more.

Then Peter said unto her, "How is it that ye have agreed together to tempt the Spirit of the Lord? Behold, the feet of them which have buried thy husband are at the door, and shall carry thee out." And in a moment she dropped, smitten by the power of God.

If the Spirit of God were working in that way today, what a lot of work there would be for the undertakers! There would not be enough of them in any of our cities to bury those who drop dead. In those early days the church walked with God in holiness and righteousness. Today sadly the church has drifted so far away from God, and there is so much sin and hypocrisy and unreality, that God (I say it reverently) does not think it worth while to deal with people in this manner. The church refuses to listen to His voice. Do not let us think of Ananias and Sapphira as so very different from other people. They are like many of us today.

We are then told, "And great fear came upon all the church, and upon as many as heard these things." Well, we too have heard them. God grant that great fear will come upon us. Fear of what? Fear that we shall dishonor the Spirit of God by pretending to be what we are not, by pretending to be genuinely devoted when we are full of hypocrisy and unreality. If the Spirit of God speaks to any of us and we are saying in our hearts, I haven't been genuine, I haven't been real—may we face God about our hypocrisy today. By His grace let us put all unreality out of our lives and turn wholly to Him as the One alive from the dead? Let us renew our consecration to God and say, "By His grace, I want to be all for Christ. I want to be real, that others may be reached by my testimony and brought to know my Savior too."

> I'll live for Him who died for me,
> How happy then my soul shall be!
> I'll live for Him who died for me,
> My Savior and my God!
>
> (Ralph E. Hudson)

The Apostolic Testimony (Acts 5:12-16)

In these verses we read of many miraculous signs done by the apostles in confirmation of the gospel message. It is interesting to note that at the beginning of any dispensation miracles are customary. (By dispensation we mean a special ministry God commits to men at a particular time.) But as the dispensation moves on and the truth God has given becomes better known, miracles in a large measure are withdrawn. So in the beginning of the church era mighty works of power were manifested.

We read, "By the hands of the apostles were many signs and wonders wrought among the people; and they were all with one accord in Solomon's porch." There was a blessed unity and God could move in a marvelous way. There was no mass effort on the part of outsiders to identify themselves with the Christian company. Men were rather filled with fear because of the judgment that had come upon Ananias and Sapphira, so people were slow to take a place in fellowship with the Christians. Would that it had always been so! The curse of Christianity today is that vast numbers of members of Christian churches have never been saved! Their hearts are in the world and they love the things of the world. This mixed multitude has always hurt the testimony of the church.

In the early church nonbelievers dared not join themselves to the Christians, but the people generally magnified the apostles as they recognized the wonderful way in which God was working through them. However, believers, "multitudes both of men and women," were added to the Lord. I call your attention to the phrase "added to the Lord." What does it mean? Well, you see, a new dispensation had come in when all who believed in the baptism of the Holy Spirit were joined to the Lord Himself. Though we do not get the doctrine of the one body until God gave it to the apostle Paul, we have the fact of the unity of the body everywhere. It is implied here where we read of people being "added to the Lord." The only way to be added to the Lord is by becoming members of His body.

"Insomuch that they brought forth the sick into the streets, and laid them on beds and couches, that at the least the shadow of Peter passing by might overshadow some of them." This is a thoroughly oriental picture and very interesting. Even today in the Middle East people imagine a man's shadow carries his influence. Parents will run to draw their children away from the shadow of someone they dislike; while on the other hand, should some honored person pass by, they will endeavor to have the children come within his shadow, hoping thereby to bring good fortune on them. These people were so impressed by the power that Peter possessed that, when he was passing along a certain street or road, they brought their sick into the streets so that his shadow might fall on them. We are not told that anyone was healed in that way. Their action shows us their appreciation of Peter. It is also suggestive because while in the Orient it speaks of one's influence, it raises the question: What about our influence? Are we so walking with God that people like to come in contact with us? Or is there so little of Christ about us, are we so self-centered and worldly that no one would think of bringing people within our influence to be blessed and helped? There is a shadow influence even today.

I have often told how my oldest son at one time had an eclipse of faith until one day several of us were invited to spend an afternoon with William Jennings Bryan in his Florida home, and I was asked to bring my son. During that visit, for two or three hours we discussed the Word of God and exchanged thoughts on precious portions of Scripture. The young man sat apart and said very little, but as we left that place he turned to me and exclaimed, "Father, I have been a fool! I thought I couldn't believe the Bible, but if a man like that with his education and intelligence can believe, I am making a fool of myself to pretend I cannot accept it." So much for the shadow ministry of William Jennings Bryan. I wonder if we know anything of the shadow ministry. As people come in contact with us, even if we do not utter a word, is there something about us that makes them say, The more I see of that person the more I want to know God? I think that is what the beautiful picture of Peter's shadow suggests.

We are told, "There came also a multitude out of the cities round about unto Jerusalem, bringing sick folks, and them which were vexed with unclean spirits: and they were healed every one." God's power was working mightily. But again this stirred the ire of the leaders of the people. This time they took a more stringent stand. So in the next section we will see how the chief priests attempted to hinder the work.

Arrest and Liberation of the Apostles (Acts 5:17-28)

The leaders of the Sadducean party were very indignant because the apostles continued to testify of the resurrection. They did not believe in the resurrection, and yet here were the disciples preaching it. In truth the resurrection was the deathblow to all the philosophy and theology of the Sadducees. They were exceedingly disturbed. This message was being carried throughout the land. They therefore arrested the apostles and shut them up in prison. But an angel of the Lord came and opened the doors and told them to go and "speak in the temple to the people all the words of this life." Here was direct angelic, supernatural intervention.

So they went early in the morning in obedience to the command laid on them. Word of what was going on soon reached the high priest. Filled with amazement he called together the Sanhedrin of Israel and commanded that the apostles be brought before them. The officers went first to the prison, but returned saying, "The prison truly found we shut with all safety, and the keepers standing without before the doors; but when we had opened, we found no man within." Then they went to the temple and there they found the apostles preaching Christ, and brought them the second time before the chief priests. They reproved them saying, "Did not we straitly command you that ye should not teach in this name? and, behold, ye have filled Jerusalem with your doctrine, and intend to bring this man's blood upon us." They meant: "You are trying to give people the impression we are responsible for His death!" What had these same leaders said only a few weeks before in Pilate's judgment hall, when Pilate asked, "What shall I do?" They cried, "Let him be crucified...His blood be on us, and on our children." But now they say, "You are trying to bring this man's blood upon us." Oh, no, Peter was not trying to do that. But he was trying to show them that God had made a way through the shedding of the blood of the Lord Jesus Christ by which all their sins and guilt might be washed away if they would but trust in the Savior they had rejected.

Peter's Testimony (Acts 5:29-32)

Peter refused to stop teaching in the name of Jesus. He had received a commission from the Lord Himself to go into all the world and preach the gospel. He said, "We ought to obey God rather than men." Notice that the Christian has his responsibility to human government. As long as rulers do not attempt to thwart the purposes of God, the believer is to be subject to the powers-that-be. But when human government would hinder his obeying the Lord's voice, then it is for the child of God to answer with Peter, "We ought to obey God rather than men," and to be prepared to take the consequences.

Peter took this as an opportunity to preach to the leaders in Israel. The boldness of this man is amazing. Consider how cowardly he had been before—afraid to confess Jesus to the young girl on the porch, and later even cursed and swore that he did not know Him. Now you see him facing the most august assembly of Jewish leaders and philosophers, challenging them in the name of the Lord Jesus Christ. How can we account for it? It is accounted for by the fact he had received the Holy Spirit of God who had baptized him into Christ. He had anointed Peter, empowered him, as Jesus had promised. There was now no fear in him.

"The God of our fathers raised up Jesus, whom ye slew and hanged on a tree." Peter did not beat around the bush. He did not attempt to mollify these dignitaries in Israel. They were guilty. They had stirred up the rabble and so Peter faced them with their sin; not that they might be condemned but that they might be saved by turning to God in repentance.

"Him hath God exalted...to be a Prince and a Savior." That is the message of the gospel. That is the word we are to bring to all men everywhere today. We look toward the throne of God and there by faith we see the man Christ Jesus, who shed His precious blood for our redemption, sitting on the right hand of the Majesty in Heaven. There He is in the presence of God the Father, ever living to make intercession for us, and through His name the message of salvation is sent out into all the world.

The Lord Jesus Christ is the Savior. He is not simply a helper—be clear about that. Many believe that if we do our best, our part, the Lord Jesus will make up the rest. That is not the gospel at all. Somebody has suggested that in many places today the old hymn "Jesus Paid It All" might well be changed to read:

> Jesus paid a part,
> And I a part, you know;
> Sin had left a little stain,
> We washed it white as snow.

That is not the gospel. Christ did not say, "When you have done your best, I will make up the rest." Jesus is not a crutch, a makeshift. He is the Savior. He does it all!

I have often told about the man who had been converted and got up in a meeting to testify what the Lord had done for him. The leader, who was quite a legalist, said, "Our brother has told about God's part, but he forgot to tell his part before he was converted. Brother, haven't you something more to tell us?" The man replied: "Brethren, I completely forgot to tell you about my part. I sure did my part. I was doing my part running away from God as fast as I could for thirty years and God took after me 'til He ran me down. That was His part."

We do the sinning; He does the saving. That means He has to get all the glory. If salvation were a partnership affair, then when we get to Heaven we would sing, "Unto Him that loved us, and unto myself who did my best to put away my sin." But there will be nothing like that in Heaven. Jesus must get all the glory because He did it all.

And so Peter proclaimed Christ as a Prince and a Savior. As a Savior He is exalted to give repentance to Israel: repentance—change of mind, complete change of attitude. Well, these dear people in Israel had rejected Him. Now Christ is waiting for them to turn toward the One from whom they had turned away. That is repentance. And Gentiles also need to turn to Him from their sin and folly. When a sinner trusts in the Lord Jesus Christ, his sins are all put away and he stands before God as though he had never sinned at all.

People come to me and say, I have trusted Christ but I can't forget my sins. It may be salutary that you shouldn't forget them. It may be well for you to remember, in order that you may walk carefully. "Let him that thinketh he standeth take heed lest he fall" (1 Corinthians 10:12). But God has forgotten them! He says, "Their sins and their iniquities will I remember no more" (Hebrews 8:12). Of how many people is this true? Of all who put their trust in Jesus Christ. "To him give all the prophets witness, that through his name whosoever believeth in him shall receive remission of sins" (Acts 10:43).

That was Peter's message. That is the message we carry to the world. That is the message of the church. So often today some dear brethren forget their message is to go to the lost world. I often hear messages over the radio. I seldom manage to hear them in churches because I am constantly kept on the go. Some sermons I've heard broadcast are rhetorically beautiful and, so far as they go, true and Scriptural. Yet no mention is made about the blood of Jesus Christ, and no word is spoken about His atoning sacrifice! I hope the day will never come when I speak a half-hour without telling of Christ crucified. He is the only Savior for lost sinners, through whom forgiveness and justification are granted to all who trust Him. This is our message. It was Peter's message. "We are his witnesses of these things."

But our witness alone would not amount to very much. We do not have any power in ourselves. The power comes through the Holy Spirit whom God has given to those who repent and believe the gospel. When people repent and believe the message, then the Holy Spirit comes to seal them as God's beloved children and He indwells them, giving them power for testimony. Mark this—I shall only be given power for testimony if I do not grieve Him. The reason so many Christians are powerless is that they allow so many things in their lives, secretly or openly, to grieve the Spirit of God.

Vanity, pride, selfishness, carelessness, worldliness, unkind thoughts and feelings—all these things grieve Him. Covetousness grieves Him. The love of money grieves Him. There are so many other things we might add, which grieve the Holy Spirit of God and hinder the testimony for Christ. I wonder if we have all gone into the presence of the Lord and said, "Search me, O God, and know my heart: try me, and know my thoughts: And see if there be any wicked way in me" (Psalm 139:23-24). Then, did we wait for Him to search us, and have we dared to open our hearts to Him, and have we been honest with Him? Did we put these things out of our lives? If we were more zealous about this, we would count more for God. The Holy Spirit is given for testimony to them that obey Him, and it is as we walk in obedience that His power is revealed in our lives and words.

Gamaliel's Counsel (Acts 5:33-42)

We are told the learned doctors "were cut to the heart" by Peter's message. It sounds well, but it was not divine conviction. Their natural feelings were stirred—but with hatred. "They were cut to the heart, and took counsel to slay them." You see, instead of yielding to repentance through the Word of God, they hardened themselves and would have added sin to sin by killing the very messengers who told them of the grace of God in Christ Jesus.

But in the last section we read that there was one man among them whose name we always honor because of his kindly moderation. Of course, he should have gone farther than he did and said, "Brethren, these men are right. Let us turn to God, too, and accept His blessed Son." You will remember that Rabbi Gamaliel was the teacher of Saul of Tarsus. Saul had been brought up at his feet. Gamaliel turned to them and said in effect: "Brethren, let us not be too extreme. Take heed what you do touching these men. There have been people before who came among us with certain strange doctrines. There was a man who thought he was called of God to overturn the Roman power and deliver us from the Roman domination; and another who led a party out into the wilderness, proclaiming himself to be a divinely appointed leader. After a while their claims proved to be fraudulent. Now Jesus may be another man like them and perhaps these disciples are simply misled. By and by the truth will be made known. Of course, if they are right, we do not want to be found fighting against the truth. And if this be of God, you cannot overthrow it. Let us be careful, lest we be found fighting against God."

That was good advice. Yes, very good advice, as far as it went—but it did not go far enough. He should have said, "Brethren, let us investigate for ourselves, and if we find these men have a message from God, let us accept it with all our hearts." If Gamaliel had done that there might have been another Paul going throughout the world. At any rate, we give Gamaliel credit for his kindly spirit, and it is well to keep his counsel in mind and be very slow to judge anything that may turn out to be truly based on the Word of God.

"And to him they agreed: and when they had called the apostles, and beaten them [they weren't going to kill them, or keep them in jail; the beating showed what their feelings were], they commanded that they should not speak in the name of Jesus, and let them go."

We read, "They departed from the presence of the council, rejoicing that they were counted worthy to suffer shame for his name. And daily in the temple, and in every house, they ceased not to teach and preach Jesus Christ." They could not do otherwise. Their hearts were full of Christ and out of the abundance of the heart the mouth speaketh. And if our hearts are full of Christ and if we really know Him as our Savior, we will want to tell others about Him.

Would you not like to know Him? Would you not like to acquaint yourself with Him and be at peace? "He that believeth on the Son hath everlasting life."

CHAPTER SIX

CHECKING DISSENSION IN THE CHURCH

In Acts 6 we see brought out very vividly Satan's two master methods by which he has endeavored to hinder the work of God throughout the centuries. In the first half of the chapter we see him endeavoring to hinder by inward dissension; in the second half by outward persecution. In the Epistle to the Philippians Paul urged the believers to go on together in the unity of the Spirit. He told them that as long as they work together in love and unity they need never be afraid of the attitude from without. Even their adversaries realize it is impossible to hinder those who stand together in Christian harmony. But if that inward peace is destroyed, then the church is weakened when it has to face a godless world.

Choosing the Seven (Acts 6:1-7)

In the first four verses of Acts 6 we see Satan trying to disturb the inward peace of the church. God had accomplished a wonderful thing. Day after day and week after week ever since Pentecost, God had "added to the church daily such as should be saved." Three thousand definitely stepped out from among the multitudes who rejected Christ on the day of Pentecost; another two thousand were added shortly after. Then in Acts 5 we learned that a great many believers were added to the Lord, and it looked as though Christianity was to sweep everything before it.

Satan saw that he must busy himself if he was to hinder this work. He found access to the hearts even of God's own children and started a spirit of murmuring and complaining among them, for he knows that if he can set believer against believer, he will easily accomplish his fell purpose.

Oh, how many a church, how many a testimony for God, has been destroyed in that way! God may be graciously working, precious souls are being saved, and then some member gets an idea that he is not being appreciated. He begins murmuring and goes around in the church complaining against his brethren. Little unkind things are said reflecting on others, and so a spirit of opposition develops. Then people wonder why the work of God does not make more progress, and why there does not seem to be more power in the ministry, and why more souls are not being saved. It is all because there is a root of bitterness inside, which is not judged. How many warnings we have in God's Word against such things! He has told us to avoid murmuring and evil speaking.

A brother was strongly denouncing another brother to a friend of mine, and pointing out his faults and inconsistencies. My friend turned to him and asked quietly, "Is it because you love your brother that you are talking like this?" The calumniator blushed with shame. It is not love that leads people to do this; it is Satan acting through God's people and leading them to take an unkind or discourteous attitude toward their brethren.

In this way Satan tried to disrupt the church at Jerusalem. In the days when so many were being saved and the Spirit of God was working so mightily, one would think that there would have been no place for murmuring or selfishness. But it was in those very days that "there arose a murmuring of the Grecians against the Hebrews because their widows were neglected in the daily ministration." The word *Grecians* does not mean "Gentiles." It should be translated "Hellenists." It signifies Jews who were born not in Palestine, but in other lands where Greek was the language commonly used. In other words, they were Greek-speaking Jews. Up to this time the Gentiles had not been brought into the church at Jerusalem. Those converted on the day of Pentecost were Jewish and the Gentiles that had been converted or proselytized were all linked with the house of Israel in some way. The Hellenist Christians had a great many Gentile ways about them because they were brought up among the Greeks. The Hebrews were the Jews of Palestine who were much more rigid observers of the law of Moses than the Hellenists. A great deal of bitterness existed between these two groups. The Hebrews of Palestine, very proud of their heritage, looked with suspicion and sometimes with contempt at their fellow Jews who were born among the Gentiles. The Hellenistic Jews, who gloried in their wider freedom, felt that the Hebrews of Palestine were very narrow-minded and self-centered.

This spirit of dissension, which existed before their conversion, cropped up after they were saved. When people are saved, the new nature they receive does not entirely change their old nature. We still have our natural tendencies which we must judge continually in the presence of God. A brother lost his temper during a meeting and at the close apologized: "You must excuse me, it's the Irish in me." A dear brother quietly said, "God can make the Irishman behave like a Christian." We are not to excuse ourselves if we go wrong because of national characteristics.

These Hellenist Jews and the Hebrews of Palestine were converted and brought to Christ, yet Satan found a means of creating dissension among them. The Hellenist Jews said, "Our widows are neglected in the daily ministration." In other words, "If a Jewish widow born in Palestine comes for help she gets two loaves; but a Hellenist widow only one. Our widows are not being treated fairly." So they began to complain and murmur.

I have no doubt that those disciples who had charge of the food distribution tried to be fair and upright, but it is not easy to please everybody. It is so easy to imagine people treating us coldly and indifferently. We find fault with so many things for which we have no real ground of complaint.

However, the twelve immediately called the rest of the disciples together and said, "It is not reason that we should leave the word of God, and serve tables." I suppose the complainers had gone to these leaders and said, "You ought to do something about this; there must be a fairer method of administration." But the twelve answered in effect, "Brethren, we have an important job to do. Our business is to minister the Word of God." But recognizing that the care of the physical needs of the people required attention, they commanded: "Wherefore, brethren, look ye out among you seven men of honest report, full of the Holy Ghost and wisdom, whom we may appoint over this business." In other words they said, "You think that some are not acting honestly? Then you choose seven men, seven deacons of your own selection, so you will have no more reason to complain, but they should be men of honest report." It takes a man of integrity to handle the finances of the church; a man full of the Holy Ghost to care for the temporal things of the assembly as well as to preach the Word. The disciples continued, "But we will give ourselves continually to prayer, and to the ministry of the word."

Notice the order—prayer first, and then the ministry. Often the ministry of the Word seems so powerless and weak because there is so little prayer behind it. A man of God must be a man of prayer; he must know the importance of waiting on God in private if he is to have the power of God in public. The twelve said as it were, "Our business is to spend our time in the presence of God in order that we may receive a message from Him and present that message in the energy of the Holy Ghost, that it may be used in the building up of the saints." God grant that we too may ever have this ideal before us!

We are told that "the saying pleased the whole multitude." Apparently everybody had an opportunity to express himself. It is amazing how little of church politics you find in the selection of these seven men. I do not know of any worse form of politics than that wherein someone tries to dominate or control a certain situation in the church. There was nothing of that here.

One might have expected the people to say, "We must be sure to have three Palestinian Jews, three Hellenists, and then we will let these six decide on the seventh one." That's the way we might do it today. But they did not do that at all. When the matter was put up before the whole church they met together and chose seven Hellenistic Jews! Every one of them had a Greek name: Stephen, Philip, Prochorus, Nicanor, Timon, Parmenas, and Nicolas. Nicolas was not even a Jew, but a Gentile who had been a proselyte to Judaism and a convert of Christianity. Instead of having a mixed committee, one not likely to dominate the situation for any one group, they said, "We will make up a committee entirely of the party that is doing the complaining." Imagine their putting these brethren in charge of the care of physical needs.

"And the word of God increased, and the number of the disciples multiplied in Jerusalem greatly." When dissension is checked within, then Satan's work is hindered without, and the work of God continues in great power and blessing. My brethren, is there not something here that ought to speak to every one of our hearts? Are you praying for a revival and blessing in the church of God? Do you ever go into the presence of God and say, "Lord, revive me. Is there something in me that hinders a revival; has this tongue of mine been working overtime to hinder the work of the Spirit of God?" If we have, we may all say, "God, give me grace to judge it in the presence of the Lord, that the Holy Spirit may have free course and the Word go forth with great power."

The Persecution of Stephen (Acts 6:8-15)

We are told in a later Epistle of Paul's that "they that have used the office of a deacon well purchase to themselves a good degree, and great boldness in the faith which is in Christ Jesus" (1 Timothy 3:13). And we find in Acts 6:8 that one of these men who had been appointed as a deacon to serve tables fulfilled his ministry so blessedly that God said to him, "Stephen, I have a wider ministry for you; I have something more for you to do." We read, "Stephen, full of faith and power, did great wonders and miracles among the people." This is the first time we read of any member of the church, other than the apostles, doing miracles. God put His hand on Stephen and He used him to perform miracles and wonders. If you are faithful in a little place, God will have a much larger place for you. If you are faithful in things that are small, He will put you in a place over things that are large (see Matthew 25:23). People want to do such big things, but they are often not willing to do the little things.

Stephen had been true and faithful in serving tables and so God said, "I want you to go out and preach." But this led to renewed persecution. The devil had not been able to disrupt the work by inward dissension, so he decided to try another method with Stephen. We read: "There arose certain of the synagogue, which is called the synagogue of the Libertines, and Cyrenians, and Alexandrians, and of them of Cilicia and of Asia, disputing with Stephen. And they were not able to resist the wisdom and the spirit by which he spake." These objectors argued with him; they would rise up in the meetings to ask questions and find fault. But Stephen, full of faith and the Holy Ghost, was more than a match for them all. When they could not accuse him openly they acted underhandedly. "They suborned men, which said, We have heard him speak blasphemous words against Moses, and against God." We may be sure of this: Stephen never said one blasphemous word against either Moses or God.

But these false witnesses, goaded on by others who had been opposing the truth of God, "stirred up the people, and the elders, and the scribes, and came upon him, and caught him, and brought him to the council." What were the blasphemous words? Well, they tried lamely to suggest something: "We heard him say, that this Jesus of Nazareth shall destroy this place, and shall change the customs which Moses delivered us."

Had Stephen said that? Certainly not. Had they heard anything like it? Yes, for Jesus Christ had prophesied that Jerusalem and the temple would be destroyed (as they were in A.D. 70). Also, Jesus Christ had declared the new dispensation would succeed the old (as it did in the providence of God). And so they were simply misusing the words that had been reported from the lips of Jesus Christ. You know the old saying, "Half a truth is a whole lie." If you take someone's words out of their context and turn them around you can easily make him out a falsifier.

We are told of Stephen that "all that sat in the council, looking stedfastly on him, saw his face as it had been the face of an angel." I wish I could have a photograph or picture of Stephen standing before the council, listening to all those false accusations, and noticing the expressions of rage, ridicule, and indignation on the faces of his accusers. Yet he stood there, looking at them with a radiant countenance, full of love, trust, peace, and confidence, undisturbed by all the bitter things that were being said. His heart was not filled with malice because of their hatred toward him, but joy in the realization that he was there as Christ's faithful servant.

In the next chapter we read of his defense, but we leave him now facing the council with a countenance like an angel. Stephen has been with the Lord for many years but he has never lost that countenance. He is in glory, still with the face as that of an angel.

We remember the story that our Lord told of the nobleman who went into a far country to receive for himself a kingdom and to return. But his citizens hated him and sent a message after him saying, "We will not have this man to reign over us" (Luke 19:14). Evidently when the Lord Jesus related that parable He looked forward to this very day. He had been crucified and had gone into the far country. Now after some months the Word of God had been preached to Israel, but nationally they were unchanged, as proved by their attitude toward Stephen.

CHAPTER SEVEN
STEPHEN'S DEFENSE AND MARTYRDOM

A t the close of the sixth chapter we saw Stephen standing before the Jewish Sanhedrin, where he was called into account for preaching Jesus crucified and raised again from the dead. One might have thought that his glorious face, lit up as it was by the light of Heaven, would have softened the hearts of those who sat in judgment upon him, but it seemed to have the opposite effect. It stirred up more hatred against him and against the gospel he preached.

The Promise to Abraham (Acts 7:1-8)

The high priest put the question to Stephen, "Are these things so?" That is, "Did you really say that Jesus of Nazareth was to destroy the temple and change the customs Moses delivered?"

In Acts 7 we have Stephen's defense. We might say we see Stephen led by the God of glory up to the glory of God. You will notice verse 55, "But he, being full of the Holy Ghost, looked up stedfastly into heaven, and saw the glory of God."

He begins his defense by relating God's dealing with their great progenitor Abraham; how God led Abraham out of the land of the Chaldeans and brought him into the land of Canaan, and definitely promised the land of Canaan to him and to his seed after him. But Abraham died without possessing any of it, except the grave in which he buried his wife Sarah. Yet Stephen had the confidence that eventually Abraham would possess the land of Canaan, which God promised to him. It is true he has passed on to a better country, "for he looked for a city which hath foundations, whose builder and maker is God." But nevertheless, the promise remains, that land shall yet be the dwelling place of the seed of Abraham.

The Egyptian Bondage (Acts 7:9-16)

In this section our attention is drawn to some remarkable facts. Stephen showed how God permitted the people of Israel to go down to Egypt, at first to be favorably received and then to fall into sad bondage and slavery. He reminded his hearers how they were eventually delivered. But here he emphasized the patriarchs' relationship to their brother Joseph. They hated Joseph because he was their father's favorite. He was hated also for his dreams that told of his coming glory, and so they sold him to the Ishmaelites who carried him down into Egypt.

Joseph is a type of Christ. He was rejected at first, but the day came when his brethren bowed before him and recognized his authority. The story of Joseph pictures Christ's first and second advent. Our blessed Savior when He came the first time was rejected. His own people spurned Him, refused Him, and the Gentiles put Him to death on Calvary's cross. But that is not the end of the story. He is coming again and will be manifested in power. The day will come when His own earthly people will bow before His feet and recognize Him as their Brother, Jesus who is also their Savior and their Lord.

The Wilderness Experience (Acts 7:17-50)

Stephen proceeded to tell of the deliverance from Egypt through Moses, who was rejected the first time and then later received. It is easy to follow the logic in Stephen's mind. He is pointing out to the people of Israel that invariably in their history they rejected their deliverer the first time and accepted him the second time. The story of Moses is somewhat different. Moses' life divides into three sections of forty years each. He spent forty years learning the wisdom of the Egyptians and forty years unlearning it and learning instead the wisdom of God. After that, he was forty years leading the Israelites through the wilderness until they came to the borders of the land of Canaan.

Stephen emphasized that from the beginning there was a great love in Moses' heart for his people and he longed to see them freed from bondage. He went out and tried to help alleviate their suffering and distress, but they did not want his help. They said, "Who made thee a ruler and a judge over us?" They rejected him and he had to leave Egypt and go to the far side of the desert, where he remained for forty years. In the meantime his people were enduring greater and greater suffering, all because they had rejected their redeemer.

What a picture of Israel down through the centuries! God raised up Jesus in accordance with His prophecy by Moses: "The Lord thy God will raise up unto thee a Prophet from the midst of thee, of thy brethren, like unto me; unto him ye shall hearken" (Deuteronomy 18:15). And so Jesus came, "to preach the gospel to the poor...to preach deliverance to the captives, and recovering of sight to the blind, to set at liberty them that are bruised." But they did not understand; they spurned Him and said, "We will not have this man to reign over us." "We have no king but Caesar." So God took Him up on high. We read in Hosea 5:15: "I will go and return to my place, till they acknowledge their offense, and seek my face: in their affliction they will seek me early." Has any nation suffered as Israel has suffered? Has any nation endured as much? In Lamentations 1:12 we read: "Is it nothing to you, all ye that pass by? behold, and see if there be any sorrow like unto my sorrow, which is done unto me, wherewith the Lord hath afflicted me in the day of his fierce anger."

You may ask, Why this affliction—why has God permitted this suffering to come upon the people with whom He chose to enter into covenant relationship? It is because in the time of His visitation, when the Deliverer came, they spurned Him. Israel had to stay forty years longer in Egypt because they did not recognize Moses as their deliverer, but in due time they did receive him. Forty years in Scripture is the full period of testing and trial.

God met Moses in the wilderness at Mount Horeb by the burning bush—in itself a symbol of the nation of Israel. The bush burned continuously but was not consumed; and Israel has suffered continuously but remains today. And Israel will remain when the last of the Hitlers and anti-Semites have passed away because God has said, "This people have I formed for myself." But when will they be brought into the place of blessing? When the great Prophet comes the second time, then "they shall look upon me whom they pierced, and they shall mourn for him, as one mourneth for his only son, and shall be in bitterness for him, as one that is in bitterness for his firstborn" (Zechariah 12:10).

Stephen showed that Moses, in his rejection at first, and acceptance the second time, is a type of the Lord Jesus Christ.

> This is that Moses, which said unto the children of Israel, A prophet shall the Lord your God raise up unto you of your brethren, like unto me: him shall ye hear. This is he, that was in the church in the wilderness [that is, the congregation of the Lord of old in the wilderness] with the angel which spake to him in the mount Sinai, and with our fathers: who received the lively oracles to give unto us: To whom our fathers would not obey, but thrust him from them, and in their hearts turned back again into Egypt (Acts 7:37-39).

Israel's history down through the centuries has been that of forgetting God and turning to the ways of the Gentiles, all of which accounts for their continual suffering.

Egypt is a type of the world, and it is quite possible for Christians in their hearts to turn back to Egypt—the world—and not know what crucifixion with Christ means. Many are not able to say with Paul, "God forbid that I should glory, save in the cross of our Lord Jesus Christ, by whom the world is crucified unto me, and I unto the world" (Galatians 6:14). It is one thing to recognize we are dead to the corrupt world, dead to the licentious world, dead to the vulgar world; it is quite another thing to recognize that the cross of Christ comes also between the believer and the esthetic world. A great many of us who are not tempted by the corruption of the world, fall under the spell of the culture and refinement of the world. We love the world's songs, its plays, its art; the result being that our hearts are largely in the world instead of wrapped up in God Himself. We may learn a lesson from the experiences of Israel as we continue to read the charge Stephen gave.

The children of Israel said, "Make us gods to go before us: for as for this Moses, which brought us out of the land of Egypt, we wot not what is become of him" (Acts 7:40). You see, Moses had gone up into the holy mount to receive the tables of the covenant from God and they could not see him. They wanted a leader they could see. It is easier to walk by sight, than by faith. "They made a calf in those days, and offered sacrifice unto the idol, and rejoiced in the works of their own hands. Then God turned, and gave them up to worship the host of heaven." He allowed them to sink into idolatry and experience the result of its dreadful corruption.

Stephen continued by quoting from the Old Testament prophet Amos 5:25-26:

> O ye house of Israel, have ye offered to me slain beasts and sacrifices by the space of forty years in the wilderness? Yea, ye took up the tabernacle of Moloch, and the star of your god Remphan, figures which ye made to worship them: and I will carry you away beyond Babylon (Acts 7:42-43).

The reason given here for the captivity in Babylon was that the people made the calf in the wilderness. Even in that distant past they cherished false gods and had never judged that sin. This is a solemn thought. Let us never forget: Sin never dies of old age! It goes on working like leprosy, until it is dealt with in the presence of God. They never judged that sin and it led them deeper and deeper into idolatry for which they were eventually driven into captivity.

Stephen's Final Indictment (Acts 7:51-60)

And so Stephen rehearsed the history of Israel up to the building of the temple by Solomon and showed how God all along had displayed His grace but they had been continuously rebellious against Him. Then he turned on the audience and cried, "You are just like your fathers were!" It took courage for Stephen to say this. It was like the prisoner putting the judge on the docket. There sat the leaders of Israel to judge him, but this devoted servant of God spoke the word that judged them! "Ye stiffnecked and uncircumcised in heart and ears, ye do always resist the Holy Ghost: as your fathers did, so do ye." What a tragic indictment that was, and how true it still is! God through the Holy Spirit has spoken to us as a people in many, many ways, but we have rejected His testimony, spurned His Word, and resisted the Holy Spirit. God give us grace to humble ourselves before we are broken in judgment. For we must either bow in penitence under the mighty hand of God or be humbled in the day when His judgments are poured out on us.

Stephen continued:

> Which of the prophets have not your fathers persecuted? and they have slain them which showed before of the coming of the Just One [that is, of the Lord Jesus]; of whom ye have been now the betrayers and murderers: Who have received the law by the disposition of angels, and have not kept it (52-53).

There they stopped him. He hadn't finished; he had a great deal more to say. He doubtless intended to go on and present the claims of the Lord Jesus Christ, but they would hear no more. "Cut to the heart," they ground their teeth in hatred of him.

"But he, being full of the Holy Ghost, looked up stedfastly into heaven, and saw the glory of God, and Jesus standing on the right hand of God." This is very significant. We are told in the Epistle to the Hebrews that when Jesus had by Himself purged our sins, He sat down on the right hand of the Majesty on high; but here, as Stephen looked up, he saw the Lord standing. What does it mean? It is just as though the blessed Lord in His great compassion for Stephen had risen from His seat and was looking over the battlements of Heaven to strengthen and cheer the martyr down on earth. Stephen exclaimed, "Behold, I see the heavens opened, and the Son of Man standing on the right hand of God." That revealing vision should have broken them down, brought them to repentance, and shown them they were fighting against their own best interests. Instead (so hardened were they in their sins), "they cried out with a loud voice, and stopped their ears, and ran upon him with one accord, And cast him out of the city, and stoned him: and the witnesses laid down their clothes at a young man's feet, whose name was Saul."

Thus Saul comes into the picture. He was to take up the story that Stephen had to drop.

They stoned Stephen, as he called on the Lord, "Receive my spirit." "And he kneeled down, and cried with a loud voice, Lord, lay not this sin to their charge." Oh, the love that filled that man's heart! "Don't judge them for this." It was like the beloved Master saying, "Father, forgive them; for they know not what they do."

And with these words he fell asleep—and that is what death is to the Christian, falling asleep. The fear of death is gone,

> [For Christ] also himself likewise took part of the same; that through death he might destroy him that had the power of death, that is, the devil; And deliver them who through the fear of death were all their lifetime subject to bondage (Hebrews 2:14-15).

CHAPTER EIGHT

THE GOSPEL'S ENTRY INTO SAMARIA

G od sometimes has to act through disagreeable circumstances in order to compel His saints to work in accordance with His plan for them. We have seen, in studying this book of Acts, that at the very beginning the Lord Jesus Christ laid out a program for the evangelization of the entire world. He said, "Ye shall receive power, after that the Holy Ghost is come upon you: and ye shall be witnesses unto me both in Jerusalem, and in all Judea, and in Samaria, and unto the uttermost part of the earth." Up to the present then we have found the gospel going out in the city of Jerusalem and throughout Judea, but the disciples were very, very slow in fulfilling the rest of the program. God, however, waited in wondrous grace for them to fulfill His mandate. He desired that any in Israel who were prepared to bow their hearts in repentance should receive the message first and then it was to go out into the rest of the world. So He permitted what we call the transitional period, before the work was carried to the nations generally.

I remind you that when I use the words *transitional period* I am referring to a period that must be understood as in the mind of man—not in the mind of God. The moment the work of the cross was finished and the Holy Spirit came to empower believers to preach the gospel to the uttermost parts of the earth, God's mind was toward all men everywhere, but it took His servants some time to understand His viewpoint. He was very patient with them.

Persecution Increases (Acts 8:1-4)

The apostles had been preaching for a number of years in Jerusalem and Judea, and many Jews had been brought to a saving knowledge of the Lord Jesus Christ. But so far no one had carried the message beyond the confines of Israel.

Following the death of Stephen, God allowed greater persecution to break out in Jerusalem and Judea in order that His Word might be scattered abroad, that His purpose might be fulfilled. "There was a great persecution against the church which was at Jerusalem; and they were all scattered abroad throughout the regions of Judea and Samaria." Thus Christians went out into the whole land of Palestine—"except the apostles"—the very ones who had been commissioned to preach to every creature. For some reason they remained behind in Jerusalem while the rest of the disciples (those who had been converted under them) fled from the persecution and carried the gospel wherever they went, but at first only to the Jews.

We note that Stephen was buried by godly Jews, perhaps not actually by the disciples themselves, for the term may refer to pious Jews who repudiated the act of stoning Stephen.

But now Saul, the bitter persecutor, "made havock of the church, entering into every house, and haling men and women committed them to prison. Therefore they that were scattered abroad went everywhere preaching the word." Thus many were hearing the gospel who might otherwise have been left in ignorance of it.

Philip in Samaria (Acts 8:5-25)

The Philip referred to in these verses was not Philip the apostle, but one of the seven deacons who had been appointed to help in distributing bread among the Christian converts. He was another man who used the office of a deacon well! He was set apart to minister in the temporal affairs of the church but he had been so faithful, true, and conscientious in carrying out his responsibilities that the Spirit of God committed to him a greater ministry (see 1 Timothy 3:13). We saw that the same was true of Stephen also. The Spirit sent Philip out to preach Christ to the people of Samaria. I call your attention to his message. He did not go to them with what some people call "the social gospel," and he did not go to talk to them on political subjects. Philip had one message and one Person to present to the people: the message of redemption and the Person of Christ who accomplished that redemption. The message of God's servants today should be the same as his, for "the preaching of the cross is to them that perish foolishness; but unto us which are saved it is the power of God" (1 Corinthians 1:18).

These poor, despised Samaritans, hated by the Jews because of their religious differences, "with one accord gave heed unto those things which Philip spake, hearing and seeing the miracles which he did." God granted mighty signs to accompany him as he ministered the Word, "For unclean spirits, crying with loud voice, came out of many that were possessed with them: and many taken with palsies, and that were lame, were healed. And there was great joy in that city."

It was a wonderful awakening. Undoubtedly the city of Samaria was largely prepared for it because our Lord when on earth passed through Samaria on various occasions and ministered to the people. Many indeed had already been brought to accept Him as Messiah. Therefore, when these Jewish missionaries came to them and told them that the same Christ who had died for them was living to save them, they gave heed. Moreover, they saw how the mighty God was working in healing the sick and demoniacs; and many who believed were baptized.

But we are told, "There was a certain man, called Simon, which beforetime in the same city used sorcery." This Simon Magus was what we would call a magician, a charlatan, who had "bewitched the people of Samaria, giving out that himself was some great one." Such men as he were very common in the Orient not only before and during the days when our Lord was here on earth, but afterwards, when the gospel was first being carried to the different nations of the world outside of Palestine. This sorcerer was operating inside the land of promise; not exactly among the Israelites, but among these people whom the Jews considered a mongrel nation. Probably Simon was himself a renegade Jew and had heard of the great works of Jesus. At any rate, he claimed to be a miracle worker and by his trickery and so-called magic had deceived the people: "To whom all gave heed, from the least to the greatest, saying, This man is the great power of God."

"But when they believed Philip preaching the things concerning the kingdom of God, and the name of Jesus Christ, they were baptized, both men and women." Philip's message naturally turned them away from Simon. Now that they had heard the truth, they turned away from the false. Simon therefore decided he had best join this new movement. So we read, "Then Simon himself believed also: and when he was baptized, he continued with Philip, and wondered, beholding the miracles and signs which were done." It is important for us to remember there is a belief that results in salvation, but on the other hand, there is a belief that may not result in salvation. In other words, it is possible to accept many facts concerning Jesus Christ from a merely historical standpoint. One can believe a great deal about Him and yet not be saved. But you cannot believe in Jesus as your personal Savior without being numbered among the redeemed. These Samaritans heard Philip and trusted the Savior he proclaimed. Even Simon listened and believed many things Philip said, and came forward to be baptized. Philip baptized him because it was God's appointed way of separating His people outwardly from the unsaved. In the beginning it was God's way of separating the remnant of Israel from the nation that was under His judgment. In Samaria it was God's way of separating believers from the prevalent religious system.

Because Simon was baptized does not necessarily mean that he was born of God. I know there are people who believe baptism and salvation are one and the same thing. Simon was a man who seemed just like the others, but there was no real faith in his soul, no true repentance toward God. I am afraid there are a great many people in Christendom today who have been baptized and have given intellectual assent to the truths of God's Word but have never faced their sins before God. They have never committed themselves to Him and trusted Christ as their own Savior. If you are resting on the fact that you have joined a church, or been baptized, or partaken from time to time in the communion of the Lord's supper, face your condition honestly before God! Ask yourself: Have I, as a repentant sinner, turned to God in faith? Have I trusted Christ as my Savior? Is He the Lord of my life? If these things are not true, if you cannot answer these questions in the affirmative, then the fact that you have been baptized and are outwardly linked with the people of God does not make you a Christian. You are not yet saved, nor born again.

We see in Simon a baptized man, a religious professor, who had not been regenerated. He simply wanted a place in the Christian company. He despaired of winning these people back unless he could come in among them and pose as a Christian leader. Then he hoped to gain them to himself. So "when he was baptized, he continued with Philip, and wondered, beholding the miracles and signs which were done."

Notice that up to this time matters in Samaria had been moving along just as in Jerusalem at the beginning. But these Samaritan believers had not yet received the Pentecostal blessing, the outpouring of the Holy Spirit. We read,

> When the apostles which were at Jerusalem heard that Samaria had received the word of God, they sent unto them Peter and John [two of their outstanding leaders]: Who, when they were come down, prayed for them [the Samaritan believers], that they might receive the Holy Ghost: (For as yet he was fallen upon none of them: only they were baptized in the name of the Lord Jesus.) (Acts 8:14-16)

The expression "in the name of" always implies "by His authority." It does not mean they were not baptized in the name of the Father and of the Son and of the Holy Spirit, for that is what Jesus told His disciples to do (Matthew 28:19). They were baptized in the name of, or by the authority of, the Lord Jesus. But they had not yet received the Holy Spirit; they had not been baptized into the body of Christ.

When these disciples came down, they laid their hands on them, thus identifying this new church in Samaria with the work in Jerusalem. So when they laid their hands on them, they received the Holy Spirit, and doubtless there were many outward signs.

Why did not these Samaritans receive the Spirit of God the moment they professed faith in the Lord Jesus Christ? Later in Acts, when we read of Peter going to the house of Cornelius, we are told that the moment Peter spoke the words, the Holy Ghost fell on all them that heard the Word. But here we have an interval between the time the Samaritans accepted the message preached by Philip and the time they received the Holy Spirit. The reason, I think, is perfectly clear. For something like five hundred years the temple at Jerusalem and the temple at Mt. Gerizim had been rival sanctuaries. The Jews in the south and the Samaritans north of Jerusalem had each claimed to be God's chosen people, and there was intense rivalry between them. One can understand that if the Spirit had immediately fallen on these Samaritan believers, when they received the Word, then the strife between the Jews and Samaritans might have been perpetuated. There might have been down through the centuries two different groups of Christians, each claiming to be the true church. But when the apostles came from Jerusalem and identified themselves with the believing Samaritans, and God gave the Holy Ghost to them in answer to the prayers of the apostles, the work was recognized definitely and openly as one. There was only one body, whether Jews in Judea or Samaritans in Samaria. All were joined into one body of which the risen Christ was the Head. There was not the same danger of rivalry between two groups when the gospel was brought to the Gentiles whose pagan religion was very different from Judaism.

And now Simon was looking on, and when he saw what was taking place he offered the apostles money, saying, "Give me also this power, that on whomsoever I lay hands, he may receive the Holy Ghost." This shows how little Simon had entered into the truth of the gospel. If he had understood, he would have known God gives freely, without money and without price. No spiritual blessing can ever be purchased. I think Christendom today has largely forgotten that. I have heard of people on their deathbeds calling in preachers or priests and offering to turn over properties if their sins might be forgiven and a place assured them in Heaven. It is a delusion! "The wages of sin is death; but the gift of God is eternal life through Jesus Christ our Lord." And the Holy Spirit coming to indwell believers is as truly a gift of God as the blessed Son He gave to die on the cross was His gift for the redemption of guilty man.

So when Simon offered the apostles money for the power of the Holy Spirit, Peter looked at him with indignation and said, "Thy money perish with thee, because thou hast thought that the gift of God may be purchased with money." Notice the strength of that! If the gift of God could be purchased with money, it would not be a gift! God is saving men without money on the basis of the finished work of His beloved Son. And because Jesus has been glorified, He has sent forth the Holy Spirit to empower believers to proclaim the gospel.

Peter continued, "Thou hast neither part nor lot in this matter: for thy heart is not right in the sight of God." Peter, filled with the Holy Spirit, was able to see through all the pretense and camouflage, through all the outward profession of this man Simon Magus. Philip, the deacon, was deceived by him. He did not have the gift of discerning of spirits, but Peter saw into the very depths of the man's being and declared, "Thy heart is not right in the sight of God." Many of us do not have that ability of discerning, but we can at least see that if anyone thinks he can purchase the gift of God, that heart is not right in the sight of God. Such an one may not be as great a hypocrite as this man Simon, but he has not yet faced things honestly in the sight of God.

Peter called on Simon to repent. "Repent therefore of this thy wickedness." We have pointed out that this word *repent* means to "change the mind," that is to change the attitude. Peter was saying in effect, "You need not go on like this. Change your attitude. Face things honestly before God. Repent of your wickedness, and pray to the Lord (the best versions read, the Lord Jesus Christ) if perhaps the thought of your heart may be forgiven."

Peter continued, "For I perceive that thou art in the gall of bitterness, and in the bond of iniquity." There is something exceedingly solemn here: a man outwardly in fellowship with the church of God, but whose heart is not right with God. There are many like this; many who need the same admonition that Peter gave to Simon:

"Repent of this thy wickedness!" Simon did not seem to be very much affected. Instead of turning to the Lord himself, he said, "Pray ye to the Lord for me, that none of these things which ye have spoken come upon me." And that is the last we hear of him in the pages of Holy Scripture. We hear about him a great deal in early church writings—that he became the first antichrist, and went from place to place opposing the gospel. But he turned here to Peter and said, "I want you to pray for me." Did you ever hear of people doing that? He said, "Peter, I put my case in your hands." A lot of people are doing that today. If you do not go directly to Christ, Peter cannot do anything for you, nor can any of the saints; not even the virgin Mary, the mother of our blessed Lord. Remember, there is one mediator between God and men, the man Christ Jesus. Why not go directly to Him and put your case in His hands!

This incident closes with verse 25 in which we are told that, when they had testified and preached the Word of the Lord, the apostles returned to Jerusalem. On their way there, they preached the gospel in many villages of the Samaritans. Thus we see them reaching out to the second group of which our Lord had spoken (Acts 1:8). As we pursue our study of Acts, we will see the river of grace ever widening until it reaches the uttermost part of the earth.

The Conversion of the Ethiopian (Acts 8:26-40)

God's ways are not our ways. He often interrupts our plans and our service in very remarkable ways that we find perhaps difficult to understand. I think we have such a case here. Just when things seemed to be at their best, when revival was spreading through the Samaritan villages, the Lord laid His hand on Philip and spoke to him through supernatural methods ("the angel of the Lord"), saying, "Arise, and go toward the south unto the way that goeth down from Jerusalem unto Gaza, which is desert." One would not have been surprised if the record stated that Philip sought to reason with the angel, and that he might have said, "See the wonderful work going on here! I do not think that my work is finished by any means. Should I leave these fruitful fields and go to a desert—a desert actually and spiritually, too?"

But there was no objection; he went immediately at the command of the angel and was led to a man in a chariot. Now you must not think of this as if Philip had just met a single individual driving a chariot across the desert. Undoubtedly what Philip saw was a great caravan—soldiers, merchants, retinue—and in the midst a chariot (which would stand out over everything else), the chariot of the treasurer of Candace queen of Ethiopia. The man in that chariot had gone to Jerusalem on a spiritual quest. He was an Ethiopian Gentile, not a Jew; but he had it in his heart, apparently, to know the God of Israel and had come all the way from Ethiopia to Jerusalem to worship the true God. He was probably a proselyte to Judaism. He had accepted the revelation God gave Israel so far as he understood it. But you can imagine his heartsickness when he came to Jerusalem and found there nothing but cold formality. If he had been asking in his heart, "How may I, a poor sinner, come into fellowship with God?" there was no answer. He was returning to his home a disappointed—and doubtless disillusioned—man. Yet he had obtained in Jerusalem one thing that was of great importance—a portion of God's holy Word.

He had acquired the book of the prophet Isaiah. The Ethiopian was so interested in it, so anxious to find out what it had to say to his own heart and conscience that, as the horses jogged along dragging the chariot across the desert, he read from that book. How wonderfully God times things! The man had read to a part that filled his mind with questions and stirred his heart, and at that very moment he saw a stranger coming across the sands to the side of his chariot. For the Spirit had said to Philip, "Go near, and join thyself to this chariot." The man was reading aloud the words we find in Isaiah 53.

Philip, leaning over the side of the chariot, said, "Do you understand what you are reading?" The Ethiopian looked at him, doubtless in amazement, saying in effect, "How can I? I am a poor ignorant man from Ethiopia. Oh that I had someone to explain the words to me!" He invited Philip to come and sit with him and then pointed to the passage: "He was led as a sheep to the slaughter; and like a lamb dumb before his shearer, so opened he not his mouth: in his humiliation his judgment was taken away: and who shall declare his generation? for his life is taken from the earth." The form in which these words come to us shows that the manuscript the Ethiopian held was not the original Hebrew. He probably could not read the Hebrew of the Jews: he was reading Greek, for this is from the Greek translation of the Old Testament—the Septuagint. The Greek idiom had become almost universal for business transactions.

As the eunuch pondered the words he wondered who the one could be who silently stood like a lamb dumb before his shearer. Who was this man whose judgment was taken away and evidently died a sacrificial death for others? He turned to Philip and asked earnestly, "I pray thee, of whom speaketh the prophet this? of himself, or of some other man?" No, the words did not refer to the prophet himself, even though Isaiah had been a great sufferer for the testimony of the Messiah. We are told in Jewish history that he was sawn asunder for his faithfulness. Jewish scholars tried to apply this passage to the prophet Jeremiah, saying he was the one despised and rejected of man. But on the other hand, the greatest of Jewish doctors down through the centuries have declared these words refer not merely to some prophet or ordinary servant of God, but to His supreme Servant, the Messiah, who was to come in due time for Israel's deliverance.

Philip understood this Scripture and knew the truth of God. So he "opened his mouth, and began at the same scripture, and preached unto him Jesus." What a wonderful message to give to a poor seeking soul! And oh, how many thousands through the centuries since have been brought face to face with the Savior through Isaiah 53.

I think this Ethiopian accepted Jesus the first time he ever heard of Him. There is no evidence that he had heard previously. Doubtless many questions were asked and answered. Philip probably told the whole story—how Jesus came to earth, was born of a virgin, lived His holy life, was anointed by God, went about healing the sick, raising the dead, and preaching the kingdom of God. Finally He fulfilled the prophecy of Isaiah and died on Calvary's tree, bearing the weight of our iniquities. Then, Philip would have gone on to say how Christ was buried with the rich—in Joseph's tomb—and how He came out of the grave and commissioned His disciples to carry the gospel message, baptizing those who believe in the name of the Father, and of the Son, and of the Holy Ghost. I imagine that it was at that climax of the message that the Ethiopian stopped him and said, "Wait! Look! Here is water; what doth hinder me to be baptized?" It was his way of saying, "I believe! I acknowledge Christ as the Savior; I want to confess Him publicly as my Savior."

Scholars generally agree that Acts 8:37 is not recognized as part of reliable Scripture. But inasmuch as it was found in many manuscripts dating back to the early Christian era, it tells us the attitude of the early church concerning this question. "Philip said, If thou believest with all thine heart, thou mayest. And he answered and said, I believe that Jesus Christ is the Son of God." This is the confession that God calls on every sinner to make. "If thou shalt confess with thy mouth the Lord Jesus, and shalt believe in thine heart that God hath raised him from the dead, thou shalt be saved. For with the heart man believeth unto righteousness; and with the mouth confession is made unto salvation" (Romans 10:9-10).

And so we are told that the eunuch commanded the chariot to stand still, and a most informal and lovely service took place. One can imagine the people in that caravan gathering around, looking on in wonderment and surprise as Philip and the Ethiopian descended from the chariot, laid aside their outer garments and "went down both into the water...and he baptized him."

Philip's work is now done. We read in the next verse that "When they were come up out of the water, the Spirit of the Lord caught away Philip, that the eunuch saw him no more." The Ethiopian did not need the servant any more—he knew the Master. He did not need the evangelist, for he knew the One of whom the evangelist preached—Jesus Christ, the Savior of sinners. So "he went on his way rejoicing."

You see, it takes so little to save a sinner! It may seem like a long process, but the moment the poor lost sinner looks into the face of Jesus and trusts Him as Savior, he is a new creature. If the Ethiopian had possessed one of our hymnbooks he would have doubtless gone on his way singing:

Oh happy day that fixed my choice
On Thee, my Savior and my God!
Well may this glowing heart rejoice
And tell its raptures all abroad.

'Tis done; the great transaction's done—
I am my Lord's and He is mine;
He drew me, and I followed on,
Charmed to confess the voice divine.

(Philip Doddridge)

Many hundred of years were to roll by before such a hymn as that was to be written. But I am sure it expresses the joy in the heart of this dear man who had gone to Jerusalem only to find an empty temple, yet on his way back found the Lord of the temple through the prophet Isaiah and Philip the evangelist.

In the meantime, Philip, who had accomplished his work, "was found at Azotus: and passing through he preached in all the cities, till he came to Caesarea." And thus the message was going out farther and farther as the stream of grace broadened and deepened and thousands more were brought into a saving knowledge of Jesus Christ.

CHAPTER NINE

THE CONVERSION OF SAUL OF TARSUS

E very conversion is a miracle, and nobody becomes a Christian apart from conversion. Our Lord Jesus said, "Except ye be converted, and become as little children, ye shall not enter into the kingdom of heaven" (Matthew 18:3). Little children receive the testimony in the simplicity of faith, and we are called on to do the same. It is remarkable to see, as we look back over the history of the church, how many enemies of the cross have been subdued by the sight of the Lord Jesus Christ who gave His life for them—and not the least of these is Saul of Tarsus.

God's ways are beyond our understanding and He does not undertake to explain them to us. If we had been members of that early church in Jerusalem, we would have been thrilled over the testimony of Stephen for it looked as though he was destined to become a great leader. Through his eloquence, persuasiveness, and his tender way of presenting the gospel, he might have appealed to many, and many *were* converted through him. On the other hand, bitter hatred and enmity were stirred against him as the servant of Christ, and he was stoned to death. When we read of Stephen's death we are introduced to Saul of Tarsus, a young, calloused, bigoted Hebrew who hated the very name of Jesus: "And the witnesses laid down their clothes at a young man's feet, whose name was Saul."

In Tarsus was a large Jewish colony, and this man Saul, as a student of Gamaliel, had been brought up according to the strictest ideas of the Jews. He tells us later on that he was a "Hebrew of the Hebrews; as touching the law, a Pharisee" (Philippians 3:5). And there he stood that day, looking on as Stephen was put to death. It seemed to be nothing to that hardened young man that the dying martyr's face shone as if it were the face of an angel and that he died praying for blessing on his murderers. God answered that prayer!

The church must have felt that Stephen's death was a terrible blow to the Christian testimony, but God has a way of burying His workmen, yet carrying on His work. He raises others to take the places of those He calls home to Heaven. No one ever thought this cynical, young man was to take the place of Stephen and carry on when Stephen was gone. At his death, Stephen had said, "Behold, I see the heavens opened, and the Son of man standing on the right hand of God." Now, the next time the heavens are opened, Saul of Tarsus sees the blessed One on the right hand of God and is won by Him forever.

Saul's Conversion Experience (Acts 9:1-22)

As Acts 9 opens we see Saul hurrying to Damascus, with only one dominant desire: to root out all that he found "of this way." You will note this expression occurring a number of times in the book of Acts. That was apparently the only name given to early Christianity: the Way. That is what Christianity is; it is a way! It is not just fire insurance for eternity, not simply a method of saving us from eternal judgment; it is a way of blessing, righteousness, and gladness right here on earth. Saul of Tarsus thought to destroy all who were of this way. There is something about Christianity that will not allow it to die. Tertullian said in the second century, "The blood of the martyrs is the seed of the church." Destroy one Christian and ten will take his place. It has been that way all over the world and that, in itself, shows the divinity of the gospel.

Saul's conversion experience came as he was hurrying along the Damascus road, whether on horseback or afoot I do not know. He has so often been pictured on horseback; but I have an idea he was riding a donkey, because the Pharisees had a great prejudice against riding horses. We read, "suddenly there shined round about him a light from heaven: And he fell to the earth, and heard a voice saying unto him, Saul, Saul, why persecutest thou me?"

He never got over this revelation of the mystery of the body of Christ—that every member of the church is a member of the glorified Head in Heaven. If one touched a believer on earth, immediately it was felt up there in Glory. Jesus did not say, "Why do you persecute My disciples?" He said, "why persecutest thou *me*?"— for to persecute one of His own is to persecute Him.

Paul cried out, "Who art thou Lord?" And the answer came back, "I am Jesus." He used His personal name, the name meaning "Jehovah the Savior." It was the name the angel gave Him before His birth: "Thou shalt call his name JESUS: for he shall save his people from their sins." That was the name our Savior bore through all His earthly ministry, and when he hung on the tree Pilate wrote that name on a tablet and it was placed above His head. And now that He is in Glory, we read, "At the name of Jesus every knee should bow, of things in heaven, and things in earth, and things under the earth; And that every tongue should confess that Jesus Christ is Lord, to the glory of God the Father."

Jesus said to Saul, "It is hard for thee to kick against the pricks." Saul was like a refractory ox kicking against the driving goad! And that reveals to us that this seemingly hard, indifferent young man was all the time struggling with his conscience. Deep inside he was hearing again the voice of the dying martyr, Stephen. In effect, Jesus said, "Saul, you are making a mistake. You are kicking against the goads." There was something moving within him, troubling him through all those days of persecution. Perhaps one reason for this was that Saul was not the first of his family to be saved. In Romans 16 he gave certain names and he called them "my kinsmen...who also were in Christ before me." Doubtless they prayed for their kinsman and God was working in his heart.

Saul trembled, and said, "Lord." The implied meaning is that Paul accepted Christ as Lord there and then on the Damascus road. We are told "No man can say that Jesus is the Lord, but by the Holy Ghost" (1 Corinthians 12:3). And we know "that if thou shalt confess with thy mouth [Jesus as Lord], and shalt believe in thine heart that God hath raised him from the dead, thou shalt be saved"

(Romans 10:9). In other words Saul said, "Lord, henceforth I am Thine, Thy bondservant; I belong to Thee; Thou art my Lord. Lord, give me instruction now. What wilt Thou have me to do?" From the moment of his conversion he was submissive, ready to yield himself wholly to the One who died to redeem him.

Saul arose from the earth; and when his eyes were opened [that is, the lids—he was still blind, blinded by the glory of the light that shone from the Savior's face], he saw no man: but they led him by the hand, and brought him into Damascus. And he was three days without sight, and neither did eat nor drink (Acts 9:8-9).

The Lord had instructed him to "Arise, and go into the city." It is sometimes a blessing to a man to go through a period of soul exercise. We would often like to hurry people into confession of Christ, but sometimes they are not yet ready; the heart exercise is not deep enough; conscience-probing has not been sharp enough. And so God allows some people to go through weeks, sometimes months, of soul exercise and then He lets the light break. For Saul of Tarsus there were to be three days before his sight was restored and he learned of the fullness of the joy of his salvation.

The men who were with him on the road heard the sound, but they thought it was thunder. They could not distinguish anything articulate. Do you know how some modernists try to explain Saul's conversion? They say he had an epileptic fit! Charles Spurgeon has well exclaimed: "O blessed epilepsy, if it effects a conversion like this!" Others say Saul had a sunstroke. What a mercy if every modernist were to be sunstruck if it would change him into a flaming messenger of the cross!

And there was a certain disciple at Damascus, named Ananias; and to him said the Lord in a vision, Ananias. And he said, Behold, I am here, Lord. And the Lord said unto him, Arise, and go into the street which is called Straight, and inquire in the house of Judas for one called Saul, of Tarsus: for, behold, he prayeth.

Prayer is always an evidence of the working of the Spirit of God
in a man's soul. We are not told anywhere in the Bible that men have
to pray to be saved. They are to believe. But on the other hand, we
always recognize this: when God is dealing with a man the natural
thing is for him to cry out in prayer. Does your heart cry out to God?
St. Augustine uttered these words in the fourth century when writing
to one in great soul distress, "You said 'I am longing for peace and I
am crying to God day and night.' The fact that thou art seeking Him
is proof thou hast found Him, for He reveals Himself to those who
seek Him." Am I speaking to anyone who has been seeking Jesus,
the sinner's Savior, and who fervently prays for light? Oh, then, you
do believe in Him and you pray because of your faith in Him!

When Ananias received God's message he felt he had to reason
with God about it. Is not God making a mistake, sending him to
Saul of Tarsus? Does it not look as though God is delivering Ananias
himself into the hands of the enemy? No wonder Ananias talked
back. He said, "Lord, I have heard of this man,...he hath authority
from the chief priests to bind all that call on thy name." But the
Lord replied, "Go thy way [do what I tell you, Ananias]: for he is a
chosen vessel unto me, to bear my name before the Gentiles, and
kings, and the children of Israel: For I will show him how great
things he must suffer for my name's sake."

Notice that all the Lord Jesus had said to His apostles He now
reiterated to this new convert. The Lord had commanded the twelve
apostles to go into all the world and preach the gospel to all nations—that is, all the Gentiles. The word *Gentile* is the same as
nations; it is a different translation of the same word. But the apostles
hesitated and did not seem to have the faith to reach out. God said
in effect, "Now I am going to send this man as My special representative," and He gave him the same commission.

Then Ananias instantly obeyed and "entered into the house; and
putting his hands on him said, Brother Saul." I like that! Notice the
affection in this term. This bitter enemy of the cross, now subdued
by grace, is addressed as "Brother Saul." Ananias continued:

> The Lord, even Jesus, that appeared unto thee in the way as thou
> camest, hath sent me, that thou mightest receive thy sight, and

be filled with the Holy Ghost. And immediately there fell from his eyes as it had been scales: and he received sight forthwith, and arose, and was baptized.

By his baptism he cut himself off from unbelieving Israel and took his place in identification with the Christ the nation had rejected, and with the Christ he himself had spurned until now. After spending some time with the Christians in Damascus, Paul went away for a little while to Arabia and came back to Damascus (Galatians 1:17). "And straightway he preached Christ in the synagogues, that he is the Son of God" (Acts 9:20). This is a stronger, clearer note than we have had so far in the book of Acts. Peter proclaimed Him as the Servant; but Saul now as the Son of God. "But all that heard him were amazed, and said: Is not this he that destroyed them which called on this name in Jerusalem, and came hither for that intent, that he might bring them bound unto the chief priests?" What has happened? The miracle of conversion! The same miracle that always occurs when a poor sinner looks to the Lord Jesus Christ.

Saul never forgave himself for persecuting the Christians. God forgave him; the Christians forgave him; but he never forgave himself. Years afterwards, when he looked back to these times, he said, "I am the least of the apostles, that am not meet [worthy] to be called an apostle, because I persecuted the church of God (1 Corinthians 15:9). And when he said, "This is a faithful saying, and worthy of all acceptation, that Christ Jesus came into the world to save sinners"—he added brokenheartedly—"of whom I am chief" (1 Timothy 1:15). He felt there had been no greater sinner than he, for he tried to root out the church of God from the earth. He tried to destroy all who professed the name of Jesus. But God had mercy on him because he did it ignorantly in unbelief. Oh, the boundless mercy of God!

How he delights to take up a great sinner and make him a great saint! This book may fall into the hand of someone who is an avowed enemy of Christ. Perhaps the same feelings that filled the heart of Saul of Tarsus fill your heart. But let me assure you that the One who saved Saul of Tarsus is looking down in compassion on you.

All your bitterness, opposition, and hatred of the gospel message does not change His love for you. Oh, that you might get a vision of the risen, glorified Christ and be brought as a captive in the chains of love to that blessed Savior's feet, that you might then become a modern Saul of Tarsus, to go forth and preach the gospel of Christ! Many, many times has this experience been duplicated in the history of the Christian church.

I've heard people say, "I do not believe in sudden conversions." To be perfectly frank, there is no other kind. I do not mean by that that everyone has as marked an experience as Saul of Tarsus had. But I do mean that in the life of every person who is ever saved there comes a definite moment when he trusts the Lord Jesus Christ, turning from all confidence in self. And that is conversion. It may take place after long years of unrest and soul-searching, or as in the case of Saul of Tarsus, it may take place in a moment by a mighty convicting work in the soul, bringing one to an end of himself who has never before been very much concerned about the message of the gospel.

We see both kinds all about us. There are those who are brought up, for instance, in Christian homes and all their lives hear the gospel story and perhaps they grow to young manhood or womanhood without definitely committing themselves to Christ. And yet many could say that they have never known a time in their conscious lives when they did not have some conviction of spiritual things. But there had to come a definite moment when they trusted Christ for themselves. That is conversion.

And then so many other people who have lived wild, reckless, careless lives, having no interest whatever in things of God, could say as one of the old hymns puts it:

> I once was far away from God
> On ruin's dark and fatal road,
> And little dreamed I'd see the day
> When I should tread the narrow way.

And yet these people, brought suddenly to a recognition of their lost, sinful condition and led to definite faith in the Lord Jesus, in a moment become new creatures in Christ. There are many such. It was so of Saul of Tarsus. His was really a model conversion.

"But Saul increased the more in strength, and confounded the Jews which dwelt at Damascus, proving that this is very Christ." Following his conversion he became a witness. And that is the will of God for all who are saved. If we know the Lord Jesus Christ for ourselves, we should immediately join the ranks of those who are witnessing to others of His saving power. It is not the will of God that all should preach in a public way, but it is the will of God that all who know the Savior should speak of Him to others and seek to win their fellows to Christ. I am afraid there are a great many Christians (I do not doubt the reality of their conversion when I speak as I do) who are just content to be going to Heaven themselves and who show very little interest in the souls of those about them. It was otherwise with Saul of Tarsus. No sooner was he saved himself than he began telling all who would listen the wonderful truth that had been revealed to his own soul, that Jesus was indeed the Christ of God, the promised Messiah and the Son of God.

The New Fellowship (Acts 9:23-31)

Saul preached Christ in Damascus, in the very city to which he had gone intending to throw into prison those who loved the Savior's name. But we are told that "after many days were fulfilled, the Jews took counsel to kill him." Having rejected their own Messiah, they rejected this man who sought to awaken them to a sense of their responsibility to His claims. But we are told that Saul knew of their plans. They "watched the gates day and night to kill him," hoping that as he went in or out of the city they might be able to waylay and slay him. But the disciples, learning of it, "took him by night and let him down by the wall in a basket." It was a rather humiliating way for this servant of Christ to leave the city of his first labors, wasn't it?

I remember standing at that wall of the city of Damascus, and I looked up to a little house in the wall and a window there. The guide was absolutely certain that that was the window through which they lowered the basket with the apostle in it. Well, I do not know whether that is true or not, but as I looked at it I could just imagine what it must have meant to this one-time proud, haughty Pharisee, now crouched up in a basket and dropped down over the wall. You would have thought he would never have referred to it again. And if he had had the pride and conceit that some of us have, it would have been among the buried annals. But we hear him speaking of it many years afterward (2 Corinthians 11:33).

From Damascus he went on to Jerusalem, and undertook to search out the little companies of believers and to join himself to those whom before he had persecuted. We read, "When Saul was come to Jerusalem, he assayed to join himself to the disciples: but they were all afraid of him, and believed not that he was a disciple." We do not wonder that they were afraid of him. The last they had seen and known of him he was going from house to house trying to find those who professed the faith of the Lord Jesus Christ and deliver them over to be persecuted for His name's sake. "Oh," they might have said, "we don't dare let this man into our assemblies; he is an enemy, perhaps he is a spy just waiting to turn us over to the authorities."

But Paul had a friend who knew and understood. We read, "Barnabas took him, and brought him to the apostles, and declared unto them how he had seen the Lord in the way, and that he had spoken to him, and how he had preached boldly at Damascus in the name of Jesus." The testimony of Barnabas authenticated the testimony of Saul. In other words Barnabas said, "Yes, I know all about it. You do not need to be afraid of him now. He was once the enemy of the truth, but a great change has taken place. Saul of Tarsus has been born again."

I can not too often stress the importance of that second birth. It is being forgotten in so many places today. People imagine they may become Christians by outward reformation, or by joining a church, or even by what they call "religious education." They think that you can take a child and educate him along religious lines and he will grow up a Christian. But that is all a delusion. Jesus said, "Except a man be born again, he cannot see the kingdom of God." And the apostle Peter said, "Being born again, not of corruptible seed, but of incorruptible, by the word of God, which liveth and abideth forever.... And this is the Word which by the gospel is preached unto you" (1 Peter 1:23,25). Saul of Tarsus had believed the gospel. He was born again. He would never again lift a persecuting hand against God's people. He was saved. And now he longed for association with others of like precious faith. His heart was welling up with love for them now.

In Jerusalem he found a recognized fellowship of believers. This was the new creation company. This fellowship is called in 1 Corinthians 1:9, "the fellowship of [God's] Son." We read there, "God is faithful, by whom ye were called into the fellowship of his Son." "The fellowship" is a beautiful name for the people of God. Once we were just so many units, individual units. We were not particularly interested in one another. It was every one for himself. But grace reached our hearts, and that introduced us into a wonderful fellowship where we had common interest, and from now on we were members one of another.

This fellowship is called very distinctly, "the church of God." I have heard it said sometimes by persons who had not fully considered the matter that the church had no existence during the period of transition as depicted in the book of Acts, that it came into full existence only after the apostle Paul was in prison. However, referring to his unconverted days Paul wrote, "I persecuted the *church of God*" (1 Corinthians 15:9, italics added). So we see that the church of God was there before he was converted. He used the same expression in the Epistle to the Galatians, written years after his own conversion (1:13): "For ye have heard of my conversation in time past in the Jew's religion, how that beyond measure I persecuted the church of God, and wasted it." And from the day of Pentecost to the present time, the church of God has been a distinct company in this world, made up of those who know and love the Lord Jesus Christ. The church of God includes all believers.

The Scriptures also speak, however, of "churches of God"—that is, local companies of believers. In Galatians 1:21-22 Paul wrote, "Afterwards I came into the regions of Syria and Cilicia; And was unknown by face unto the churches of Judaea which were in Christ." And in the second verse of that chapter he wrote, "unto the churches of Galatia." Used in the plural, the term *churches* refers to local companies in various places, made up of those who professed faith in the Lord Jesus Christ. In writing to those who had been brought to God from heathenism, he said, "For ye, brethren, became followers of the churches of God which in Judaea are in Christ Jesus: for ye also have suffered like things of your own countrymen, even as they have of the Jews" (1 Thessalonians 2:14).

It is important to see the distinction between "the church of God" to which all Christians belong and the "churches of God" in different communities. A church of God is a company of Christian people. These people may have different doctrinal standards, different views as to ordinances and sacraments, different conceptions of church government, and so on. But where you find believers in the Lord Jesus Christ gathered together seeking to honor Him, coming together for worship, for praise, for testimony, for prayer, there you have a local church of God in any given community.

These churches of God were scattered, by the time Paul was converted, not only in Jerusalem but all over Judea. And in a little while we find them also among the Gentiles. In Acts 5:11 we have the term *the church* used for the first time, in the original manuscripts at least: "Great fear came upon all the church, and upon as many as heard these things." In Acts 2:47 we read "Praising God, and having favour with all the people. And the Lord added *to the church* daily such as should be saved" (KJV). You will notice that in other versions the words "to the church" are omitted. Probably these three words are not to be considered part of the original text of Scripture, though they do clarify that this verse is referring to a particular company of believers constituting the church in Jerusalem.

Another term is used throughout the book of Acts, and in fact through all the New Testament, and that is "the kingdom of God." Wherever these early Christians went preaching the gospel of the grace of God, they carried with them the proclamation that Christ is the rightful King and Lord of all. They called on men everywhere to subject themselves to Him. And those who believed the gospel, those who received the Lord Jesus Christ as their Savior, those who acknowledged Him as their Master now were brought into His kingdom. God "hath delivered us from the power of darkness, and hath translated us into the kingdom of his dear Son" (Colossians 1:13).

His kingdom was set up in their hearts. It is a moral thing. "The kingdom of God is not meat and drink, but righteousness, and peace, and joy in the Holy Ghost" (Romans 14:17).

In Acts 9 we read of a company of people in Jerusalem who honored Christ while living in the midst of a sinful world. They crowned Him Lord of all, and they constituted His kingdom. And still that glorious kingdom is in the world today. Some day it will be openly revealed, when our Savior comes again. Now it is "the kingdom and patience of Jesus Christ" (Revelation 1:9). When He returns it will be the day of the kingdom and glory. I think it is helpful to us as believers if we get some of these terms clearly in mind. We are members of the church of God; we are members also of churches of God. We belong to this glorious fellowship of the redeemed, and we have been translated into the kingdom of the Son of God's love.

More than that, Saul of Tarsus was chosen of God later on to open up a new and wonderful revelation that had never been made known before; that is, that believers are not only members of the church of God, but the church of God is also the body of Christ. All believers are members of that body and He is their glorious Head in Heaven. What a wonderful fellowship that is!

The outward expression of this fellowship is seen in the Lord's table. In 1 Corinthians 10:16-17, we read, "The cup of blessing which we bless, is it not the communion?" The word *communion* is the same as the word *fellowship* in the original text: "Is it not the [fellowship] of the blood of Christ? The bread which we break, is it not the [fellowship] of the body of Christ? For we being many are one bread and one body." We eat and drink together as those redeemed to God by the precious blood of His Son in remembrance of Him who gave His life for us.

Now it was into this fellowship that Saul, the one-time enemy of the cross of Christ, had been brought. What a wonderful thing it must have been for Saul of Tarsus to sit for the first time with these Christians at Jerusalem and enjoy communion with them, to partake of the loaf and the cup in commemoration of the Savior whom for so long he had rejected!

I remember reading in a missionary record of a young man in New Guinea who had been away to school and had gotten a good education, then returned to his own island and to his own village after his conversion. On the Lord's day the group of missionaries and believers were gathered together to observe the Lord's supper. As this young man sat by one of the elder missionaries, the missionary recognized that a sudden tremor had passed through the young man's body. The young man had laid his hand on the missionary's arm, indicating that he was under a great nervous strain. Then in a moment all was quiet again. The missionary whispered, "What was it that troubled you?" He answered, "The man who just came in killed and ate the body of my father. And now he has come in to remember the Lord with us. At first I was so shocked to see the murderer of my own father sit down with us at the table of the Lord, I didn't know whether I could endure it. But it is all right now. He is washed in the same precious blood." And so together they had communion. Does the world know anything of this fellowship? It is a marvelous thing, the work of the blessed Holy Spirit of God.

I think of Saul of Tarsus seated there with that little group of believers around him. And I think of them looking over and saying, "That is the man that arrested my father. That is the man that threw my mother into prison. That is the man that tried to make me blaspheme the name of the Lord Jesus. There he sits, a humbled contrite believer, receiving the bread and the wine in commemoration of the Lord who died." What a wonderful fellowship!

We read that Saul went in and out among them at Jerusalem. He enjoyed to the full these privileges of fellowship. "And he spake boldly in the name of the Lord Jesus, and disputed against the Grecians." The term *Grecians* here means not only Greeks, but Hellenistic Jews—Jews born within the nations of the Gentiles. But they, instead of responding to the message, went about to slay him. God permitted Saul now to know something of the persecutions that he had caused others.

When the brethren realized that his life was in danger if he remained in Jerusalem, they brought him down to Caesarea, the seaport, and sent him to Tarsus, his own native city. And now with Saul out of the way the churches prospered. That seems a strange thing. You would have thought they might have prospered more with the ministry of this wonderful man of God among them. But now he was the object of the intense hatred of the Pharisaic party that he had once represented. And the Christians realized that it was better that he go elsewhere to labor than remain in Jerusalem. And so we are told, "Then had the churches rest throughout all Judaea and Galilee and Samaria." Observe the three districts. By this time churches had been established throughout Judea, far north in Galilee, and in the intermediate district of Samaria. And they "were edified; and walking in the fear of the Lord, and in the comfort of the Holy Ghost, were multiplied."

Have you ever noticed the Bible arithmetic in the book of Acts? In 2:41 we read the Lord *added* those that believed. And in 2:47 the Lord *added* those that were being saved. In 5:14 certain ones were *added* to their company, and they became about five thousand men. And then in 6:7 and 9:31 (KJV) the number of believers were *multiplied*. This is Bible arithmetic. First addition, then multiplication. I am afraid sometimes it is not like that today. In fact, I know a great many churches where there seems to be subtraction rather than holding their own, let alone addition or multiplication. My dear brothers and sisters, if our companies are not being added to, and if believers are not being multiplied, I'll tell you the reason: It is because the church is not walking in the fear of God and the comfort of the Holy Ghost. When the Spirit of God has His way in the hearts and lives of believers, then unsaved people are going to be reached and won for Christ. If we are not seeing people converted it indicates that something is wrong. If believers are truly moving forward with God, if He is having His way in their lives, then their testimony will really count for Him. Let us face this honestly and ask ourselves, "What am I doing to win souls that the work of the Lord may progress and believers may be added to the Lord?"

The Practical Side of Christianity (Acts 9:32-43)

We are coming to the close of Peter's later Judean ministry. In Acts 10 and 11 we will see him used of God to open the door to the Gentiles; and in chapter 12 we have his arrest and marvelous deliverance from prison. From there on, Peter fades into the background and Paul takes the prominent place.

I was half asleep on a warm afternoon while we were traveling through Palestine when suddenly the train stopped with a jerk. As I woke up with a start and looked out the window, I saw the name "Lydda." It carried me back two thousand years. At this town of Lydda Peter was engaged in ministering the Word, "And there he found a certain man named Aeneas, which had kept his bed eight years, and was sick of the palsy." I think every one of the different diseases mentioned in Scripture was intended by God to illustrate in some way the effects of sin. Palsy was a disease very common in Palestine during the days of our Lord's sojourn on earth, and afterwards. It illustrates the utter helplessness of the sinner.

The Lord Jesus often ministered to people with palsy. You will remember the palsied man who was let down through the roof by his four friends, and the Lord Jesus gave him not only healing of his body, but forgiveness of his sins (Mark 2:1-12). You will recall the poor man who had lain by the pool of Bethesda for thirty-eight years. He was sick five years before even the Lord came from Heaven! Jesus said to this poor, helpless man, "Wilt thou be made whole?" The impotent man answered him, "Sir, I have no man, when the water is troubled, to put me into the pool." Jesus spoke the life-giving word that gave strength to those palsied limbs and the man sprang to his feet and went away carrying his bed (John 5:1-17).

Here in Acts 9 we have another palsied man in all his helplessness. If you have not trusted Christ, you are just like him. You have no ability to save yourself; you can't take one step toward God. if this man was ever to be healed, someone must come to him, and that is just what Christ Jesus did. We read, "When we were yet without strength, in due time Christ died for the ungodly" (Romans 5:6). He comes to us where we are and speaks the word that gives life to poor, helpless sinners.

Peter evidently saw in this man a spirit of expectation. The man may have been a Christian—we do not know. "Peter said unto him...Jesus Christ maketh thee whole: arise, and make thy bed. And he arose immediately." One may ask, "Why do we not have many miracles like this today?" God has never promised in His Word that all miracles and signs would remain in the church to the end of the dispensation. He was speaking to the disciples when He said, "In my name shall they cast out devils;...if they drink any deadly thing, it shall not hurt them; they shall lay hands on the sick, and they shall recover" (Mark 16:17-18).

Many of the apostles found that these signs accompanied their ministry, but we never read that the same power was given to other believers. In the early church there were far more evidences of the miraculous power of the Spirit of God to heal than we perhaps see today, but there was greater reason for it. Men knew less of the human body and its ailments and how to minister to them than they know today. Down through the centuries God has given remarkable enlightenment and skill in dealing with physical ailments and God does not always do for us what we can do for ourselves. He does not always work miracles. He can bless the medicine and the skill of the physician and surgeon, and these are as much an answer to prayer as if He wrought a miracle. After all, every case of healing is from God. The doctor's ability does not count for anything at all unless God blesses his efforts for the building up and renewing of the bodies He made.

There is another point to remember. When the church went forth in the beginning, in its purity, "terrible as an army with banners," it was the delight of the Lord to give signs to accompany it. But we must remember we live in a day when we can look back over fifteen hundred years or more of grave departure from the Word of God, fifteen hundred years in which apostasy has been making tremendous strides in the Christian church, fifteen hundred years of ever-increasing worldliness and corruption. It has been said that "the corruption of the best thing is the worst corruption"—and we can see why the Lord might withdraw some of His great gifts. Suppose He gave some of these gifts today in abundant measure. To what section of the church would He give them? He could not give them to all. Would there not be a great danger of increase in spiritual pride on the part of any section specially honored?

There are reasons why God withholds certain things. I have sometimes illustrated it like this: A young man is engaged to a beautiful young woman and has full confidence in her. He delights in lavishing presents on her. Given a position across the sea, he goes away, and from his new station sends beautiful and precious gifts to this lady of his heart in the homeland. But then he learns the one he has trusted is proving unfaithful to him. She is seen with other lovers and found here and there with them in questionable places. When the heart-breaking news comes to him, do you not think it would dry up the stream of gifts? He would not feel the same about her. Will you look at that example as a little parable? When the church was in its first love, the Lord Jesus delighted to grace her with many gifts, but the church has been unfaithful. We have drifted far away from the principles of those early days and the Lord has had to deal with us in much more reserve than in the beginning.

There are those who say today that miracles passed away with the apostles. That is not true. Many wonderful miracles have occurred in answer to prayer during the last nineteen hundred years, and here and there throughout the world today God still acts in wonderful grace. Again and again God puts forth His hand in healing power, and many given up by doctors have marvelously recovered as God's people have prayed. Other signs and wonders too have accompanied Christianity. It really behooves us to be careful and not go to either of two extremes. Let us not insist that the working of the Spirit of God through miracles and signs is past; on the other hand, let us not say that He will always so act if we ask Him to do so. The measure in which He delights to work is left with Him.

Peter said to Aeneas, "Arise!" and the man arose immediately. It was a real testimony to the people in the neighborhood. "And all that dwelt at Lydda and Saron saw him, and turned to the Lord." God used the miracle of healing to direct the attention of needy souls to Christ Himself, and they came not only for physical help, but also for spiritual blessing.

The next miraculous healing we read about occurred in Joppa, a place not far from Lydda, and on the sea coast whereas Lydda is inland. "Now there was at Joppa a certain disciple named Tabitha, which by interpretation is called Dorcas: this woman was full of good works and almsdeeds which she did" (Acts 9:36). I want to fix your attention on this verse for a few moments for we are given one of the very real evidences of a truly converted person. She was deeply interested in doing good to others. It is marvelous to see how God in His grace exercised people's hearts into sharing their possessions to supply others' temporal needs. Christianity is not a means simply of getting into Heaven, nor is it only a system of doctrine, but it is a wonderful manifestation of divine life and love in the midst of a world of sin and wretchedness.

I am afraid sometimes we forget that side of our faith; many professing believers are so terribly self-centered. They seem to be looking constantly for some new religious thrill or new spiritual experience. They are always looking inside and always seeking blessing for themselves. They stream to the altar when the invitation is given. If you gave the invitation a hundred times a year, they would come a hundred times.

That isn't the ideal Christian at all. The ideal Christian is one who is resting in Christ for his soul's salvation and his great concern becomes the salvation of others. He is interested in making Christ known and in doing good in a temporal way to others. John insisted on this, and James asked, "If a brother or sister be naked, and destitute of daily food, And one of you say unto them, Depart in peace, be ye warmed and filled; notwithstanding ye give them not those things which are needful to the body; what doth it profit?" (2:15-16)

Dorcas loved the Lord and displayed this love in a very practical way. She was not satisfied with reading her Bible only. She had a consecrated needle and used it for the blessing of other people, and the Spirit of God has preserved this record that we might learn from it and never forget her. Some of you dear Christian women who are not satisfied with your life, get busy and try to help and bless other people, and you will be surprised to see how your own spiritual condition will improve! You will get on wonderfully well when you start thinking about others. I do not go quite so far as a preacher a few years ago, who said, "Anyone whose chief concern is the salvation of his own soul hasn't got a soul worth saving." Every soul is valuable. But I would say this: Anyone constantly occupied with his own spiritual experience and never concerned about blessing other people will never have an experience worth being occupied with.

Dorcas must have been a most genial person. I can't imagine her as one of those sour pusses we sometimes see today—going around with long, melancholy faces and a holier-than-thou attitude. I think her face gleamed with the love of Christ. I do not think she had a dainty little handshake, but I believe she had a pump-handle handshake. She was always interested in other people—really a warm-hearted Christian.

But this dear woman died. Her spirit went home to be with Christ and her body lay there in an upper room. The Christians felt Dorcas should go to Heaven, but they wanted her here. For some of us they would not worry very much. They would just look pious and say, "The Lord has taken him." But they would not be very anxious to have us come back. These dear believers, however, were exceedingly sorry to lose this wonderful Christian character.

"And forasmuch as Lydda was nigh to Joppa, and the disciples had heard that Peter was there, they sent unto him two men, desiring him that he would not delay to come to them." They probably thought, *We do not know what he can do, but we shall send for him.* "Then Peter arose and went with them. When he was come, they brought him into the upper chamber: and all the widows stood by him weeping, and showing the coats and garments which Dorcas made, while she was with them." Can't you just see that picture? The lifeless body of the dear one lying on the bed while her friends, gathered around, mourn for her. One exclaims, "Look at this coat. I didn't know where I was going to get a winter coat; but she cut a coat that her grandfather left and made it over for me!" And others were showing one thing and another. "Dorcas made it for me!" These garments seemed to have a mute voice, and Peter heard their crying and "put them all forth, and kneeled down, and prayed; and turning him to the body said, Tabitha, arise. And she opened her eyes; and when she saw Peter, she sat up. And he gave her his hand, and lifted her up, and when he had called the saints and widows, presented her alive." What a rejoicing they must have had!

She is one of the special saints of the New Testament. Her name has been enshrined in countless Dorcas societies—groups of Christian women who come together to do what she did and emulate her ministry to the poor and needy.

This is one of the ways the gospel of Christ commends itself to the needy. Do you realize what we call social service really began, after all, with Christ and His apostles? Many talk today of the social gospel and try to distinguish it from the saving gospel. There is no such distinction, for the gospel that saves the individual also brings blessings to the needy.

In all the reading I have done I have never read of any hospital for the treatment of the sick being established in the world before Christ came. We have no record of an asylum for the mentally sick people before Jesus came. Before He came the mentally deficient or insane were driven from their homes and left in tombs or in desert places. They were looked upon as demoniacs. People sometimes considered them inspired and listened to their strange ravings for some new revelation. But there was no asylum in which they could be treated and tenderly cared for.

There was no such thing as a leprosarium in the world until after Jesus came. The leper was doomed to wander in the wilderness, and it was only during the Christian era that the first home for lepers was opened. Ever since then the church of God has been ministering to those suffering from that horrible disease.

There was no such thing as an orphanage until after Jesus came. The Greeks, Romans, Egyptians, and Assyrians, with all their boasted civilization, never thought of opening an orphanage. Instead, orphan children, unless adopted by some of their relatives, were exposed to the elements and left to die, or else were sold into slavery. Many little boys and girls were given over to a fate worse than death before Jesus came. It was a Christian who started the first orphanage, and it is Christian people who have been interested in these things ever since. There was no such thing in all the world as international relief—until Jesus came. You can search all the records and you will never read, for instance, that during the famine in Egypt the people of Rome took up an offering to help the starving people; nor during a pestilence in Syria did the people in Greece raise a fund to assist those in distress in Syria. It was not very long after Jesus came that the Christians in Achaia and other parts of the Grecian world were sending to those in need in Judea. The Red Cross would never have come into existence were it not for Jesus; for, after all, what is the symbol of the Red Cross? It is the blood-red cross of Christ! We need to remember that all these agencies had their birth in the gospel of the grace of God.

Dorcas stands out before us as a special picture of one who lived her faith by ministring to the temporal needs of those around her. May we all learn to emulate her concern for others.

The last verse of Acts 9 introduces us to the events recorded in the next chapter: "And it came to pass, that he [Peter] tarried many days in Joppa with one Simon a tanner."

CHAPTER TEN

THE CONVERSION OF CORNELIUS

We turn now to one of the great crisis chapters in the book of the Acts, which deals with the conversion of the first Gentiles. We have been following the ministry of Peter and the other apostles in Jerusalem, Judea, Samaria, and Galilee. But our Lord had commissioned them to go to the uttermost parts of the earth. On a number of different occasions before He left them to go back to Heaven, he laid out His program for world evangelization. "Go ye into all the world and preach the gospel to every creature," was part of His commission (Mark 16:15). Again He commanded them: "Go ye therefore, and [disciple] all nations, baptizing them in the name of the Father, and of the Son, and of the Holy Ghost: Teaching them to observe all things whatsoever I have commanded you" (Matthew 28:19-20). Lastly He bade them begin at Jerusalem, then go to Judea and Samaria and to the uttermost part of the earth (Acts 1:8).

The amazing thing is that not only months, but years went by, before they carried out the last part of the program. So slowly may good men, even godly men, apprehend God's plans and act in accordance with them. We do not read of any apostles going to the Gentiles with the gospel message until one of the Gentiles actually sent for Peter and asked him to come. That is the way God came in and rebuked the dilatory methods of these dear servants of His. Somebody might say, "The apostles were slow to understand His program." There can be no question of it. In Galatians we find years afterward that the apostle Peter had to be withstood at Antioch

137

because of his attitude toward Gentile Christians. The apostles were not infallible. Some say Peter was the first pope, but he himself made no such claim. He was a man of God, an apostle of Jesus Christ; but a man of like passions as ourselves, and was subject to the same mistakes and blunders. God had to reach out beyond Jewish limits, stirring the heart of a Roman soldier to get Peter to go to the Gentiles with the gospel.

Cornelius's Vision (Acts 10:1-8)

In these verses Cornelius is introduced to us and we learn something of his spiritual condition and the command given to him. He was captain of a Roman cohort of a hundred men and was stationed in the city of Caesarea, not far from Joppa. He is described as a devout man, God fearing, and we are told all his family shared with him this fear of God. Many people have, I think, mistaken Cornelius' condition. There can be no question that he was already a regenerated man; that is, born again. Of all unsaved men we read, "There is none that seeketh after God" (Romans 3:11).

Although Cornelius had turned to God, he was not a proselyte to Israel. Had he actually become a proselyte to Israel, he would have been recognized as on the same ground as a Jew, but Peter spoke of him as one in whose house it was not lawful for a Jew to eat bread. So Cornelius was a pure Gentile, standing outside of the Jewish circle. But he had doubtless been influenced by what he had heard and seen in the testimony of his Jewish neighbors and had given up the idolatry of his fathers. That he had turned to God in repentance was very evident; he was born again.

More than this, we are told a little farther on that an angel of God appeared to him in a vision and said, "Thy prayers and thine alms are come up for a memorial before God." That is significant in illustrating this man's spiritual condition. In the eleventh chapter of Hebrews we read that without faith we cannot please God; therefore if this man pleased God and God accepted his prayers and almsgiving, it is evident he had already turned to Him. What was lacking? He was like other people who turned to God before Jesus came.

He did not have the light and knowledge that came through God's Son. He knew God as Creator and prayed to Him; the new nature manifested itself in his almsgiving. But he had no assurance of salvation, and he could not have it until he received definite word from God, for assurance comes by the Word of God. So the angel said, "Send men to Joppa, and call for one Simon, whose surname is Peter: He lodgeth with one Simon a tanner, whose house is by the sea side." The angel of God knew exactly where Peter lived. It is a good thing God knows where we are living. "He shall tell thee what thou oughtest to do. And when the angel which spake unto Cornelius was departed, he called two of his household servants, and a devout soldier of them that waited on him continually; And...sent them to Joppa."

Peter's Preparation (Acts 10:9-18)

Before the servants of Cornelius reached the apostle, God had to break down his prejudices in order that he might be ready to go into a Gentile home to proclaim the gospel message. "On the morrow, as they went on their journey, and drew night unto the city, Peter went up upon the housetop to pray about the sixth hour." The flat roof of a house in the Middle East forms a good place where one may retire in order to be alone for quiet and meditation. Peter prayed so long he became hungry. In that condition he fell into a trance and saw a most remarkable vision: "He...saw heaven opened, and a certain vessel descending unto him, as it had been a great sheet knit at the four corners [by sheet is meant what we might call a vast tarpaulin of some kind], and let down to the earth." It was a picture of the heavenly calling.

It was God's way of showing Peter that He was going to give to all men the opportunity to enter into one blessed fellowship, to spend eternity with Him in Heaven. But in this sheet Peter saw all types of animals including four-footed domestic beasts, wild beasts, creeping things, and fowls of the air. The domestic animals would even include the ceremonially unclean hog. And creeping things, according to the Old Testament, were considered unclean. After hungry

Peter looked on this heterogeneous collection of beasts and birds and creeping things, he heared a voice say, "Rise, Peter; kill, and eat."

Peter, though a Christian, was still very punctilious as to clean and unclean food and he rebelled, "Not so, Lord; for I have never eaten any thing that is common or unclean." Notice the contradiction implied in that expression, "Not so, Lord." In one breath Peter acknowledged Him as "Lord" and in the same breath he refused to do as he was commanded. I wonder if some of us are like this. We know what His will is for our lives, we confess Him with our lips as Lord; but we draw back from full obedience and say, "Not so, Lord." What a strange, incongruous thing this is! If He is not Lord of all, He is not Lord at all! And if He is Lord, it is not for us to say, "Not so," but to give him wholehearted obedience. Peter thought he was being obedient to the express word of God, which in the old covenant forbad the eating of unclean animals. He did not yet realize he had passed completely out of one dispensation into another.

Our Lord Jesus Christ had said, "Whatsoever thing from without entereth into the man, it cannot defile him; Because it entereth not into his heart, but into the belly, and goeth out into the draught, purging all meats" (Mark 7:18-19). By this He did away with the ceremonial distinctions as to clean and unclean meats. So God answered Peter, "What God hath cleansed, that call not thou common [or unclean]." And in order that this might be impressed on his mind, the same vision was given to him three times and then the vessel with its strange company of beasts was received up into Heaven.

What a remarkable picture! It illustrates how God can now receive in grace all kinds of men and women. I have heard my mother tell that when my own dear father was dying, this passage was running through his mind and he kept repeating, "A great sheet and wild beasts, and—and—and..." He could not seem to remember the next word but went back and started over, and once more came to that same place. A friend bent over and whispered, "John, it says, 'creeping things.'" "Oh, yes," he said, "that is how I got in. Just a poor good-for-nothing creeping thing, but I got in—saved by grace." No matter how low, vile or utterly useless and corrupt or unclean, the soul that trusts Jesus is in the sheet let down from Heaven and will have a place in glory by and by.

Peter meditated on this vision. God had to give him a special revelation to prepare him for his ministry to the Gentiles. He had to show him there is no longer any difference between Jew and Gentile. All stand on common ground before God; all have to be saved by grace. "While Peter doubted in himself what this vision which he had seen should mean, behold, the men which were sent from Cornelius had made inquiry for Simon's house, and stood before the gate, And called, and asked whether Simon, which was surnamed Peter, were lodged there."

Peter's Journey (Acts 10:19-33)

After the three men approached Peter with their request he did a most unprecedented thing for a Jew: he invited them in and gave them lodging. The day before he received the vision he might have thought these Gentile strangers utterly unfit to associate with. It is delightful to see the confidence with which he went on to carry out the Lord's command and give the gospel message to a Gentile family.

When he reached the house of Cornelius a whole company of Gentiles eagerly waited to hear his message. Peter and the few Hebrew Christian friends who accompanied him were the first to proclaim the gospel to a strictly Gentile audience. As Peter came in, we get an idea of the spirit of Cornelius when we see this devout Roman soldier bowing down at the apostle's feet. Think of it: A Gentile centurion, a Roman soldier, bowing down reverently before a Jew who had once been just a poor fisherman! It shows how grace was working in Cornelius. Peter reached out to him and said, "Stand up; I myself also am a man." He meant, "I have no right to such reverence as this. Do not put me in a place that does not belong to me." Would that those who profess to be his successors acted in the same way!

And as he talked with him, he went in, and found many that were come together. And he said unto them, Ye know how that

it is an unlawful thing for a man that is a Jew to keep company,
or come unto one of another nation; but God hath showed me
that I should not call any man common or unclean.

Peter's faith had laid hold of the import of the vision and he was
ready, with confidence, to give the gospel to these Gentiles. What a
delightful state of affairs, to find a whole company waiting eagerly
for the Word! It was not necessary to advertise a meeting to be held
in the house of Cornelius; everybody was there ahead of time, waiting for the preacher.

Peter's Sermon (Acts 10:34-43)

I think it was easy for the preacher to preach that day with such
an enthusiastic audience before him. "Then Peter opened his mouth."
I like that. If any young preachers are reading this, let me caution
you—Don't mumble! Open your mouth and give out the Word so
people can hear.

"Of a truth I perceive that God is no respecter of persons." He
had learned his lesson. He had learned that there is no difference
between Jew and Gentile: for the same Lord over all is rich unto all
that call on Him, for all have sinned and come short of the glory of
God. "But in every nation he that feareth him and worketh righteousness, is accepted with him." That is, wherever a man is found,
in all the world, who turns in repentance to God and takes the place
of a lost sinner and trusts God for deliverance, He will make Himself responsible to give that man light enough to be saved.

Peter was the one sent to convey the message to Cornelius,
"preaching peace by Jesus Christ." That epitomizes the message of
the gospel. Into a world torn by the effects of sin, trouble, distress,
bloody warfare, grief, pain, sorrow, and death, God sends His messengers, "preaching peace by Jesus Christ." When we trust that
blessed Savior, we have peace with God; and when we learn to
bring our daily troubles to Him, the peace of God keeps our hearts
and minds through Christ Jesus. This is the message the world needs
today—peace through Jesus Christ.

"That word, I say, ye know, which was published throughout all

Judaea, and began from Galilee, after the baptism which John preached; How God anointed Jesus of Nazareth with the Holy Ghost and with power *who went about doing good*" (italics added). These last five words epitomize the life of Jesus. He has left us an example that we should follow in His steps. Let us never be content with a mere intellectual faith or the thought that we belong to this or that church, but be sure that ours is the faith which worketh by love. Let us too go about doing good.

"And we are witnesses of all things which he did both in the land of the Jews, and in Jerusalem; whom they slew and hanged on a tree." The Jews did not understand their actions and He Himself prayed for them, "Father, forgive them, for they know not what they do." Let me say a word here. Because the Jewish people long ago had part in the crucifixion of the Lord Jesus Christ, do be careful not to entertain the unworthy thought that we Gentiles have a right to blame them. The Lord prayed for them, for their forgiveness. The Gentiles were as guilty as the Jews. He prayed for them too. We need to remember that through Christ being immolated as the great sin offering, God is able to proclaim peace to all men everywhere who will trust in Him. God raised Him from the dead and that was God's token of His satisfaction in the work His Son had accomplished, for Jesus "was delivered for our offenses, and was raised again for our justification."

> Him God raised up the third day, and showed him openly; Not to all the people, but unto witnesses chosen before of God, even to us, who did eat and drink with him after he rose from the dead. And he commanded us to preach unto the people, and to testify that it is he which was ordained of God to be the Judge of quick and dead (Acts 10:40-42).

Let us never forget that unless we know Christ here as Savior, someday we shall have to face Him as Judge.

Peter then came to the very climax of his message in one wonderful verse: "To him give all the prophets witness, that through his name whosoever believeth in him shall receive remission of sins." The word was so clear, the gospel was so plain, and it was all so simple, that Cornelius and his household understood what they heard.

The Effect of the Sermon (Acts 10:44-48)

Peter preached the word and, while he was preaching, Cornelius and all his household received the message in faith. Peter did not have to urge and plead and entreat. He preached the word and the whole congregation broke down. God, who reads the heart, saw that every one of them received and believed the message that Christ had died for them, and their sins were remitted. God set His seal on them by giving the same Pentecostal blessing that He had given at Jerusalem to His own blessed disciples. We are even told that they spoke in tongues. This is the second occasion when this strange gift was given, so far as the record goes, though the same things may have occurred in Samaria. We are not told they spoke there in tongues, but they may have done so.

Peter, when he saw the evident blessing of the Lord, turned to the little company of Hebrew Christians who had come down with him from Joppa and he said, as it were, "What shall we do about it?" God had received them and given evidence that all were for-given. "Can any man forbid water, that these should not be bap-tized, which have received the Holy Ghost as well as we?" I have heard people say sometimes that if you are baptized with the Holy Ghost you do not need to be baptized in water. It is not a question of what you need—it is a question of what God has commanded. So Peter commanded them to be baptized in the name, or by the au-thority, of the Lord Jesus.

They were so radiantly happy now that they asked him to stay with them for a while. I can just imagine what a delightful time they all had together as day after day people gathered around Peter and he opened up the Word. He told them more about God's wonderful grace and led them into the marvelous truths of the gospel. Yet all the time in the back of Peter's mind was the burning question— How am I ever going to square myself with the home assembly? How will I ever tell them? As we consider the next chapter we will see Peter's presentation of the case to the brethren at Jerusalem.

CHAPTER ELEVEN
PETER'S DEFENSE

No one, I think, can read the account of Acts 11 thoughtfully without realizing how prejudices control and dominate the hearts of men. Most of us are more prejudiced in religious matters than we realize. Sometimes what we call "conscience" is, after all, only prejudice. We profess we cannot have any sympathy with this or that person (because he does not see as we do) on account of our consciences. Whereas, if we were honest, we would have to admit that our lack of sympathy is due in large part to our prejudices. Remember the old saying—"Orthodoxy is my doxy; Heterodoxy is someone else's doxy."

Notice too how things have changed during the Christian era. In the early days the prejudice was on the side of the Jews, who looked with contempt on the Gentiles. There was good reason for this. God had said, "This people have I formed for myself; they shall show forth my praise" (Isaiah 43:21). On another occasion he said, speaking of the Jews, "You only have I known of all the families of the earth: therefore I will punish you for all your iniquities" (Amos 3:2). Thus in a special sense God recognized Israel as His peculiar people, and He Himself put a hedge about them to keep them from mingling freely with the pagan who worshiped idols and indulged in all the unclean things that accompany idol worship. God called the Jews to separation from the sins of the Gentiles. So we need not be surprised that when the time came to carry the message of the grace of God to the Gentile world, even the Hebrew Christians looked with disfavor on reaching out into the pagan world with the proclamation of the gospel.

Now singularly enough, the shoe is on the other foot. Today it is the Gentile, and often the professing Christian among the Gentiles, who looks with disfavor on the Jew and, in many instances, has no sympathy with Christian missionary outreach to Israel. I have often heard it said, "The Jew had his chance; he refused Christ and therefore we have no further responsibility toward him." That is not the attitude of the Lord Jesus Christ. He commanded His disciples to go first of all to the lost sheep of the house of Israel. Paul said his ministry was to the Jew first, then also to the Gentile.

Some five or six years rolled by after Pentecost before the early Hebrew Christians began the work of evangelizing the Gentiles. And how often it is today that we find little spiritual effort on the part of the Gentiles to evangelize Jews! We are so easily controlled and dominated by our prejudices that we forget "there is no difference: For all have sinned and come short of the glory of God."

Destroying Prejudice in the Early Church (Acts 11:1-18)

After Peter's mission to the Gentile home of Cornelius he was put on trial, as it were, when he returned to the church at Jerusalem. He was called upon to defend himself for going to the Gentiles with the gospel. The disciples in Jerusalem did not yet have a vision broad enough to reach out to their Gentile neighbors from whom many of the Jews had suffered so much. We can realize why they hesitated, but in so doing they ignored their Lord's express command.

The apostles outside of Jerusalem received the news as a wonderful thing. "The apostles and brethren that were in Judaea heard that the Gentiles had also received the word of God." It seemed almost unbelievable. God, then, was reaching out beyond the confines of Israel to poor, lost, ruined sinners of the nations. This word came back to Jerusalem and the brethren there were perplexed about it. "When Peter was come up to Jerusalem, they that were of the circumcision [that is, converted Hebrews] contended with him, Saying, Thou wentest in to men uncircumcised, and didst eat with them." We remember that when our Lord was here on earth, the same charge was brought against Him when He ate with publicans and sinners, and He had to defend Himself for letting His grace go out to the needy. Peter also had to defend himself for going to the Gentiles with the message of the gospel.

Peter then related the whole story and left the verdict to them to decide whether he had been divinely guided. He explained that while he was praying he had seen a vision. In other words, this was not a mere notion of Peter's. It was not that he had himself decided to leap over national barriers and go to the Gentiles. Rather while he was waiting on God, seeking the mind of God, there came to his soul a revelation of God's grace in relation to a needy world.

He related his vision of a sheet filled with all types of animals. His Jewish audience recognized that according to Levitical law many of the animals were clean but others definitely unclean. The Jew was punctilious about eating only the things ceremonially clean, but the Gentile indulged himself as he would, eating many things considered unclean by the Jews.

"And I heard a voice saying unto me, Arise, Peter; slay and eat." I think I can understand something of Peter's feeling of revulsion— a strict Jew, looking at that heterogeneous collection of beasts, saying, "I cannot select my food from them." But a voice answered him from Heaven, "What God hath cleansed, that call not thou common." What did this mean? One thing it meant was that the day had passed when one had to distinguish between clean and unclean beasts. Our Lord Jesus Christ had declared that not that which enters into the mouth defiles the man. So it is left to us now to select those foods that are most suitable for our well-being.

However, there is a deeper meaning in the sentence, "What God hath cleansed, that call not thou common." He was referring to the whole world of sinners. In days gone by, the Gentiles were considered unclean. You will remember how the Jews were forbidden to mingle with the Gentiles in marriage. In the days of Ezra, when people failed in this matter and intermarried with the Gentile people, Ezra called them to separate from their wives and put away their children, for they were unclean. It was heartbreaking, but it was the will of God (Ezra 9).

What does it mean then, "What God hath cleansed, that call not thou common"? It means that, through the atoning blood of the Lord Jesus Christ, even the Gentiles have a way of access to God. Although outside the nation of Israel, they are entitled now to participate in the riches of God's grace. Even though they are strangers to the covenant of promise, they can know the salvation He has provided through the Lord Jesus. The apostle Paul said that he was "the minister of Jesus Christ to the Gentiles, ministering the gospel of God, that the offering up of the Gentiles might be acceptable, being sanctified by the Holy Ghost" (Romans 15:16). And we can go to all men everywhere now and say to them, "No matter what your record, whether you are Jew or Gentile, whether you have been punctilious about keeping the law or whether you have been utterly lawless, Christ died for all men, and the grace of God, proclaiming peace for all men, goes out to sinners everywhere." God's Word says, "Whosoever will, let him take the water of life freely."

This was the message the Lord was teaching Peter. There are no longer any ceremonial distinctions to be observed; God is waiting in grace to save whosoever will. Peter said the animals were presented to him three times. The same proclamation was made three times in order that he might be assured it was in very truth the mind of God. It often takes quite a little while to get something new into our understanding. "And, behold, immediately there were three men already come unto the house where I was, sent from Caesarea unto me. And the Spirit bade me go with them, nothing doubting." And so Peter started off to the household of Cornelius where he had that wonderful experience of which we read in Acts 10.

"Moreover these six brethren accompanied me, and we entered into the man's house." That was wisdom on the part of Peter. He was going to do an unprecedented thing and he wanted plenty of witnesses who could testify when he got back to Jerusalem that he did everything according to the mind and will of God.

There are a few points I want to emphasize regarding Cornelius. First, God could have given Cornelius the gospel through the angel that came to him. But it did not please Him to propagate the glad tidings in that way. He prefers to reach sinners through redeemed men and women, and this is a very wonderful and serious thing for us to consider. I am sure, of the myriads upon myriads of angels surrounding the throne of God, any one of them would count it a privilege to come down and stand at any crossroad in all the land and proclaim the gospel of the Lamb of God. But God has passed angels by, and has entrusted the message of His grace to sinners saved by that grace. How have we responded to that—we, to whom this wonderful privilege has been given? Will we rise to our privilege? Are we making known the gospel as we should to a lost world? In the next place, I want you to realize this: Cornelius was a man whose prayers and almsgiving had been accepted by God, therefore he must have been on the ground of an Old Testament believer. He was already quickened, but was not what the New Testament calls "saved." When we speak of being saved we mean far more than being safe. All down through the centuries those who turned to God in repentance were quickened by the Spirit of God, and in that sense were children of God and went home to Heaven at death. But they did not know positively that they were justified before God. They could not know for certain that their souls were saved. All these precious truths awaited revelation in the new dispensation.

Cornelius was a God-fearing, earnest man with no knowledge of peace with God. He was longing to be assured that he was accepted of Him. He sent to Peter to know how he and his household might be saved; in other words, how they might come into the full glad knowledge of forgiveness of sins. What a vast number of people in Christendom today are very much like Cornelius. They are undoubtedly God-fearing, and in their hearts believe in the Lord Jesus Christ, and therefore have knowledge Cornelius did not have; but they have no assurance of salvation. I am sorry to say it, but this is largely due to the preaching they hear in many places.

In Acts 10 we find the content of Peter's message. It was Jesus Christ, living His wonderful life here on earth, going about doing good, crucified for our sins, raised from the dead, and ascended on high to God's right hand. That was the message Cornelius needed to hear.

It is strange to hear people who profess to believe the Bible say they do not think anyone can know he is saved until the day of judgment. The Word of God says, "For the preaching of the cross is to them that perish foolishness; but unto us which are saved it is the power of God" (1 Corinthians 1:18). There are people who are saved and know they are saved. And there are others who really love the Lord but somehow or other have never dared to step out on His testimony, and so still are in doubt as to their salvation.

Cornelius and his household heard the Word and believed and they were saved, and immediately "the Holy Ghost fell on them, as on us at the beginning"—that is, on the day of Pentecost. Then Peter said in effect, "I realized, when I saw this, what God had done—that He had broken down the middle wall of partition. When I understood that God had accepted them and given them the gift of the Holy Ghost, what could I do about it?" "Then remembered I the word of the Lord, how that he said, John indeed baptized with water; but ye shall be baptized with the Holy Ghost" (Acts 11:16).

When the brethren in Jerusalem heard all this, they had nothing to say against it, but "held their peace, and glorified God, saying, Then hath God also to the Gentiles granted repentance unto life." Thank God that fact remains blessedly true. No poor sinner in all the world need feel he has gone so far there is no salvation for him. God grants forgiveness to all who will believe His Word, to those who will change their attitude toward the God against whom they have sinned.

Who and What Is a Christian? (Acts 11:19-30)

Acts 11:19-20 carries us back several years to the time immediately following the martyrdom of Stephen. We remember that it was after Stephen's death that Saul, on his way to Damascus, was miraculously and marvelously converted to preach the faith he had once persecuted. He had already been preaching perhaps three years and had visited Jerusalem, but because the Jews tried to kill him, had gone back to his native city Tarsus.

In these intervening years we find that the brethren who had fled from Palestine on account of the persecution there preached the gospel message to the Jews only. The Lord's commission had been very definite, "Go ye into all the world, and preach the gospel to every creature," but their Jewish prejudices hindered them from realizing that the same message was also for Gentiles. However in His time God overruled and they began to reach out to the nations. We read, "Some of them were men of Cyprus and Cyrene"; that is, although Jews, they had been born in these countries and had been accustomed to mingle with the Gentiles. So when they returned to their homelands they went to the Greeks and preached the Word.

Antioch was a great Greek city in Syria and there the gospel was first freely proclaimed to the Gentiles, with the result that many were saved. "And the hand of the Lord was with them." There was a great difference between these Greeks to whom the Gospel was preached in Antioch, and Cornelius to whom Peter carried the Word. Cornelius and his household feared the Lord. They knew God but did not understand the gospel of the new dispensation. It was otherwise with these Greeks. They were out and out idolaters, living in all the sins of paganism. What a day it must have been when the gospel of the grace of God was preached to those men! God worked in power and they were broken down and turned in faith to the Lord Jesus Christ.

"A great number believed, and turned unto the Lord." I wish we could always keep to the simplicity of things as we find them here. What led them to the Lord? The proclamation of the grace of God. Nothing else. They did not have to depend on all the other things to which preachers resort today in order to attract the people. They simply went to the heathen and preached Christ and Him crucified. God set His seal on that message and brought many to a saving knowledge of His blessed Son.

When the news of this reached Jerusalem, it created quite a stir among the brethren. They had already sat in judgment on Peter for going to the Gentiles. They did not take a stand of direct opposition, but sent Barnabas, a trusted man, to make sure it was really a work of God and not simply some human effort. Barnabas was the man who, we are told in an earlier chapter, had large properties in Cyprus, his native island. He had sold those properties and brought the money and laid it at the apostles' feet to be used in helping the needy brethren (Acts 4:36-37). He was characterized not only by sincere faith in the Lord Jesus Christ, but by his love for others. So he was sent to investigate and report to them as to the character of the work in Antioch.

"When he came and had seen the grace of God, [he] was glad." How can anybody see the grace of God? Grace is God's undeserved favor granted to poor lost sinners who put their trust in the Lord Jesus. Strictly speaking, we cannot see grace any more than we can see love, or its antithesis, hate. Then what did Barnabas see? We see the effects of hate in the unkind things it does, and we see the grace of God manifested in the changed lives of those who have received and believed the gospel message. This is how the gospel is propagated. The gospel proves itself by what it does. We hear a great deal about the need of a new gospel for a new age, but the old gospel still works, and works in power. When men and women believe it and receive it in their hearts, they become new creatures in Christ Jesus. Licentious, wicked, unclean people become chaste, holy, and clean; unrighteous people become faithful, honest, and true. This is how the grace of God is seen.

If we profess to believe in the Lord Jesus Christ, let us be careful to reveal the reality of our faith by godly lives. The world is looking on to see what the gospel we talk about has done for us. Christian men and women should so live and walk before the world, should so act in their behavior one to the other, that unsaved people will have to confess they see the grace of God in them.

Barnabas went to Antioch and saw the grace of God, and he ministered to them "and exhorted them all, that with purpose of heart they would cleave unto the Lord." How young converts need that encouragement! It is not merely a matter of receiving Christ as Savior. When one does that, thank God, he is saved; but from that moment on we need to cleave to the Lord with purpose of heart. Our Lord has warned us that "no man, having put his hand to the plough, and looking back, is fit for the kingdom of God" (Luke 9:62). May God enable us to plow a straight furrow—to go forward in the path of devotion to the Lord! How do we cleave to Him? With purpose of heart.

Let me give a few suggestions to young believers. In the first place, give the Word of God its proper place in your heart. Do not let a day go by in which you do not spend some time in your Bible. You cannot grow in grace without that. You are newborn babes and you need to be fed, and the Word is not only for our food but for our enlightenment. We cannot find our way through this world without the instructions we get from the Word of God. Not only should you be careful to meditate on the Word of God each day, but see that you spend some time daily waiting upon God in prayer. Prayer is the Christian's vital breath. A believer who is not given to prayer will never really count for God in this world. We are told to be faithful in prayer, to pray without ceasing.

Next, if we are going to cleave to the Lord, we should cultivate Christian fellowship—seek the association of those of like precious faith. None of us is strong in ourselves, and we need one another. We are to exhort each other, to be helpers of one another in the faith.

Then let us be unsparing in self-judgment. We need to keep account with God. When conscious of failure and sin, when we have yielded in any sense to temptation, let us not go on getting deeper and deeper into things that are wrong, drifting farther and farther from God. Turn at once to the Lord, face the matter in His presence. Remember, "if we confess our sins, he is faithful and just to forgive us our sins, and to cleanse us from all unrighteousness." This is what is meant by cleaving to the Lord with purpose of heart—recognizing His authority over our lives and His ownership of all we have and are.

So Barnabas exhorted these young Christians to be faithful to the Lord, in order that their lives might really count for God.

Moreover, we are told this of Barnabas: "He was a good man." I would like so to live that this might always be said of me. It means far more than for people to say, "He is cultured," or, "He is talented." One may be talented, cultured, educated and yet not be good. "The steps of a good man," we are told, "are ordered by the Lord," and so we are to seek to be good men. "He was a good man, and full of the Holy Ghost and of faith," a man who walked with and counted on God. This was the man to help these new converts. As a result of his ministry, "much people was added unto the Lord."

But Barnabas was also a self-effacing man; he realized his own limitations and was glad to recognize a man with greater ability than he had himself. As he ministered, he thought, *There is another man who can help in a better way. I am going to bring that man here.* "Then departed Barnabas to Tarsus, for to seek Saul." He had been interested in Saul. Saul had come to Jerusalem and wanted to join himself to the brethren there, but they were afraid of him and feared that he intended to turn them over to the authorities. But Barnabas spoke up and told how Saul had seen the Lord in the way, and that He had spoken to him, and that he had preached boldly at

Damascus in the name of Jesus. So the believers at Jerusalem lost their fear of him and received him into their fellowship.

Barnabas appreciated what had taken place in the life of Saul of Tarsus, and recognized his remarkable ability. He knew he was a chosen vessel to give the gospel to the Gentiles. Barnabas might have said, "I can go on ministering here with nobody interfering with me." But no, he said, "I would do better to fade out a little and get a more capable man to take my place"—and off he went to Tarsus. I would like to have been present during his interview with Saul. So far as we know, Saul was in retirement, as though he had failed to qualify as a preacher of the Word, after he left Jerusalem. We do not read of any work he was doing. But I think one day he was sitting in his home feeling a bit gloomy, thinking to himself, *The Lord cannot use me. People are not willing to receive my message*—when suddenly there was a knock at the door!

"Welcome, my old friend Barnabas, I am glad to see you."

"Saul, I have come to take you to Antioch, to help the church there."

"Why, what do you need me for?"

"There is a great opportunity there, and I feel sure you are the man for the job."

Then I can hear Paul saying, deprecatingly, "Oh no; I am not worthy—I persecuted this way even unto death."

But Barnabas assured him, "You are the very man for the place. Come with me!"

And "he brought him unto Antioch." I like that. It suggests to me that Saul was not ready to go until Barnabas persuaded him, in a kindly way. And so Saul went and "it came to pass, that a whole year they assembled themselves with the church, and taught much people." Saul and Barnabas, laboring together in Antioch for a whole year! It was there the believers first received the name which this new covenant company has borne throughout the centuries.

"And the disciples were called Christians first in Antioch." In some commentaries you will read that the Antiochians were given to conferring nicknames, and someone among them is supposed to have derogatorily made up the word *Christian* from the name *Christ*. But I question that very much. Thomas Newberry, one of the great

Greek scholars of the last century, wrote that the Greek word translated "called" really means, "oracularly called," or "divinely called." The disciples were first divinely called Christians at Antioch. This was God's name for them. Now that the work of evangelizing the world had really begun, God said, as it were, "I am going to give you the name by which I want My people known"—and He gave them the name *Christians*. We do not find the word used often in the Bible, but it soon became known all over the world. Later on, when Paul was defending himself before Agrippa, the king suddenly interrupted him and said, "Almost thou persuadest me to be a Christian." That was the name by which the new company had become known. In the First Epistle of Peter we read, "If any man suffer as a Christian, let him not be ashamed; but let him glorify God on this behalf."

Who and what is a Christian? We often use the term in a very loose way today. We speak of Christians as we do of Mohammedans or Jews, as denoting a group of people who profess certain religious views. We think of almost anyone born in a country like America as a Christian. I remember handing a gospel booklet to a man on a train and he turned to me and asked, "What did you give me that book for?" I replied, "I thought you might be interested. May I ask, are you a Christian?" "Well," he replied indignantly, "take a good look at me—do I look like a Jew or a Chinaman?" "You look and talk like an American." "Then," he responded, "that is your answer."

No, there are millions of Americans who are not Christians, and thousands of church members who are not Christians. What is a Christian? The disciples were divinely called Christians—those who received the Word of God in their hearts. They received the gospel and therefore were born again through the power of the risen Christ in Heaven. They were Christians because they belonged to Christ.

A Christian is Christ's representative here in this world. Many years ago, when studying Cantonese, one of the branches of the Chinese language, I found the word used for a Christian was *Yasuyan*. *Yasu* was their word for Jesus, and *yan* was man. Whenever my teacher would introduce me, he would say I was a "Jesus man." That is what a Christian really is. It is his high privilege to represent

Christ in this world. He belongs to Christ, is united to Christ, and now should seek to live out the life of Christ before men. That is what Paul meant when he said, "I am crucified with Christ: nevertheless I live; yet not I, but Christ liveth in me: and the life which I now live in the flesh I live by the faith of the Son of God, who loved me, and gave himself for me" (Galatians 2:20). God give us the grace to be consistent Christians! There is no greater testimony to the power of the gospel than that.

In the final verses of Acts 11 we have a beautiful little illustration of Christian love in action.

> And in these days came prophets from Jerusalem unto Antioch. And there stood up one of them named Agabus, and signified by the Spirit that there should be great dearth throughout all the world: which came to pass in the days of Claudius Caesar. Then the disciples, every man according to his ability, determined to send relief unto the brethren which dwelt in Judaea: Which also they did, and sent it to the elders by the hands of Barnabas and Saul (27-30).

These Gentile brethren, converted to Christ in Antioch, heard of the need and distress of their Christian brothers in Judea and they wanted to help them. They did not have to be urged, or pleaded with. They knew their brethren in Judea were in need and they gladly helped.

What started men thinking beyond the boundary lines of their own nations? It was the love of Christ shed abroad in their hearts by the Holy Spirit. Here is perhaps the first instance in history of people putting together their money in order to send relief to men of another nation. Christianity is the truest philanthropy! Christianity teaches men formerly driven by selfishness to find real joy in ministering to those in less comfortable and less agreeable circumstances than their own. How could it be otherwise? We owe everything for eternity to the One who came from the heights of glory to lay down His life for our sins, and surely "we ought to lay down our lives for the brethren."

CHAPTER TWELVE
THROUGH THE IRON DOOR

We have in Acts 12 the closing scene in Peter's Judean ministry. When we open the next chapter, he recedes into the background and Paul becomes the leading figure. There had been persecution before, and at that time all the disciples had been scattered abroad—except the apostles. We read in Acts 12:1, "Now about that time Herod the king [this was Herod Agrippa I, the grandson of the Herod under whom our Lord Jesus was born] stretched forth his hands to vex certain of the church. And he killed James the brother of John with the sword."

You will remember there were three apostles most intimately linked with our Lord's earthly ministry—Peter, James, and John. These three were together with Christ on the mount of transfiguration and in the house of Jairus when Jesus raised from the dead the daughter of that synagogue leader. These three were in the garden of sorrow when He bowed before the Father and cried, "If thou be willing, remove this cup from me: nevertheless not my will, but thine, be done." Now one was taken away by death—James the Great (to be distinguished from James the Less, the Son of Alphaeus). Herod saw that the death of James pleased the enemies of the gospel so he proceeded to take Peter also.

"Then were the days of unleavened bread," following the Passover, and since Herod did not want to start a riot at such a time he decided to imprison Peter until after the feast of weeks. The KJV says "Easter," but in the original it is "Pentecost." Then he intended to bring him forth and put him to death. But now we find God's people using that resource which He has given His own in every trial: "Prayer was made without ceasing of the church unto God for him." What a wonderful privilege!

People say sometimes, "Why do we need to pray? Does not our gracious God know all about us and what we need far better than we do?" But we learn from God's Word that He has chosen to do in answer to prayer what He might not do apart from prayer. He gives in answer to prayer some things He will not give apart from it— "Ye have not, because ye ask not." So prayer is the resource of God's needy people—prayer for ourselves, prayer in behalf of others.

Here you have the whole church in Jerusalem praying for Peter. And while they were praying, God was working. Things had gone on until it looked as though there was no hope for Peter. God had permitted him to remain in prison many days. He gave no sign, yet all the time He was working. We often say that man's extremity is God's opportunity. Peter had come to the last night he was to live on earth—if Herod's judgment was to be carried out.

"Peter was sleeping between two soldiers, bound with two chains: and the keepers before the door kept the prison." This suggests absolute hopelessness. There was nothing Peter could do to free himself—and in that sense this becomes an illustration of the sinner's condition. We can see pictured here every one of us in our unconverted days—asleep, indifferent, bound in the chains of our sins, guarded by Satan's emissaries, doomed to die. This is the state of man without Christ. Peter was a man who could do nothing for himself, when suddenly a messenger came from Heaven. Thank God, He has sent us a messenger—His own blessed Son! "And, behold, the angel of the Lord came upon him, and a light shined in the prison." We read in Psalms, "The entrance of thy words giveth light." That is why we preach the gospel and proclaim the way of salvation to men who are sleeping in sin, so they may be brought to the Light and realize their needy condition, and then go on to follow the gleam.

The angel "smote Peter on the side." I do not know whether Peter enjoyed that or not! He was sleeping soundly, comfortable even in his chains. And so it is when we seek to bring people to see their lost condition, many of them say, as the sluggard in the book of Proverbs, "Yet a little sleep, a little slumber, a little folding of the hands to sleep." Oh, unsaved man or woman, sleeping in your sins, hear me! A little more sleep, a little more slumber—and you will wake up in a lost eternity! "Awake thou that sleepest, and arise from the dead, and Christ shall give thee light."

Peter was awakened roughly by the angel who said, "Arise up quickly. And his chains fell off from his hands." As he acted in obedience to the angel's command, though he thought it a vision or a dream, his chains fell off. So it is today when men hear the Word and act on it. "Verily, verily, I say unto you, He that heareth my word, and believeth on him that sent me, hath everlasting life, and shall not come into condemnation; but is passed from death unto life" (John 5:24). One of our own dear brethren told me that after having been bound by the chains of strong drink, and useless to himself and everyone else, he came under the spell of the gospel. "I heard the Word, and in one moment my chains fell off. I have never again walked the drunkard's pathway." That is what the gospel can do for anyone who accepts the message.

"And the angel said unto him, Gird thyself, and bind on thy sandals." In other words, "You are a free man. Now act as a free man." The angel continued, "Cast thy garment about thee, and follow me." First then, the sinner must be awakened; then he is brought to see his true condition and, trusting in his Deliverer, he is to follow Him. In other words, we are to follow Christ because we are saved. We are saved through what He did on Calvary's cross.

And he went out, and followed him; and wist not that it was true which was done by the angel; but thought he saw a vision. When they were past the first and the second ward, they came unto the iron gate that leadeth unto the city; which opened to them of his own accord (Acts 12:9-10).

If Peter had passed through that iron gate the following day in his chains, he would have gone out, under the Roman guard, to the place of execution—to die. That is what Herod intended. But Peter, obeying the word of God, having received the message of the angel, walked through the wards until he came to the iron gate. He might have said, "I have no power to open that portal." But in a moment it opened by itself and Peter went through, not to die, but to live and to spend many years in service for the Lord Jesus Christ.

And so it is today: If you and I had passed through the iron gate of death in our sins we would have gone out into everlasting judgment. But thank God, Christ has died for us and therefore His death becomes our death. The iron gate is open and we pass through the gate in Him.

"And they went out, and passed on through one street; and forthwith the angel departed from him." Now Peter is alone and for the first time he realizes what has taken place. Up to this moment he thought he was in a dream, but "when Peter was come to himself, he said, Now I know of a surety, that the Lord hath sent his angel, and hath delivered me out of the hand of Herod, and from all expectation of the people of the Jews." So you have two illustrations here: The illustration of God dealing in grace with sinners sleeping in chains and, on the other hand, you see His marvelous power in delivering His servant in answer to prayer. For while the church was praying, God was working. That is the way it always is. Do you know why we do not see a greater demonstration of divine power among us? Because there is so little prayer. The church was praying and God sent His angel and delivered Peter.

When Peter had considered the situation I think he reasoned something like this: "Let me see, where had I better go? I am a marked man, and if I stay in the streets I shall be caught again. I think I shall go to the prayer meeting!" That is a good place for a man to go! Peter knew they were having a prayer meeting at the house of Mary, the mother of John Mark, the author of the second Gospel. His mother was apparently very wealthy, and had a large house in Jerusalem in which she set aside one room for prayer.

But now we have a remarkable story of people praying—without really expecting an immediate answer. We are told that "As Peter knocked at the door of the gate, a damsel came to hearken, named Rhoda"—that is, Rose. I think the gate was probably like one of those doors which you and I have seen in old fashioned barns, where either the upper or lower half opens and the other half still remains locked. Little Rose opened one half and looked out and saw Peter. She became so excited she forgot to open the other half! They were praying, "Lord deliver Peter," but when Rhoda ran in and told them that Peter stood at the gate, they said to her in effect, "You're mad. Nonsense! Don't tell us that—we know he is bound in the prison." They argued with her, declaring he could not be there. What an indictment against even praying Christians! Little Rhoda "constantly affirmed that it was so." But they said, "It is his angel." (They used the word *angel* for *spirit*.) In other words, "It is his spirit. He has already been executed. Poor Peter has been slain and you have seen his spirit!" And all the while Peter continued to knock. I have heard of spirits rapping, but I don't think any ever continued to knock like Peter. By and by someone decided they had better go see what it meant. "and when they had opened the door, and saw him, they were astonished." They should have been expecting him: they should have said, "We are praying you might be freed and here you are! God has answered prayer."

Have you never had an experience like that where you prayed and prayed and asked God for something, then when He came in grace and answered, you could hardly believe it to be true? You thought there must have been a mistake somewhere. It shows how we dishonor God with our lack of faith. "But he, beckoning unto them with the hand to hold their peace, declared unto them how the Lord had brought him out of the prison." And knowing that Herod would be desirous of apprehending him again, Peter said, "Go show these things unto James, and to the brethren. And he departed and went into another place"—just where, we are not told.

"Now as soon as it was day, there was no small stir among the soldiers, what was become of Peter." When they came to change the guard, I suppose they said, "Whatever has happened to Peter? Last night he was sleeping between two soldiers, bound with two chains, and the keepers before the door kept the prison, but now he has disappeared!" When word reached Herod, he was furious. He examined the keepers and, tyrant that he was, ordered their execution.

Then Herod went into Caesarea—and here we have an incident of which Josephus also wrote. He tells how the citizens of Caesarea, at odds with Herod, sent for him. To them he delivered a great speech. They then made some kind of treaty and burst into round after round of applause, exclaiming, "It is the voice of a god, and not of a man." Instead of denying that and saying, "I am just a mortal man; I am not to be worshiped or adored," Herod complacently took all the honor to himself. Because he dared to receive the glory that belongs to God, God smote him. Josephus tells how he was smitten with an incurable disease and died within a few days. Dr. Luke (for remember he was a physician who knew all the facts and understood the malady) told exactly what it was: "And immediately the angel of the Lord smote him, because he gave not God the glory: and he was eaten of worms, and gave up the ghost." And so Herod, this bitter enemy of the church of God, perished.

This ends the record of the special work God had given Peter to do in connection with Israel and the opening of the door of faith to the Gentiles. From this time on we see the river of grace becoming wider and wider, deeper and deeper, reaching to the uttermost parts of the earth. "The word of God grew and multiplied." Barnabas and Saul, who had gone up to Jerusalem, bringing assistance to those afflicted by the famine, "returned from Jerusalem [that is, they went back to Antioch in Syria where that mighty work of God had already begun] and took with them John, whose surname was Mark." This young man was intimately related to Barnabas and so he went along with Barnabas and Saul to enter into the ministry.

Acts 12 is a good reminder of the words of the psalmist—"Call upon me in the day of trouble: I will deliver thee, and thou shalt glorify me" (Psalm 50:15).

CHAPTER THIRTEEN
THE BEGINNING OF WORLD EVANGELISM

The church in Antioch was an excellently cared-for church! We do not see anything in the New Testament of that which is so common today: one lone minister set over a congregation; but we find the Spirit of God giving gifts as it pleased Him. In one congregation there might be a number of men ministering the Word, and that without jealousy one of another, each seeking to minister the gift God had given him.

A Missionary Church (Acts 13:1-3)

In the church of Antioch we find five ministering the Word. First of all, there was Barnabas, the Levite, who had sold all his patrimony and put everything he had into the work of the Lord. He was seeking now to minister to the people at Antioch.

Then "Simeon that was called Niger"—that is, "Simeon the black man." We wish we knew more about him. He is the one outstanding man in the New Testament who comes before us as a servant of God from the Negro race. There was no racial prejudice in this church. People of different color skin and of different religious background were found happily worshiping together—Jews, Gentiles, people of various races. This is all we read of Simeon, yet it is enough to tell us that the grace of God was working in a mighty way, breaking down carnal prejudice.

Then we read of Lucius of Cyrene. The name is probably Gentile, evidence that God had already begun to gift these Gentile believers in a special way.

And then Manaen. We have no way of ascertaining his background, but we know that he was brought up with Herod the tetrarch, who was part Samaritan and part Idumean. Though nurtured in the royal court, in all the corruption of those days, he occupied a much higher position than Herod ever obtained—a minister of the gospel of the Lord Jesus Christ.

Last of all we have Saul, the former persecutor, a Pharisee of the Pharisees, a Hebrew of the Hebrews. He had tried to root Christianity out of the earth, but had been so marvelously converted that now he sought to further the Christian cause by preaching the faith he had once endeavored to destroy.

"As they ministered to the Lord, and fasted, the Holy Ghost said, Separate me Barnabas and Saul for the work whereunto I have called them." We do not know just how the Holy Spirit revealed His will: whether it was a deep impression made on the hearts of Saul and Barnabas, or whether, on the other hand, it was a deep impression on the members of the church. But certainly they began to talk about it and said, "These men ought to reach out and go to the regions beyond. God has given us abundant witness here, and now we should think of those who have never heard the gospel story." In either event, the Spirit of God revealed His mind.

He still speaks to men, impressing them with the deep need of a lost world. The history of missions is a story of the miraculous working of the Spirit of God down through the centuries. One can think of many whose names will shine brightly before the judgment seat of Christ because they were aroused by the Spirit of God and obeyed the call to carry the message of Christ to the lost, both at home and abroad. These spiritually impressed men and women felt they could not go on in the ordinary walk of life but must give their talents to reach those who had never heard the name of Christ. So they went out to the ends of the earth carrying the gospel message of the grace of God. It was so here in the beginning of world evangelism as the Holy Spirit said, "I want Barnabas and Saul for a special ministry. I want them to go out into the world with the message of salvation."

The church united in this effort. There was nothing unusual. They fasted and prayed, and laid their hands on them, and sent them away. Some have thought of this as the ordination of Barnabas and Saul as gospel ministers. That is absurd on the face of it. Both had been preaching the gospel many years. This laying on of hands was an expression of the fellowship of the Antiochian church with these men as they started the work of world evangelization.

In the Old Testament sacrificial system, the offerer, recognizing his need of atonement and feeling oppressed by his sinfulness, placed his hand on the head of the offering. In this way he identified himself with the offering. Isaac Watts expressed the meaning of that when he wrote in one of his hymns:

> My faith would lay her hand
> On that blest head of Thine,
> While, as a penitent, I stand
> And there confess my sin.

So today when a poor sinner reaches out the hand of faith and places it, as it were, on the head of the Lord Jesus Christ and says, "I recognize that the Son of God loved me and gave Himself for me; I am identified with Him in His sacrifice"—then his soul is saved.

As the brethren in Antioch laid their hands on Saul and Barnabas, they identified themselves with their missionary efforts. They said in effect: "Brethren, we are one with you in this missionary enterprise. You go out into the regions beyond, and we shall stay by you here at home. You go down into the dark caverns of the earth, and seek to find the gold and precious things that shall adorn the crown of the Lord Jesus Christ in the ages to come, and we will hold the ropes and look after your temporal needs and pray." This should always be the attitude of those at home toward those who carry the message to the uttermost parts.

Evangelism in Cyprus (Acts 13:4-13)

"So they, being sent forth by the Holy Ghost, departed unto Seleucia; and from thence they sailed to Cyprus." Notice that while the church had full fellowship with them in their going out, we are not told they were sent by the church. They did not get their commission from the church, but from the risen Lord who had told them to go into all the world.

Some people talk as though this question of missions is a mere matter in which the church may decide whether it is wise or not, but that is not the case. The Lord answered that question plainly and clearly when He said, "Go ye therefore, and teach all nations, baptizing them in the name of the Father, and of the Son, and of the Holy Ghost: Teaching them to observe all things whatsoever I have commanded you: and, lo, I am with you alway, even unto the [consummation of the age]."

Some years ago there was a great missionary rally in the Royal Albert Hall in London, England, and a clergyman turned to the Duke of Wellington (the "Iron Duke," whose armies had defeated Napoleon) and asked, "My lord Duke, do you believe in missions?" "What are your marching orders?" asked the Duke. "Of course, the Bible says to go into all the world," answered the clergyman. "Then you have nothing to say about it. As a soldier you are to obey orders." And that is true of the church down through the centuries to the end of the dispensation. It is the Lord who commands us to go; it is the Lord who sends His workers out, and the church is to have fellowship with them to the utmost of its ability.

Seleucia was a city on the sea coast. From there the two apostles sailed for Cyprus. Doubtless the heart of Barnabas was burdened for Cyprus. Born there, it was his former home. We can understand him saying, "I should like to go first to my island home and tell the people there about the matchless grace of God as revealed in Jesus Christ." We read, "And when they were at Salamis, they preached the word of God in the synagogues of the Jews," but at first did not find an opening to go to the Gentiles.

Verse 5 refers to John Mark, cousin of Barnabas and son of Mary of Jerusalem, a wealthy woman with a large house where many of the early services were held. John Mark was the author of the second Gospel. At this point he joined their journey.

"And when they had gone through the isle unto Paphos, they found a certain sorcerer, a false prophet, a Jew, whose name was

Bar-jesus." As *bar* means "son," his name really meant "Son of Jesus." He was a renegade Jew who had gone out among the Gentiles pretending to be a marvelous wonder-worker, and thereby trying to profit. He undoubtedly had heard of the Lord Jesus Christ and His miracles. That name had been mentioned here and there throughout the world. He said in effect, "I am the son of Jesus and I am able to work wonders, even as He did." He was there with the proconsul of the country, Sergius Paulus. Paulus is exactly the same name as Paul, and it is interesting to note that from this time on we never read again of Saul; it is as though Paul took the name of his first illustrious convert.

> Sergius Paulus, a prudent man; who called for Barnabas and Saul, and desired to hear the word of God. But Elymas the sorcerer...withstood them, seeking to turn away the deputy from the faith. Then Saul (who also is called Paul,) filled with the Holy Ghost, set his eyes on him, And said, O full of all subtilty and all mischief, thou child of the devil, thou enemy of all righteousness, wilt thou not cease to pervert the right ways of the Lord? (Acts 13:7-10)

The word translated "child" is slightly different; in the original it is the word *son*. In withstanding Elymas the sorcerer, Paul was acting for God because this man was seeking to hinder the salvation of the soul of Sergius Paulus.

It is a serious thing to trifle with the souls of men. How inexcusable it would be if one professed to be a physician and tried recklessly to minister to sick people, using medicines which he did not understand, some of which were deadly poisons! He would be subjected immediately to the law and there would be severe consequences. There have been such men in days gone by. But if it is a serious thing to tamper with the human body, it is far more serious to tamper with the souls of men. Because Elymas was trying to do just that, Paul spoke to him as he did, calling him "Son of the devil."

The Spirit of God never used a term like that of ordinary unsaved men. The Lord Jesus said of certain ones of His day, "Ye are of your father, the devil." He did not address everybody like that, but only those men who deliberately and definitely set themselves to oppose the divine program. In the First Epistle of John, the apostle spoke of Cain and Abel, and said, "In this the children of God are manifest, and the children of the devil: whosoever doeth not righteousness is not of God, neither he that loveth not his brother."

All men by nature are children of wrath, but no man is called a "child of the devil" unless he deliberately gives himself to Satanic propaganda and takes a stand as a positive enemy of God. That was the position Elymas the sorcerer took and Paul invoked a judgment on him for that: "Behold, the hand of the Lord is upon thee, and thou shalt be blind, not seeing the sun for a season. And immediately there fell on him a mist and a darkness; and he went about seeking some to lead him by the hand." The physical judgment that fell on him was the expression of the darkness of this man's soul.

When Sergius Paulus saw this and saw how Elymas was confounded before the messenger of the true gospel, we are told he "believed, being astonished at the doctrine of the Lord." And so he was the first Gentile convert on their first missionary journey. He was a man of position and authority and his conversion doubtless meant a great deal in the island of Cyprus. The people generally would say, "The proconsul has accepted the new message. He has received the gospel and now believes in this Jesus whom Paul and Barnabas preach." Many were no doubt impressed.

We are told, in verse thirteen, they came back to the mainland. They had finished their work in Cyprus for the time being. Cyprus, however, was visited later by Barnabas, who spent some time there.

"Now when Paul and his company loosed from Paphos, they came to Perga in Pamphylia." This was a mountainous country, difficult to reach. And we are told that "John departing from them returned to Jerusalem." The Spirit of God does not tell us why he did not go on with them, yet it does not seem hard to read between the lines. We shall see later on that the apostle Paul felt there was no legitimate reason for this young man to leave them. John Mark, you know, was the son of a rich woman. That isn't always the best start in life—to be born with a silver spoon in your mouth! He had been sheltered and perhaps coddled all his days, and when his cousin Barnabas went into missionary work he was impressed and desired to go along too. But when he found himself in difficult circumstances, perhaps he contrasted his discomforts with the calm and agreeable atmosphere he had left in Jerusalem. He might think, "Mother would never let me suffer like this." So, when at Perga as he looked at that high mountain range and thought of the stress and strain of what lay ahead, a great spasm of homesickness came over him and he decided to give up the work.

Paul did not approve of that. He felt this business of missions was not merely a junketing trip. It was not a matter of going to foreign lands just to see strange people and places. It was a tremendously serious matter, calling for true soldierly bearing, and he felt John Mark had failed in this and was unworthy of confidence. Barnabas, who was related to John Mark, did not quite share this view. Later God allowed him to rectify his action, and he became a devoted servant of the Lord Jesus Christ.

So we have here the beginning of Christian missions. We can thank God that, through the centuries since, this work has continued. For a period the church seemed to forget its responsibility, but during the last 150 years there has been a greater awakening in the church of God toward missionary effort. Again we thank God for having put upon the hearts of so many a burden for the lost world.

Paul's Sermon at Pisdian Antioch (Acts 13:14-43)

After Paul and Barnabas departed from Perga they made their way over the mountains, and at last reached the principal city of that district, another Antioch. Do not confuse Antioch in Pisidia with Antioch in Syria. The Syrian Antioch, directly north of Palestine, was where the first great Gentile church was formed; the Pisidia Antioch was considerably farther north, and there another mighty work of God began.

When Paul and Barnabas reached Antioch in Pisidia, they went into the synagogue and sat down. Paul always put the Jews first. Everywhere he went there were generally to be found little congregations of Hebrews. He knew they had the Scriptures, and he felt his first responsibility was to go to them and present the One for whom they had long waited. And so the two went in and took their places. After the law and the prophets had been read, the rulers of the synagogue, perhaps recognizing Paul and Barnabas by their dress as teachers or rabbis, said, "If ye have any word of exhortation for the people, say on." There was a great deal more liberty in the synagogues than you will find in some Christian churches today, which never allow a stranger such opportunity.

There were two classes of people in the synagogue—men of Israel and those that feared God. The latter group was composed of proselyte Gentiles who had accepted the God of Israel as their God and sought to order their lives in accordance with the law of Moses. Paul addressed both. In this marvelous sermon of his, which we have with a great deal of fullness, he traced out something of Israel's history and God's promise, and then showed how in a wonderful way that promise was fulfilled. Then he stressed the responsibility of all the people to accept the Savior whom God had provided.

First he pointed out how graciously God had tolerated the failures of His people Israel in the wilderness. In spite of all their murmurings against Him, He had provided bread from Heaven and water out of the smitten rock. At last He brought them into the land of promise and consented to dwell in the sanctuary they had prepared for Him.

How patient He has been throughout the years! As we look back over the history of the church, we have nothing to boast of. You say, Israel failed very grievously. They did—but we, the church in this dispensation, have failed even more inasmuch as our privileges are greater than theirs. How sad much of the history of the church is, but God has endured our conduct in the wilderness when we have acted like fretful, irritable children. He has dealt with us in such lovingkindness not only collectively but individually. Too many of us can look back over the years and see how we failed the Lord, but He has never failed us. He has undertaken for us so graciously. How our hearts ought to thank Him for His lovingkindness. How He has sustained us! What a gracious God we have!

Paul reviewed the history with which these Jews at Antioch would be thoroughly familiar from their study of the Old Testament Scriptures. And then he went on to speak of David, their great poet and shepherd king, who was a prototype of this greater Son, the Lord Jesus Christ.

Skeptics have questioned the description of David as a man after God's heart. They ask, What about the dreadful sins David committed? David faced those sins and repented and God forgave him. That is a great deal more than some of David's critics can say. But it was when God found David as a shepherd lad He said, "I have found...a man after mine own heart, which shall fulfill all my will." That is, David would fulfill God's will in regard to the kingdom and ruling the people of Israel (see 1 Samuel 13:13-14).

God promised to raise a savior for Israel from the seed of David. He said to David that He was going to give him a Son who would sit on His throne and that it would be established forever. Those words could not refer to King Solomon nor to any other of David's line, until at last Jesus of Nazareth was born in Bethlehem of Judea. In His veins flowed the blood of David, for Mary the mother of Jesus was a direct lineal descendant of King David through Nathan. Mary's husband Joseph, who was not actually the father of Jesus, was also of David's line. The title to the throne really belonged to him, so by virtue of Joseph's position Jesus had title to the throne of David.

Always before the glad and glorious message of the Savior Jesus, comes the message of John the baptist. It is the message of repentance for the remission of sins. In other words, men will never really believe in the Lord Jesus Christ and receive Him in their hearts as Savior until they turn to God first of all as repentant sinners.

One reason we have so many shallow conversions today, so many church members who have never really known the grace of God, is because there is so little preaching of the need for repentance. Jesus Himself said, "They that be whole need not a physician, but they that are sick." If men do not realize their sinfulness and lost condition before God they will never appreciate the saving grace of God as revealed in Christ. So the call to repentance should never be divorced from the message of faith—repentance toward God and faith in the Lord Jesus Christ.

John's ministry was utterly self-effacing. He came not preaching himself, nor attempting to attract men's attention to himself. But he proclaimed the coming One, the One of whom he said, "Behold the Lamb of God, which taketh away the sin of the world." This should be the attitude of every true messenger of God—preaching not ourselves, but Jesus Christ and Him crucified. This is the message we can bring to all men everywhere today. Whether you are a Jew or a Gentile, if in your heart you have any fear of God and you desire to know His way and be obedient to His will, we come to you to say: "To you is the word of this salvation sent."

There is no man so ignorant or so degraded beyond the salvation God has provided through the cross of the Lord Jesus Christ. But not until men confess their sin and bow at the Savior's feet in repentance will this salvation actually become theirs, "even the righteousness of God which is by faith of Jesus Christ unto all and upon all them that believe: for there is no difference: For all have sinned, and come short of the glory of God" (Romans 3:22-23). There is not one gospel for the Jews and another gospel for the Gentiles. "There is no difference between the Jew and the Greek for the same Lord over all is rich unto all that call upon him." Therefore, whether Jew or Gentile, if men bow before God as sinners and look up to Him in faith and receive the Savior He has provided, they will know His delivering power.

Paul next takes up the story of Jesus and tells these Antiochians, Jews and Gentiles, what had taken place in Palestine. The very people who possessed the Old Testament Scriptures in which the coming of God's Messiah was so plainly foretold, fulfilled those Scriptures in condemning the Lord of Glory! That is a solemn fact. You will remember how when the wise men came from the East to Jerusalem inquiring of the birthplace of the Messiah, King Herod called the leaders of Israel and asked them where the Savior was to be born. They turned immediately to the book of the prophet Micah. They knew exactly where to locate His place of birth, and yet they spurned Him. Why? Because they loved their sins more than Christ, and that is why men refuse Him today and spurn the Word of God.

Some say, I cannot believe the Bible; I cannot believe it is the Word of God. As a rule these are not the people who know the Bible, who read it thoughtfully and carefully. But if you do read it and you still cannot believe it, it is because you are living in some sin the Bible condemns and you do not want to repent of it. Sin blinds men's eyes to the truth. Sin blinded the eyes of the people of Israel to the fact that God was revealed in Christ here on earth. And sin keeps people from receiving Him today. Jesus Himself said, "If any man will to do his will [that is, if any man desires to do the will of God], he shall know of the doctrine" (John 7:17). If you want to know the truth, you may. If you are willing to obey God, willing to judge your sin, willing to repent of it and ask Him to make the truth known, He has pledged Himself to reveal it to you. But it is a very solemn fact that it may never grip the consciences of some people for they are determined to go on in some sin the Word of God condemns.

As we read Acts 13:30 we are reminded how often in Scripture the two words *But God* appear together. You will remember in the Epistle to the Romans, after Paul wrote of man's lost and sinful condition, he said, "But God"—and then you go on to read what God has done (Romans 5:8). Men nailed Jesus to a tree, friends laid Him in Joseph's new tomb; *but God*, by His omnipotent power, raised Him from the dead!

"And he was seen many days of them which came up with him from Galilee to Jerusalem, who are his witnesses unto the people" (31). Remember, when Paul uttered these words there were scores of those living who had actually seen the Lord Jesus Christ in resurrection glory and could give testimony concerning this. It was not done in an isolated corner, but it was something witnessed by a vast number of people.

In verse 33 (KJV) you might omit the word *again*. The translators have put it in, but it is not found in the best Greek text, and it is not needed here. It actually makes confusion.

Paul reminded his hearers that David had predicted that the Savior was to die and then be raised from the dead; for in Psalm 16 we read, "For thou wilt not leave my soul in hell; neither wilt thou suffer thine Holy One to see corruption." So the body of the Lord Jesus lay in the grave three days but it did not see corruption. It came forth in resurrection life, a testimony to the victorious power of God over death and Hell and all foes.

Based on this declaration of the death and resurrection of the

Lord Jesus Christ, Paul gave us one of the grandest gospel statements that we have in all the Bible:

> Be it known unto you therefore,...that through this man is
> preached unto you the forgiveness of sins; And by him all that
> believe are justified from all things, from which ye could not be
> justified by the law of Moses (Acts 13:38-39).

What a wonderful declaration! Forgiveness of sins and justification from all things—offered to all who believe in the Lord Jesus
Christ! Forgiveness and justification stand absolutely in contrast
one to the other. Man cannot do what Paul declared God would do
through Christ Jesus. You could not forgive a man and justify him
at the same time. If you forgive him he is guilty, and you cannot
justify him. If a man is justified he does not need forgiveness.

You can imagine a court scene—you are on trial and the jury
decides you are innocent of the charge against you and they bring in
the verdict. "Not guilty!" It means you are justified. As you walk
out of the courtroom, suppose someone comes up and says, "That
was an interesting session this morning. I think it was very gracious
of the judge to forgive you." You look at him with indignation.
"Forgive me! The jury cleared me. I am justified, I am not forgiven,
for I did not need pardon for a crime I had not committed."

But it is otherwise with God in His dealing with sinners. We are
all guilty and have come short of the glory of God. We have all
failed again and again, and there is no hope until we come into His
presence and acknowledge our sins. Then, if we confess our sins,
He is faithful and just to forgive us our sins, and to cleanse us from
all unrighteousness. But is that all? No, we are now linked up with
divine life by the Christ who died and rose again, and we now stand
before God on altogether different and new ground, and God can
say, "I justified that man; from henceforth I look on him as though
he had never committed any sin at all. I hold him clear of every
charge. Christ has settled for everything."

That is the gospel message. "There is therefore now no condemnation to them which are in Christ Jesus," and, "by him all that
believe are justified from all things, from which ye could not be

justified by the law of Moses." The law of Moses said, "Cursed is every one that continueth not in all things which are written in the book of the law to do them." The law of Moses can only condemn. We cannot be justified by the deeds of the law. But the gospel of the grace of God tells us that He who never violated that law, God's own blessed Son, went to Calvary's cross and bore the judgment of the law and was made a curse for us that we might be the righteousness of God in Him. And when we trust Him, we stand before God cleared of every charge, in Him. This is justification. Oh, how full it is!

But now Paul had a solemn word of warning for these people in Antioch in Pisidia:

> Beware therefore, lest that come upon you, which is spoken of in the prophets; Behold, ye despisers, and wonder, and perish: for I work a work in your days, a work which ye shall in no wise believe, though a man declare it unto you (40-41).

In other words Paul said: "When this message of the gospel comes to you it brings with it added responsibility. You will never be the same again after you have heard the message. If you accept it, you are justified from all things; if you reject it, your condemnation becomes greater than it ever was before because you are in possession of light and knowledge you did not previously have." And so I say today to everyone who has heard the gospel message, you may take these words to heart, receive Christ, and so be justified, or reject these words, spurn the Savior, and endure instead the unspeakable judgment that will fall on all who have heard the message of grace only to refuse it. He who hears the gospel for the first time becomes more accountable than he has ever been before.

Well, what were the results of this great sermon in the synagogue in Antioch in Pisidia? There was a real awakening. Most of the Jews were earnest, honest seekers after the truth, and as they realized their condition they desired to know more about the gospel. Many of the proselytes questioned Paul and Barnabas who took the opportunity to open up the Word of God to them, and lead them to acceptance of Christ as their Savior. They then persuaded them to go on in the grace of God, learning more and more of God's sovereign goodness.

The Effect of the Gospel Message (Acts 13:44-52)

It is always of interest to notice the various ways in which the gospel message affects different people. When Paul preached that great sermon in the Jewish synagogue at Pisidian Antioch, we are told that many of the Jews and religious proselytes opened their hearts to the truth and received the Lord Jesus Christ and took their stand definitely on His side. But there was another group that did not receive the truth. These became violently antagonistic.

"The next sabbath day came almost the whole city together to hear the word of God." The people's interest was great and they thronged the synagogue in such numbers it aroused the envy and enmity of the unbelieving Jews. It grieved them that so many were anxious to listen to these strange teachers who had come to their city. They could not accept peaceably the interest shown, so began to contradict the things spoken by Paul, and even to blaspheme. So intense was the opposition, the apostles saw that they must go elsewhere. It was useless to continue ministering to the Jewish population of that city—they would go to the Gentiles.

We read that the apostles said to these dissident Jews, "It was necessary that the word of God should first have been spoken to you." It was God's way to give the message first to His earthly people, Israel, those who had the Old Testament and the promise of the Messiah. It was incumbent on the apostles to tell them first that the prophecies had been fulfilled, that Messiah had come and had laid down His life and risen from the dead, and that through Him God now granted remission of sins to all who trusted Him. But Paul continued, "But seeing ye put it from you, and judge yourselves unworthy of everlasting life, lo, we turn to the Gentiles." What a solemn thing this is! Here were the chosen people—people who had been waiting hundreds of years for the coming Messiah—and at last when He had come, they deliberately shut their eyes to the truth. Paul said, "You [show] yourselves unworthy of everlasting life."

Let us not think only of unsaved Israel doing that. Myriads of

Gentiles are doing the same thing! Perhaps among you, my readers, are some who have heard the message of grace over and over, who know something of the corruption of your own hearts and your inability to save yourselves. You know God sent the Lord Jesus Christ into the world to redeem you, and you know that if you would turn to God and trust Him you would be saved. What are you doing about it? Is it not true many of you deliberately turn away from the true God, and thus show that you judge yourselves unworthy of eternal life?

Strictly speaking, no man is worthy of eternal life. But God in His grace is offering it to all men everywhere; and when men repent of their sin and receive the Savior He has provided, they are accounted worthy of this great gift. When they turn away from Him, trample the love of Christ underfoot and spurn the message of grace, they judge themselves to be utterly unworthy of the good things God is offering them. In other words, the man or woman who rejects the Lord Jesus Christ sins against his or her own soul. It is not merely sinning against God (there is not any greater sin you can commit than to reject the Lord Jesus Christ), but you are sinning against your own soul in that you are shutting the door of Heaven in your own face and therefore you are responsible for your own judgment.

It was this that Paul stressed in dealing with these unbelieving Jews in Antioch in Pisidia. The apostle said, in paraphrase, "You have made up your minds; you are responsible for the message you have already heard. Now we will turn to the Gentiles, to this great throng crowding the synagogue, anxious to hear. If you do not want to hear, we will go to them, 'for so hath the Lord commanded us, saying, I have set thee to be a light of the Gentiles, that thou shouldest be for salvation unto the ends of the earth.'" These words were first spoken through the prophet Isaiah, but they were spoken directly by the Spirit to Messiah Himself. Isaiah was looking down through the centuries and pictured God the Father addressing His Son, saying, "I have set thee to be a light of the Gentiles, that thou shouldest be for salvation unto the ends of the earth."

I suppose the greater number of the people reading this book have been poor lost sinners of the Gentiles. What mercy God has shown to us! Think of the darkness of idolatry and paganism into which our forefathers had sunk! But when the gospel of grace came to them who were strangers to the covenant of promise, they received it and were saved.

A dear Jewish friend said to me: "If Jesus is the Messiah, He came for the Jewish people. Then what are you Gentiles doing with Him?" I replied, "You see, you did not want Him; you spurned Him and then God said, I have set Him to be a light of the Gentiles. So He sends Him to those who are strangers to the covenant of promise. There is no difference between the Jew and the Greek: for the same Lord over all is rich unto all that call upon Him."

"And when the Gentiles heard this, they were glad, and glorified the word of the Lord: and as many as were ordained to eternal life believed" (Acts 13:48). I do not think we need attempt to look back into the counsels of God and see whether we have been *ordained* to life or not. Another clear rendering for the word *ordained* is, "as many as were *determined* for eternal life believed." Wherever you get a man determined to have eternal life, he can have it through believing on Jesus Christ. He does not have to stop and ask if he is elect or not. If he is willing to repent of his sin and come to Christ, he may have eternal life.

"The word of the Lord was published throughout all the region," but hostilities continued. "The Jews stirred up the devout and honourable women." These were probably Gentile proselytes. It is a fact that in our own country (as elsewhere), the most intense religious zealots are women. So when the Jews got hold of these women and stirred them up, they of course stirred up their husbands, "and raised persecution against Paul and Barnabas, and expelled them out of their coasts."

Then the apostles acted in accordance with the words of the Lord Jesus Christ, who said, "into whatsoever city ye enter, and they receive you not, go your ways out into the streets of the same, and say, Even the very dust of your city, which cleaveth on us, we do wipe off against you" (Luke 10:10-11). And so we read that the apostles "shook off the dust of their feet against them, and came unto Iconium." But we learn that those who were left behind "were filled with joy, and with the Holy Ghost."

CHAPTER FOURTEEN
PAUL AND BARNABAS IN GALATIA

A s Paul and Barnabas continued their first missionary journey they came to Iconium. This was the chief city of the district of Lycaonia, sometimes called southern Galatia. It is also one of the cities to which Paul addressed the Epistle to the Galatians later on. "And it came to pass in Iconium, that they went both together into the synagogue of the Jews [again they went first to God's earthly people], and so spake, that a great multitude both of the Jews and also of the Greeks believed."

I like that: "They so spake, that a great multitude...believed." If it is possible to so speak that a multitude will believe, it is possible to so speak that nobody will believe! It is possible to preach so as to convert nobody, and I think a lot of preachers have learned how to do that. Year after year nobody is converted through their ministry. Why? In the first place they do not preach the gospel, and it is the gospel that is the power of God unto salvation. And secondly, they do not preach in the power of the Holy Spirit, and it is only the Holy Spirit who uses the gospel to save sinners. Paul said, "Our gospel came not unto you in word only, but also in power, and in the Holy Ghost, and in much assurance; as ye know what manner of men we were among you for your sake" (1 Thessalonians 1:5). Notice that the preacher himself has to be right with God if he is to preach the gospel in the power of the Holy Ghost. Only then will poor sinners be won for Christ.

179

However, Paul and Barnabas had the same trouble to face in Iconium as in Pisidian Antioch: "The unbelieving Jews stirred up the Gentiles, and made their minds evil affected against the brethren." They did not immediately leave. The persecution was not so bitter that they could not go on, so they continued there giving testimony to the grace of God.

But they found the name of Jesus was divisive. It always will be. Those who accept Him are separated from those who reject Him; those who love and honor Him are separated from those who spurn and dishonor His name. When the apostles heard of the plot to kill them, they left Iconium and went to Lystra and Derbe.

Then we come to a most interesting experience which they had in the city of Lystra. First the people were ready to worship them as gods; and then they tried, as in Iconium, to stone them to death. So fickle is the mind of man!

> And there sat a certain man at Lystra, impotent in his feet, being a cripple from his mother's womb, who never had walked: The same heard Paul speak: who stedfastly beholding him, and perceiving that he had faith to be healed.... (14:8-9).

What an interesting picture! Here stood Paul preaching the word. There was that poor cripple. As Paul was preaching Christ, suddenly he looked down and saw the man looking up expectantly, earnestly. He knew in a moment that the man believed the message and believed that Christ had omnipotent power. So Paul stopped in the midst of his preaching, and "said with a loud voice, Stand upright on thy feet." The man might have answered, "I cannot rise; I have never stood erect." But there is energy in the gospel preached in the power of the Holy Spirit. In a moment the man leaped and walked. I think I can see him springing to his feet actually dancing in front of the people, crying "Is it really true? I never walked in my life before!"

Oh, the wonders of the name of Jesus! What was done for that man physically was just a picture of what the Lord has been doing for people spiritually down through the centuries. Millions of people have been unable to take one step toward God, one step toward Heaven, until the gospel came and they believed it. When they did so they found they were able to rise out of their sinfulness and helplessness and walk in the way of the Lord, glorifying Him. This is one of the evidences that Christianity is really a revelation from Heaven. It proves itself by what it does for the people who believe it.

People say, We do not see miracles today. Oh yes, you do. God is working miracles—making sober men out of drunkards, making honest men out of thieves and liars, making upright men out of scoundrels, making good Christian women out of those who have been characterless and without reputation. He has taken those who have prided themselves on their goodness and morality and led them to a place of submission where they will admit they are sinners and find new life in Christ.

Yes, it is a miracle-working gospel. The lame man leaped and walked. When the people saw it, they were amazed, "saying in the speech of Lycaonia, The gods are come down to us in the likeness of men." They were worshipers of the Greek gods and they thought two of these had appeared on earth. They called Barnabas, Jupiter (Jupiter was the guardian god of the Romans, always pictured as tall and dignified); and Paul, a little energetic man, they called Mercurius. Mercury was always represented as quick and active; the wings on his shoes denote haste in carrying messages. And so the people were going to worship them.

Jupiter had a temple in that city and the priests of Jupiter brought oxen and garlands to sacrifice to the apostles. What an experience for these two men who had just been driven out of Iconium, barely escaping death by stoning! One might say, Isn't this a wonderful triumph? Not at all! Satan was simply changing his tactics. First he tried to kill them. Now he would have them worshiped as gods. One evil was as bad as the other. Paul and Barnabas, when they heard of it,

> rent their clothes, and ran in among the people, crying out, And saying, Sirs, why do ye these things? We also are men of like passions with you, and preach unto you that ye should turn from these vanities unto the living God, which made heaven, and

earth, and the sea, and all things that are therein: Who in times past suffered all nations to walk in their own ways. Nevertheless he left not himself without witness, in that he did good, and gave us rain from heaven, and fruitful seasons, filling our hearts with food and gladness (14-17).

When Paul addressed a Jewish congregation he based everything on the written Word of God in the Old Testament. But on various occasions where we find him seeking to reach pagan Gentiles who did not know the Scripture, he makes an appeal to the omnipotent power of God as revealed in creation. He points to the heaven above and the earth below, the shining sun and stars, and says in effect: "All these bear witness to the omniscience and omnipotence of the Creator of all things. Gods such as you have imagined have not created all this. The idols you worship have not done it—but the true God who made you and the world and the universe and all that is in it." And so he challenged them as to the folly of their idolatry. He would have gone on, as he did later on Mars Hill in Athens, proclaiming the story of the Lord Jesus Christ, but they would not listen further, so anxious were they to get on with their sacrifices.

But now see how quickly they change! "And there came hither certain Jews from Antioch and Iconium, who persuaded the people" (19). In one moment this fickle people would have worshiped them as gods; a little later they were ready to stone them to death.

Then after stoning Paul, thinking him dead, they dragged that seemingly lifeless body out of the city and threw it on the refuse heap. Let the jackals devour it. And so this apparently was the end of Paul's ministry. They were finished with him. But God was not done with him.

I like to think this was perhaps the very time that Paul had the experience of which he speaks in the Second Epistle to the Corinthians (12:2-4):

I knew a man in Christ above fourteen years ago (whether in the body, I cannot tell; or whether out of the body, I cannot tell: God knoweth;) such an one caught up to the third heaven...caught up into paradise, and heard unspeakable words, which it is not lawful for a man to utter.

I believe that at the very moment they thrust Paul's body away, the real Paul—the man who lived inside of that body—was in the third heaven. God said, as it were, "I want to show you what I have in store for you." Up there Paul did not know whether he was in the body or not. If in his body, he did not know it; if out of this body, he did not miss it. He was in paradise and heard unspeakable things that are not lawful for a man to utter. How long he was there we do not know. We do read that as his body lay there on the ground the disciples stood round about, evidently making plans for the funeral, probably with tears streaming down, saying, "What shall we do? We shall have to lay his poor broken body away." But he suddenly rose up! I would like to have seen that.

It is such a graphic picture. There, gathered about the body of Paul, were Barnabas and the other believers, saying doubtless, "Is it not a pity that he had to die right in the midst of his wonderful ministry? If only he could have lived longer!" Then suddenly, I think, Paul opened his eyes, rose to his feet, brushed off his clothes and said, "It is all right. You dear brothers will have to put off the funeral a little longer!" He was ready to start again. Persecution could not thwart him. He must continue preaching the gospel of the grace of God. "He rose up, and came into the city, and the next day he departed with Barnabas to Derbe."

The next verse (21) tells us that when they had preached the gospel in that city, and had taught many, they returned again to Lystra, and to Iconium, and Antioch. It was at this time that Timothy began his journies with Paul. They visited each assembly, "confirming the souls of the disciples, and exhorting them to continue in the faith, and that we must through much tribulation enter into the kingdom of God" (22).

And when they had ordained them elders in every church, and had prayed with fasting, they commended them to the Lord, on whom they believed. And after they had passed throughout

Pisidia, they came to Pamphylia [retracing their steps down to the coast]. And when they had preached the word in Perga, they went down into Attalia: And thence sailed to Antioch [in Syria, the city they left to go on their missionary tour], from whence they had been recommended to the grace of God for the work which they fulfilled. And when they were come, and had gathered the church together, they rehearsed all that God had done with them, and how he had opened the door of faith unto the Gentiles. And there they abode long time with the disciples (23-28).

And so the first journey of the earliest missionaries of the church had come to a wonderful end. What a journey it was! How many are going to thank God through all eternity that Paul and Barnabas ever went out with the gospel message of salvation to the Gentiles!

CHAPTER FIFTEEN
THE FIRST CHURCH COUNCIL

One of the hardest things for these poor minds of ours to grasp is the freeness of God's salvation. In other words, it is so difficult for us to abide in a sense of grace, to realize that the believer in the Lord Jesus Christ is justified by faith, justified on the ground of the finished work of Christ, plus nothing else! Absolutely nothing is to be added to the propitiatory work of the Lord Jesus Christ as the ground of our salvation. This is the gospel proclaimed in the beginning and preached by God's faithful servants down through the centuries. But always there have been found those who, because of their legalistic minds, thought it too good to be true that men could be saved by grace alone and attempted to add something else to the gospel.

One comes along and says, "Yes, you are saved by faith—*but* you must be baptized to get to Heaven." We practice baptism, but not as a means of salvation. Another says, "Grace saves us—*but* it is mediated through the sacraments, and you must partake of the Lord's supper to have divine life." We observe the Lord's supper, but not as a means of salvation. Others will say, "Yes, we are saved by grace—*but* God saves men through the church, and you must join the church if you are to be saved at last." We believe in the church, but the church does not save and does not have anything to do with the forgiveness of sin.

Law and Grace (Acts 15:1-35)

In the beginning, as the apostles labored among the Gentiles, they were preaching salvation by grace alone. This troubled certain men who came down from Judea to Antioch where Paul and Barnabas were ministering that time, having returned from their first missionary journey. These men said, "Except ye be circumcised after the manner of Moses, ye cannot be saved." This was an attempt to add something to the finished work of the Lord Jesus Christ. It created so much division that a showdown was necessary and "they determined that Paul and Barnabas, and certain other of them, should go up to Jerusalem unto the apostles and elders about this question." They would go to the city where the first church had been established and find out if the gospel they were preaching was in accordance with the gospel that was being preached in Jerusalem.

When they reached Jerusalem they did not launch immediately into a discussion of the subject of law and grace. The church had a welcome meeting for Paul and his companions and they took the opportunity to give—what we call today—missionary addresses. "They declared all things that God had done with them."

It must have been most interesting to sit in that group and listen to those veteran missionaries as they reviewed the years they had served the Lord and told about some of the marvelous miracles of grace wrought among the Gentiles. One might have supposed that this alone would have answered the question whether people need anything other than grace in order to be saved. But seated there were brethren who before their conversion had been Pharisees and they had brought their Phariseeism into the church. These were, after all, honest men. It is hard for us to realize when religious conflicts arise, that a godly man may believe something altogether contrary to what we believe. Yet if we are honest before God, we need to recognize that usually he is honest too and is seeking, according to the light God has given him, to stand for what he believes to be the truth.

These men had the Old Testament—remember they did not yet have the New Testament. In the prophecies of the Old Testament Israel was recognized as God's chosen people separated from the rest of the nations. There it was made clear that as others came to a knowledge of the true and living God they came to Israel and through circumcision were admitted into the congregation of the Lord. The prophets declared men would be saved, but it was always in subjection to Israel. "The Gentiles shall come to thy light, and kings to the brightness of thy rising" (Isaiah 60:3), and "It shall come to pass, that there shall come people, and the inhabitants of many cities…saying, We will go with you; for we have heard that God is with you" (Zechariah 8:20-23). These are but samples of many Old Testament passages that declare Israel to be the vehicle through which God would save the nations.

As the legal-minded Pharisees read these Scriptures they said, "We can thank God for the conversion of the Gentiles, but they must come to God through Israel; they must be circumcised and keep the law of Moses." So we read in Acts 15:5, "There rose up certain of the sect of the Pharisees which believed [do not forget that they were sincere believers and yet they differed with others as to salvation by grace alone], saying, That it was needful to circumcise them, and to command them to keep the law of Moses." After a good deal of disputation it was decided the apostles and elders should come together and consider this matter, instead of the whole church going into session about it.

It seemed eminently fitting that Peter should be the chief spokesman on this occasion. He was recognized as the one to whom the Lord Jesus Christ had given a very special commission, "Feed my lambs…feed my sheep" (John 21:15-17). He was the one chosen of God to go down to Cornelius and preach the gospel to him and his household. So after the brethren had been gathered together to consider this matter and had a great deal of discussion, Peter rose up. He said, as it were, "Now, brethren, let me speak." (And they were willing to listen to him.) "You know how by my mouth the Gentiles heard the gospel and believed." Then he related, as he had told them before, what had occurred when he had preached the gospel to the Gentiles.

We remember that when he went and preached the gospel to the household of Cornelius he did not add works, he did not say anything about clean or unclean foods, or Jewish practices such as circumcision. He told them about the Lord Jesus Christ who lived and died and was raised again, and as he preached the gospel, "God which knoweth the hearts, bare them witness, giving them the Holy Ghost, even as he did unto us."

When the Holy Spirit came at Pentecost upon that great multitude of converted Israelites, He came in power and there were outward signs of His presence. In the same way when these Gentiles heard the Word and believed, immediately the same blessed Holy Spirit fell on them and baptized them into the body of Christ. They received the same outward signs He had given the Israelites in Jerusalem—thus demonstrating to a certainty that God accepted Gentiles on the ground of pure grace, altogether apart from the works of the law. There was no difference!

How we need to stress that *no difference* doctrine today. Paul said in his Epistle to the Romans, "There is no difference: For all have sinned, and come short of the glory of God" (3:22-23). It does not make any difference what religious standing you may have—no difference as to what part of the world you were born (whether among Christians or among the heathen)—or maybe you are a Jew—there is no difference! For all have sinned. The Greek word for *sin* literally means "to miss the mark," and all men have missed the mark. Not one man has ever lived in this world without failure and sin—except of course the Lord Jesus Christ. Another Scripture says, "There is no difference...for the same Lord over all is rich unto all that call upon him" (Romans 10:12). There is no difference—the same Savior is for everybody, and by putting their trust in Him, all men may be justified. So Peter said God "put no difference between us and them, purifying their hearts by faith."

That is what happens when people believe the gospel; it is not merely that they are justified before God—but there is new life; their hearts are purified by faith. Whereas they once loved sin, they now love holiness: whereas they once loved impurity, they now love purity. There is a complete change and reversal of attitude when people are born of God. This had taken place in these Gentiles. Who could doubt that God did the work?

Perhaps some of you have heard evangelist A. H. Stewart tell how, when greatly concerned about his soul, he was told to believe in the Lord Jesus Christ and trust Him as Savior. But he thought that way was far too easy. He went about it his own way—he joined a church, sang in the choir, and became quite a worker. He hoped in all these things to obtain peace with God, but there was no peace!

One day, while he was reading in his Bible the parable of the sower, he came to the words, "Then cometh the devil, and taketh away the word out of their hearts, lest they should believe and be saved" (Luke 8:12). Stewart threw down his Bible and said, "Will you look at that! Even the devil knows a man will be saved if he will believe!" And that day he settled it and turned to Christ and trusted Him as Savior. Yes, God saves men when they believe; He saves all sinners, no matter what their situation or condition, when they trust His Son.

So Peter said, "Why tempt ye God, to put a yoke upon the neck of the disciples, which neither our fathers nor we were able to bear?" (Acts 15:10) They were in bondage all the years they were in Judaism and they had to be delivered from this and brought into the liberty of grace. Why bring the Gentiles into the same bondage out of which they had been saved?

The breadth of Peter's vision comes out here magnificently. "We believe that through the grace of the Lord Jesus Christ we shall be saved, even as they." We would not have expected him to say that. We would rather have expected him to say, "We believe that through the grace of the Lord Jesus Christ, *they* shall be saved, even as *we*." But grace had done its work in Peter's heart so he turned it right around. In other words he said, "Do you not see, God is saving Gentiles by grace and thank God He saves Jews by grace too! He delivers the heathen from the corruption of idolatry, He delivers the Jews from the bondage of legalism."

The Christian Pharisees did not know what to say, but deep in their hearts they were probably thinking, "The Bible says these Gentiles are to come to God through Israel, and Israel is marked as separate through circumcision; therefore they must abide by the law." However, we read, "Then all the multitude kept silence, and gave audience to Barnabas and Paul, declaring what miracles and wonders God had wrought among the Gentiles by them" (12). They did not get up and try to argue the question. Very rightfully. They were visitors and did not want to be too prominent. But after Peter made this thing clear, Paul and Barnabas said in essence, "We will give you some examples how He has been changing wicked men into holy men through grace." So they gave example after example, just as returned missionaries have done through the years, telling of corrupt men changed by grace to godly men. So Paul and Barnabas gave testimony; and this helped clear the minds of the Pharisaic Christians.

After Paul and Barnabas had finished, the last man you might have expected spoke on their side: "And after they had held their peace, James answered." Who was James? The brother of the Lord. He is often called the first Bishop of Jerusalem. He was a legalist of the legalists before his conversion, which did not take place until after the resurrection of the Lord Jesus Christ. He was the leader of the Jewish party in the church, and was careful not to depart from the old ways until a fuller revelation had come. But God gave to James the special light that was needed for the moment.

"Men and brethren, hearken unto me: Simeon hath declared how God at the first did visit the Gentiles, to take out of them a people for his name" These Pharisaic brethren had the Old Testament and there they read of the day when the Gentiles were going to turn to God and be blessed through Israel in the kingdom reign of the Messiah. James explained that this, however, is not what is happening now. God is now taking out from among the Gentiles a people to His name and He used Peter first to go to the Gentiles. That is the work going on at the present time. In other words, God is not converting the world today. What is He doing? He is taking out an elect people from the world and bringing them to a saving knowledge of His blessed Son.

James said in effect, "I understand. You brethren are perfectly right, but God is working out His own plan. The day is coming when God will bless the Gentile world through Israel and they too are going to enjoy the kingdom reign of Messiah and will all be united together as one holy, happy people; but that is not what God is doing now! God is now taking out a people, Jew and Gentile, to constitute the church of God. When He completes this work, the Lord is coming back the second time. That will be the time of blessing for the whole world. He will build again the tabernacle of David, which is fallen down. He will then bring Israel as a nation into blessing again. Then all the remnant of the Gentiles will return to God— that is, in the millennial reign of the Lord Jesus Christ. Wars will cease. The Lord Jesus Christ will reign in righteousness over all the earth, and Jew and Gentile will be one happy, redeemed people, glorifying God together."

In light of this fact, James said,

> Wherefore my sentence is, that we trouble not them, which from among the Gentiles are turned to God: But that we write unto them [knowing the intense feeling of the Jewish brethren toward certain things tolerated by the Gentiles], that they abstain from pollutions of idols, and from fornication [from which every Christian should abstain], and from things strangled [which in the Jewish mind were very unclean], and from blood. For Moses of old time hath in every city them that preach him, being read in the synagogues every sabbath day (19-21).

To this they agreed, and the first council of the church ended in happy unison. What a wonderful thing it was that the Spirit of God should have so overruled, where men held such different views, as to bring them all at last to see that salvation is by grace alone through faith! How we can rejoice today that that precious truth has been preserved through the centuries and that, believing in Him, we can be a part of that great company of the redeemed some day to be revealed as the glorified church of our Lord!

Meantime, as we wait for His return from Heaven, we are to seek to get the gospel of His grace out to all men everywhere, that all may have an opportunity to know of the Savior and to find in Him life and peace, through faith, altogether apart from meritorious works of any kind.

Paul's Second Journey Begins (Acts 15:36-41)

We have already considered the many momentous events that took place in connection with his first journey. We have seen how he and Barnabas eventually returned to Antioch in Syria, from which city they had set out on their gospel tour. Then, after remaining for some time, "teaching and preaching the word of the Lord," it came into the heart of Paul to go on another journey.

We do not have in connection with this second missionary

journey the same evidences of direct divine guidance as on the first. In that instance, we are told that the Holy Ghost said very definitely, "Separate me Barnabas and Saul for the work whereunto I have called them." In this case, we are told, "Some days after Paul said unto Barnabas, Let us go again and visit our brethren in every city where we have preached the word of the Lord, and see how they do." It seems to have been a voluntary thing on Paul's part rather than the direct guidance of the Holy Spirit as on the previous occasion. And, strikingly enough, from the very start things seemed to go wrong and you find the missionaries perplexed on several occasions as to just what their task should be.

Barnabas wanted to take his young cousin John Mark along. He had taken him to Cyprus when they went on their first journey, but when they returned to the mainland Mark left the apostles. He returned to Jerusalem, evidently preferring the company of his mother Mary and the comforts of home to an itinerant missionary life. "But Paul thought not good to take him with them, who departed from them from Pamphylia, and went not with them to the work." I take it Paul considered the work of the Lord so serious he could not think of linking up again with a man who had shown so little sense of the importance of service for the Lord. These mission trips were no Sunday school picnic! They were times of severe testing, hard work, and service for the glory of God. Paul did not wish to take anyone who was not divinely guided nor ready to endure hardship. Barnabas evidently felt differently.

"The contention was so sharp between them, that they departed asunder." It is rather pitiable to read such a statement about these two devoted apostles of the Lord Jesus Christ, but the Bible never tries to hide the faults of God's servants. In that aspect the Bible is so different from many secular biographies. One would think their heroes perfect in almost everything. But the Word of God turns the light on and gives the record of their failures just as truly as of their successes and victories. This is both for our warning and our encouragement.

So these two venerable brethren could not agree in regard to this companion for their travels. They separated and for years did not labor together again. We are told in Proverbs, "A brother offended is harder to be won than a strong city" (18:19). Many of us know that the beginning of strife is as one little drop of water, which, after the break in the dike has begun, soon grows into a torrent of water that is practically impossible to stem. However in this instance, as the years went on, a kindly, considerate feeling prevailed, and in his old age Paul spoke affectionately of both Barnabas and Mark. As he wrote from his prison cell to Timothy we read, "Take Mark, and bring him with thee: for he is profitable to me for the ministry."

I am sure most of us are thankful that Barnabas gave Mark another chance. There is many a young Christian who has failed in the beginning, but gone on later to become a valuable worker in the vineyard of the Lord Jesus Christ. We who are older need to be careful of our condemnation of the younger. Barnabas gave a helping hand to Mark, however it is very evident the brethren sided with Paul and thought he was right. But Mark brought forth good fruit later on.

So we read here, "Barnabas took Mark, and sailed unto Cyprus"—the same field in which they had labored before and found conditions so congenial. But Paul chose Silas, who is called a prophet—the one who went down to Antioch to convey the decree of the Jerusalem council. He proved himself to be an able man, as well as a prophet. We read that they "went through Syria and Cilicia, confirming the churches." These were the two areas where Paul and Barnabas had labored before.

CHAPTER SIXTEEN

HOW THE GOSPEL ENTERED EUROPE

It was on Paul's second visit to Lystra, Iconium, and Derbe that the brethren commended Timothy, who had been converted through Paul, as one whom they believed to be called of God to give his life to the ministry of the Word. This young man was of mixed parentage, his mother being a Jewess, but his father a Greek. So in order not to offend Jewish prejudices, Paul circumcised him, something he would never have agreed to had Timothy been, like Titus, a Gentile. Paul took Timothy along, after the local brethren had expressed their fellowship by prayer and the laying on of hands. In answer to their prayers, God gave him some special gift, which we understand was the gift of pastor, for in after years Timothy always manifested a true shepherd heart. Later in writing to the Philippians, Paul said of Timothy, "I have no man likeminded, who will naturally care for your state. For all seek their own, not the things which are Jesus Christ's. But ye know the proof of him, that, as a son with the father, he hath served with me in the gospel."

What a splendid testimony for the older preacher to give concerning the younger! Many ministers of the gospel are far more concerned with getting on in the world, furthering their own interests, than they are about the people of God. It was different with Timothy. His one yearning desire was to be used by God for their blessing.

So Paul made no mistake in taking this young man with them. He was well reported of by the brethren that were at Lystra and Iconium, and he proved to be a valuable helper in the years that followed. "And as they went through the cities, they delivered them the decrees for to keep, that were ordained of the apostles and elders which were at Jerusalem. And so were the churches established in the faith, and increased in number daily."

Led By a Vision (Acts 16:6-15)

After they had ministered in these cities they turned north and thought of going into Asia; that is, a limited area of Asia Minor in which were located in later years those seven churches spoken of in the book of Revelation. They intended to go into this district, but they "were forbidden of the Holy Ghost to preach the word in Asia." What does that mean? Had not the Lord Jesus told them to go into all the world? Certainly. Well, was not the gospel for Asia as well as for every other part of the world? Yes. But there is often a specific time for certain work to be done, and the Spirit of God saw that the time had not yet come to enter Asia. Later on, Paul went to Ephesus, the chief city of Asia, and had a glorious ministry. Hundreds, even thousands, throughout the city were converted. But this was not yet the Lord's time. It is a wonderful thing for the servant of God to be guided by the Lord's Spirit and move each moment in His will.

So they turned aside to the district called Bithynia, just over the border, but once more they were hindered. The Spirit of Jesus in some way spoke to them and forbade them to enter. And why not? In the next verse we have the answer. "And they passing by Mysia came down to Troas." Troas was a seaport looking across the Aegean to Greece. Remember, the apostles had not yet visited Europe. So far as we know, no one had yet carried the gospel to that continent.

"And a vision appeared to Paul in the night; There stood a man of Macedonia, and prayed him, saying, Come over into Macedonia, and help us." In the morning he related the vision to his companions, and Luke wrote, "Immediately we endeavored to go into Macedonia, assuredly gathering that the Lord had called us for to preach the gospel unto them" (10). Note the pronouns *we* and *us*. Luke became a member of the missionary group at Troas, and from this time on is identified with the work. He and the others concluded it was God's way of telling Paul and his companions that the time had come to cross the Aegean to enter into Europe and carry the gospel to—shall I say?—our forefathers.

People sometimes remark, "I am not interested in missions to the heathen. There is plenty of work to be done here," piously adding, "Charity begins at home." Yes it does, but it is a pity if it also ends there. And how thankful we should be that thousands of years ago somebody did believe in missions and so carried the gospel to our forefathers that they might be brought to a saving knowledge of the Lord Jesus Christ.

The apostles decided immediately to act upon Paul's vision. "Therefore loosing from Troas, we came with a straight course to Samothracia, and the next day to Neapolis." They had landed in Europe, and from thence took the Roman military highway to "Philippi, which is the chief city of that part of Macedonia, and a colony."

A Roman colony was a city that had been granted special privileges by the Roman government because of some service rendered to the empire. All freemen in such a colony were regarded as having all the rights of Roman citizens. It was similar to a little bit of Rome in a distant country. The apostle Paul saw in this a beautiful illustration of the Christian's position in this world. Later he wrote about it in his letter to the Philippians: "Our [citizenship] is in heaven; from whence also we look for the Savior, the Lord Jesus Christ." They would understand that very well, for though they lived in Macedonia, their citizenship was in Rome; and though we live in this poor world, our citizenship is in Heaven! We belong to Heaven and have all the privileges of heavenly citizens.

"We," wrote Luke, "were in that city abiding certain days." At first, it seemed as though no one was interested in their message. Many missionaries have the same disappointment. Paul heard the man in the vision say, "Come over into Macedonia and help us," and he surely had reason to believe that when he reached Macedonia he would find some anxious people waiting to receive him. But there was nothing like that. They abode "certain days," with no one asking for help or seeking them out, with no evidence that any man or woman was a bit concerned about them.

Young people sometimes hear a fervent missionary from a distant field tell of the need of young men and young women for work in Africa or China or in some other country. They say, "I must answer the call." They arrange to leave everything here and go out to the mission field, only to find nobody wants them. And they say, "Isn't that strange? They were pleading that we come, and instead of wanting us they are ready, in some instances, to kill us." Was the missionary wrong? Did he give a false impression of conditions? Not at all! The heathen do not realize their need often until the preaching of the true God gives them a sense of their real condition. Nevertheless it is that very need that calls for someone to help.

So while the Macedonians needed help, there was no one to actually say, "We welcome you and are anxious for the message you have come to give." Finally, the apostles located a little company at a place of prayer. "And on the sabbath we went out of the city by a river side, where prayer was wont to be made." That tells us it was a Jewish prayer meeting. It was the custom of the Jews, if ten men could be gathered together, to have a synagogue in a Gentile city. But if not enough were available, they would go where they could get flowing water for their cleansing rites, and there establish a place of prayer.

So Paul went to this prayer meeting, but nobody was there but a few women! All the men were absent. How many prayer meetings are just like that! Men often think they are too busy to come together and wait upon God in prayer, but a few faithful, devoted women will carry on alone. So Luke wrote, "And we sat down, and spake unto the women which resorted thither."

Paul was not indifferent to the soul needs of these women. He was thankful to find a few in Philippi ready to hear the Word. One was a Gentile, perhaps a proselyte, of the city of Thyatira. Thyatira was one of the leading cities of Asia. The Spirit of God had forbidden Paul to go to Asia, but He had this woman from Asia waiting for Paul in Macedonia. She doubtless had learned from the people of Israel of the true and living God. Her "heart the Lord opened, that she attended unto the things which were spoken of Paul." There was no great crisis in her life. She had already been seeking the truth, and now when Paul unfolded the gospel, without any excitement, without any outward evidence, the Lord opened her heart and she received the message and trusted the Savior.

"She was baptized." Thus she took the public place of identification with Christ. "And her household." We are not told who the members of her household were, except that in verse 40 we read of "the brethren" there. Lydia was a business woman, a seller of purple, and she probably had a number of men working for her. Apparently all of them opened their hearts to the Word. Lydia offered her own home as a home for the missionaries, saying, "If ye have judged me to be faithful to the Lord, come into my house, and abide there." And we are told, "she constrained us." Thus the gospel had entered Europe and the work of evangelizing Macedonia was started.

The Apostles Persecuted (Acts 16:16-24)

Next we see Satan's efforts to patronize the gospel, and the results of this. If Satan cannot stop the work of the Lord by out-and-out persecution, he will try to hinder it by condescension. And just as soon as the church of God accepts the patronage of the world it becomes subservient to the world. The apostle Paul was very jealous that nothing be allowed which, in the slightest degree, would indicate that the church of God had any connection whatever with the powers of evil. We see this in the next incident here recorded.

"And it came to pass, as we went to prayer, a certain damsel possessed with a spirit of divination met us, which brought her masters much gain by soothsaying." It was a very common thing in the ancient world at the time the gospel was first being carried to the various countries, to find such characters as this young woman. They believed themselves to be in touch with heathen gods and thought they were actually possessed by the spirit of a god. Many people flocked to these fortunetellers for their advice in matters relating to business, or marriage, or to affairs having to do with the government of kingdoms, and so on.

After all, we have not progressed very far. Today we find the same characters. Even in our land, with all its enlightenment, there are literally thousands of people who scarcely make a move without consulting a clairvoyant, or spirit medium, someone who is supposed to have special illumination because of contact with the unseen world.

This woman in Philippi believed she was possessed of the spirit of the god Apollo. It says in the King James version that she had "a spirit of divination." The margins of some Bibles read "a spirit of Python." Python was a serpent sacred to Apollo. The people believed that Apollo himself spoke through this woman, who was thus enabled to give counsel. When under the power of this spirit she was not conscious of what she was saying; in a kind of cataleptic state, she was dead to all around her. Actually we know from Scripture it was a demon and not a god at all; yet people flocked to her for help, and actually believed she was putting them in touch with the heavenly spheres. She heard Paul preaching the gospel and undoubtedly it was suggested to her by Satan that she associate herself with him and his companions. She was just a poor female slave, and the money that came to her for fortunetelling went into the hands of men who owned her, body and spirit.

The young woman "followed Paul and us [notice Luke is still of the company], and cried, saying, These men are the servants of the most high God, which show unto us the way of salvation." That is very significant when we realize the woman was under the control of a demon. Even Satan himself believes in the reality of God's salvation and here attempts to take the position of a patron of the work of the Lord by saying, "These men...show unto us the way of salvation."

Day after day she followed them, always making the same statement, endeavoring to give the impression that she, in some sense at least, was affiliated with them. "But Paul, being grieved, turned and said to the spirit, I command thee in the name of Jesus Christ to come out of her. And he came out the same hour." We have many instances in modern days of missionaries working in pagan lands where they have come in contact with people who seem to be just as truly possessed with demons as this young woman was. On many occasions these servants of God have cast out those demons, using these same words.

I remember a dear servant of God telling of a woman who continually raved and blasphemed against God. He and others felt she was under the power of a demon, that she had worse than a diseased mind, worse than a heart at enmity against God. They finally met together in special prayer and when this woman began blaspheming God as usual, God's servant rose up and said, "I command you in the name of the Lord Jesus Christ, come out of this woman and enter no more!" The next moment the woman fell at his feet in a fit. He said it reminded him of what he had read in Scripture, "The devil threw him down, and tare him," but from that time on she was never so affected again.

Demon possession is a very real thing, and the power in spiritualism today consists in this: not that God allows spirits of the dead to come back and speak through mediums but that demons take possession of these mediums and speak through them. The church of God needs to be on guard against those who are seeking to imitate the work of the Lord. The name of Jesus drove out the demon from this woman, for Jesus is conqueror and victor over Satan's host. Whenever the power of Christ's name is invoked, He can be depended on to vindicate the glory of His name.

Now that the demon was gone out of the woman, she could no longer go off into trances, therefore her masters were indignant. The money that had come through the use of the demon's awful power over this girl no longer flowed into their coffers; their profits were gone. "And when her masters saw that the hope of their gains was gone, they caught Paul and Silas, and drew them into the marketplace unto the rulers, And brought them to the magistrates, saying, These men, being Jews, do exceedingly trouble our city." Notice they did not know anything about Christianity; they did not recognize Paul and his companion as Christians—but as Jews. So it was an outbreak of anti-Semitism. "They are Jews; get them out of the way!" Oh, how often that cry has been sounded!

If there is trouble here or there, men are always looking for a scapegoat for it. During World War II many put all the blame upon the Jews! It is so much more convenient than to confess our own sins! Our trouble comes not because of any particular people, Jew or Gentile, but results from departure from God. He is dealing in judgment with the nations of this world because of their rejection of His testimony. Let us humbly confess our sin and failure before

God and thus seek deliverance from the world's prevailing distress and grave suffering.

The possessed girl's masters put the blame on Paul and Silas, not because they were Christians, but because they were Jews, and so should be dealt with. "These men, being Jews, do exceedingly trouble our city, And teach customs, which are not lawful for us to receive, neither to observe, being Romans." I imagine the very people who accused the apostles would not have been so proud to acknowledge themselves as Romans before their country was taken over and dominated by the Romans; but now they glory in what should be their shame.

"And the multitude rose up together against them: and the magistrates rent off their clothes." This was the Eastern way of saying, "We have come to our wits' end; we don't know what to do in a case like this." Then they were taken and beaten and thrown into prison. We are not told of any definite trial, or of an opportunity given to explain matters and clear themselves of the charges preferred against them. The brutal jailer, when he received them, "thrust them into the inner prison, and made their feet fast in the stocks." Their backs were torn and bleeding as a result of the dreadful flagellation, but the jailer did not so much as wash their stripes.

The Jailer's Conversion (Acts 16:25-40)

What would we do in circumstances like that? Note what they did: "At midnight Paul and Silas prayed, and sang praises unto God: and the prisoners heard them." These dear men, afflicted, miserable, unable to sleep, could not move without anguish. Yet as they sat in that dungeon their hearts went out to God, presenting their case before Him, and assured He heard, they lifted up their voices in glad thanksgiving for His grace. And we are told, "the prisoners heard them."

What a challenge that is for us when we find ourselves in difficult circumstances! We have perhaps never yet had to endure conditions so bad; but have we learned to lift our hearts in thanksgiving to God no matter what our circumstances? We read, "In every thing give thanks." Someone may say, "I can give thanks for blessings, but not for trials and testings." But Scripture says, "In every thing give thanks"—"And we know that all things work together for good to them that love God, to them who are the called according to his purpose."

Perhaps someone is reading this who is passing through great trial. I know that some are going through deep waters, and my heart goes out in sympathy, for I too have gone through the floods and been almost overwhelmed. I too have passed through fires of afflic- tion. But I can assure you there is no circumstance in which the believer can be found where the Lord is not able to sustain him and lift him above trial and enable him to rejoice. We are told to glory in tribulations. There is a Savior for you and you may find deliver- ance, peace, rest, and joy in Him.

It does not take much character, nor much Christianity, to be happy when everything is going our way. *But* when everything goes wrong—when poverty, sickness, bereavement, or misunderstand- ing is our lot—to be able to rejoice in the Lord then is Christian victory! That is what we see in the prison experience of Paul and Silas.

They presented the first sacred concert ever held in Europe. Just two artists, the concert hall a dungeon, neither piano nor organ to accompany; yet these two artists had such effect that they brought down the house! Soon the whole prison began to shake. That was the most successful sacred concert I have ever heard of. As they sang, "suddenly there was a great earthquake, so that the founda- tions of the prison were shaken: and immediately all the doors were opened, and every one's bands were loosed."

You may think it far-fetched, but I have an idea that if there were more joy in tribulation, more triumphing in trouble in our own day, we would see more shaking by the power of God. The unsaved people of the world are watching Christians, and when they see Christians shaken by circumstances, they conclude that after all there is very little to Christianity. But when they find Christians rising above circumstances and glorying in the Lord even in deepest trial, then the unsaved realize the Christian has a comfort to which they are strangers.

You may have heard the story of the Christian who one day met another believer whose face was long as a fiddle and asked, "How are you?" The man replied, "Well, I am pretty well under the circumstances." To which the other replied, "I'm sorry you are under the circumstances. Get above the circumstances! Don't allow yourself to be under them. Christians should never be under the circumstances." Paul and Silas were not. They were above them.

As they prayed, God took hold and began to shake the prison until He had loosened the very doors open and the fetters off the prisoners' limbs. The keeper of the prison—this hard man who had thrust them into the dungeon, this man so insensible to the things of God that it looked as though no power could reach him and bring him to repentance—"awaking out of his sleep, and seeing the prison doors open, he drew out his sword, and would have killed himself, supposing that the prisoners had been fled." You see, under the Roman law he was responsible for these prisoners. If he lost them, he lost his life. So rather than face the executioner himself, he sought to take his own life, "but Paul cried with a loud voice, saying, Do thyself no harm: for we are all here."

I wonder how it was that Paul realized the condition of things. It does not seem there was any possibility of his seeing beyond that dungeon to the jailer's own apartment. Yet he appeared to know and he spoke out at the right moment. Doubtless he was guided by the Spirit of God.

How often God has guided His servants, giving the right message at the right time! Somebody told me of a poor, wretched, miserable man under the power of strong drink, fighting for long against it. He finally thought he might as well give up trying. Then happening to tune in the radio he heard a voice say something like this, "Remember, if you are absolutely hopeless, Jesus is ready to save you!" He thought, "Why, that is for me." As he continued to listen, the gospel message came in power and he dropped on his knees beside the radio and his soul was saved.

The Philippian jailer was soon to learn the joy of the gospel message. When he heard the warning cry of Paul, "he called for a light, and sprang in, and came trembling, and fell down before Paul and Silas." Their stocks became their throne and he, their jailer, lay supliant at their feet! He then "brought them out, and said, 'Sirs, what must I do to be saved?'" He knew they had something he needed, and he was anxious to learn the secret of the One who had given them not only songs in the night, but songs from a dungeon death cell. Their answer came back quick and clear—"Believe on the Lord Jesus Christ, and thou shalt be saved, and thy house." No beating about the bush. No going into a labored explanation of Christian doctrine, or of the nature of the church, or of sacraments. Clear and incisive was their message, "Believe on the Lord Jesus Christ [*put your trust in the Lord Jesus Christ*] and thou shalt be saved, and thy house."

Bishop John Taylor Smith used to tell how, when he was a Chaplain-General of the British Army, the candidates for chaplaincy were brought to him and given a hypothetical situation to deal with. "Now, I want you to show me how you would deal with a man. We will suppose I am a soldier who has been wounded on the field of battle. I have three minutes to live and I am afraid to die because I do not know Christ. Tell me, how may I be saved and die with the assurance that all is well?" If the applicant began to beat around the bush and talk about the true church and ordinances and so on, the good Bishop would say, "That won't do. I have only three minutes to live. Tell me what I must do." And as long as Bishop Smith was Chaplain-General, unless a candidate could answer that question, he could not become a chaplain in the army.

I wish that were true of our own army. What answer would you give to a man with only three minutes to live? Can you find a better one than this?—"Believe on the Lord Jesus Christ, and thou shalt be saved."

There are so many who say, "I do not understand which is the true church." Never mind! Believe on the Lord Jesus Christ. Then some say, "I do not understand the true nature of the sacrament of the Lord's supper." Never mind! Believe on the Lord Jesus Christ. "Yes, but my life has been so wicked. I feel I ought to make restitution first for the sins of my past." Never mind! Believe on the Lord Jesus Christ. "I am so afraid I might not hold out." Never mind! This is God's message to any poor sinner today: Put your trust in the Lord Jesus Christ and you will be saved, and your house. The same offer is for your house as for you. When God saves you, it is evident He wants to save your whole house.

"And they spake unto him the word of the Lord, and to all that were in his house." I think they had all been getting dressed, his wife and children, and maybe some of his servants. They all crowded in to hear these strange preachers who a little while ago were cast into prison and were now pointing them to Christ.

"And he took them the same hour of the night, and washed their stripes." I imagine he said, "I am ashamed of the way I treated you. Let me make you as comfortable as I can. Let me show my gratitude." "And was baptized, he and all his, straightway." The whole household was brought to Christ that night! The apostles found the man of Macedonia at last who in a vision said, "Come over into Macedonia, and help us."

"And when he had brought them into his house, he set meat before them, and rejoiced, believing in God with all his house."

There is just one more incident, and with this the chapter closes.

> When it was day, the magistrates sent the serjeants, saying, Let those men go. And the keeper of the prison told this saying to Paul, The magistrates have sent to let you go: now therefore depart, and go in peace (Acts 16:35-36).

Evidently the magistrates, looking into the matter, had come to the conclusion that these men were not law violators and so said, "We must get them out of the way." But Paul said, as it were, "We represent the Lord Jesus Christ and do not want to be branded as violators of the law of the land so long as we are innocent, and therefore we want to be cleared of any such charge. Let them come themselves and take us out."

It was not pride that led Paul to make this demand. It was a proper sense of the dignity of his calling as an apostle of the Lord Jesus Christ.

> And the serjeants told these words unto the magistrates: and they feared, when they heard that they were Romans [freeborn

citizens of the Roman empire were entitled to trial and should never have been cast into prison uncondemned]. And they came and besought them, and brought them out, and desired them to depart out of the city (38-39).

And so Philippi, the first city in Europe to receive the good news of salvation, seemed about to close its doors to the gospel. Instead of the magistrates saying, "Now we have set you free, go throughout our city and proclaim the glorious message," they said, "Please leave our city. We do not want your message."

"They went out of the prison, and entered into the house of Lydia: and when they had seen the brethren, they comforted them, and departed." This was the nucleus of the church at Philippi.

So the gospel entered Europe, and we can be thankful that from that day to this the message of grace is still going out in that continent. Although we live on a different continent, we enjoy the message today because it was brought to Europe so long ago.

CHAPTER SEVENTEEN

PAUL AT THESSALONICA, BEREA, AND ATHENS

In the opening verses of Acts 17 we read of Paul's ministry in the Macedonian city of Thessalonica. As we study the book of Acts it is interesting to compare the various geographical references with a map of the ancient Roman Empire. In this instance it would be seen that Amphipolis and Apollonia were on the high road from Philippi east and south toward Athens and Corinth. Passing through these two cities, the apostle and his company went on to Thessalonica, which we know today as Salonica, located on the shores of a bay and inlet of the Aegean Sea. Here, as in place after place, Paul found a synagogue of the Jews, and in accordance with his regular custom, "to the Jew first," he entered into the synagogue and, as opportunity was given him, presented his message there. We are told that "three sabbath days he reasoned with them out of the scriptures."

Using the Old Testament with which the Jews were familiar, he showed how it had been predicted by the prophets that the Messiah for whom they waited must suffer even unto death and be raised again in order to accomplish the redemption of His people. We can imagine him turning from passage to passage to prove these great facts. Then having laid the foundation, he built the superstructure of his discourse, the story of the Lord Jesus Christ Himself, showing that this Jesus whom he preached was indeed Messiah.

The result of his ministry was that a number of the Jews believed and sought further fellowship with Paul and Silas. Also a great number of Gentile proselytes or seekers after the truth accepted the testimony. Of these, quite a few were well-known women who had doubtless wearied of the unsatisfactory character of paganism. Having learned from the Jews something of the one true and living God, they were now ready to accept the Savior He had provided.

This, however, stirred the unbelieving Jews with indignation and envy. They did not want to appear openly as persecutors, but we are told they gathered a group of rabble-rousers. By artfully arousing their prejudices, they moved them to make an assault on the house of Jason where the preachers of the new message were being entertained. The mob created such an uproar that the whole city was moved. Paul and Silas however were not found, but the rash leaders of the mob took Jason and several other adherents of the Way of Life, and dragged them before the rulers of the city. They accused them by saying, "These that have turned the world upside down are come hither also; Whom Jason hath received: and these all do contrary to the decrees of Caesar, saying that there is another king, one Jesus."

Their accusation was in measure true. The apostle and his companion were indeed engaged in the business of turning the world upside down, but the reason for this was that through sin the world had been turned wrongside up. So when the gospel was preached and men believed it, things were completely reversed. But the charge that the new doctrine contained anything contrary to the decrees of Caesar was false. The king proclaimed by Paul was not one who was to contend with the Roman emperor for world dominion, though He shall indeed reign in due time. He had already declared in Pilate's judgment hall, "My kingdom is not of this world; if my kingdom were of this world, then would my servants fight." The kingdom of which He is Head is not meat or drink, but righteousness, peace, and joy in the Holy Ghost. In other words, Christ had not come to establish a kingdom in the world order, but to call on men to recognize and bow to Heaven's authority in their lives.

It is evident that the rulers of Thessalonica and those associated with them were perplexed when they heard these things. Not knowing just what action to take, they placed Jason and the other brethren under obligation to keep the peace, and let them go. Doubtless recalling the instructions of the Lord Jesus, If "they persecute you in this city, flee ye into another," the believers arranged secretly to send Paul and Silas to the next city along the highway—Berea.

A very graphic account of the entrance of the gospel into Thessalonica is given in Paul's First Epistle to the church in that city. From that Epistle we gather that he remained there considerably longer than the three sabbath days mentioned by Luke in this chapter of Acts, but just how long we do not know. At any rate, the result was that many of the Thessalonians were turned from idols to the living and true God to serve and to wait for His Son from Heaven. A careful reading of the two Epistles to the Thessalonians in connection with Acts 17:1-9 will throw a great deal of light on both the entrance of the gospel into that city and the attitude of the new converts afterwards.

Going on to Berea, Paul and Silas again first sought the synagogue of the Jews, and there found the same liberty they had enjoyed in many other places. The fact is, as already noted, the Jewish synagogues of the first century of the Christian era were much more open than many Christian churches today. When teachers came from distant places, they were recognized and accorded an opportunity to present their views. Paul always took advantage of this in order that he might bring the gospel message to his own brethren after the flesh first.

It is refreshing to note the fine attitude of these Berean Jews and proselytes. We are told that "these were more noble than those in Thessalonica, in that they received the word with all readiness of mind, and searched the scriptures daily, whether those things were so." Somebody has well said that prejudice closes the door of the mind to any truth not already known. Paul wrote to the Thessalonians, "Prove all things" (1 Thessalonians 5:21). The only way to test any system of doctrine is by the Word of God itself. Isaiah warned God's people: "Should not a people seek...To the law and to the testimony: if they speak not according to this word, it is because there is no light in them" (8:19-20).

Bearing this in mind, these Berean Jews examined the Scriptures carefully as they listened to the teaching of Paul. One can see them sitting in the synagogue with the sacred scrolls in their hands, leaning forward, listening eagerly, wonder and surprise often expressed on their faces as they looked inquiringly at each other. Unrolling the great vellum volumes, they turned from one passage to another, comparing Scripture with Scripture, until they were finally convinced that what Paul proclaimed was the truth. Then they aligned themselves definitely on the side of Christ, receiving the message in faith and acknowledging the Lord Jesus as the sent One of God.

We are not surprised to read in Acts 17:12, "Therefore many of them believed," and we have the additional words, "Also of honourable women which were Greeks, and of men, not a few." This must have been one of the most encouraging experiences that Paul ever had. We do not read of any other city wherein he was given so fair a hearing, wherein people were so honest in seeking to know whether the message preached was really in accordance with Scripture or not. How blessed it would be to find more people today characterized by the same nobility as that which distinguished these Bereans. They possessed a nobility of mind that led them to put away all prejudice and preconceived notions and to examine fairly the matters to which their attention was called, testing everything by Scripture!

But this happy state of affairs was soon brought to an end, for Satan cannot long endure the uninterrupted reception of the gospel. And so after some days—we do not know how many—certain of the unbelieving Jews of Thessalonica, having learned that Paul was preaching the Word in Berea, hurried down the highway and arrived there also. By their misrepresentations, they stirred up many of the people who had not yet been brought to know the Lord. Once more there was an uproar and an effort made to apprehend the messenger of the cross. Again the brethren had to take steps to safeguard the life of the apostle. As he was the outstanding exponent of the new faith, the indignation of the unbelievers was directed against him particularly, so the believers sent him away, we are told , "to go as it were to the sea." This would suggest a stratagem in order to throw his persecutors off his trail. Silas and Timothy remained to help the young believers and encourage them in their faith.

The last part of Acts 17 brings us with Paul to Athens, that great cultural center of ancient Greece. The men who conducted Paul to Athens returned to Berea with a message from him to Silas and Timothy urging them to rejoin him as soon as possible. Meanwhile Paul waited for them at Athens. As he went about day after day, his spirit was moved to its deepest depths as he saw the evidences of the gross idolatry to which the city was devoted. An old Greek philosopher wrote some time before Paul's day, "In Athens it is easier to find a god than a man." Images were everywhere; not only representations of all the gods of the various countries that made up what we call Greece, but the gods adored by Asiatics, Egyptians, Romans, and peoples from far-distant lands. Practically every false deity worshiped on earth could be found in Athens, and yet this was the educational center of the world. There were different schools of philosophy where great teachers lectured on the folly of idolatry and taught their adherents to scorn the superstitions of the less cultured strata of society. But these philosophers had nothing to offer in the place of the idolatry they scorned. They were simply theorists philosophizing as to the nature of the universe and man, but with no certainty of anything because they were without any divine revelation.

As Paul had opportunity, he disputed in the synagogue with the Jews and talked with the devout persons—that is, Greeks who were influenced by Judaism. As he went about in the streets and in the markets he lost no opportunity to converse with any who were ready to listen. Paul was an outstanding personal worker who did not feel that he must have a pulpit in order to disseminate the truth God had sent him to proclaim.

Information regarding his teaching soon came to the ears of some of the philosophers of both epicurean and stoic schools. Contemptuously they asked, "What will this babbler say?" The Greek word translated "babbler" means "seed-picker." It was an ironical expression implying that he was like a bird picking up odd seeds here and there, yet had no definite philosophical system behind his teaching.

Others who heard him preach of Jesus and the resurrection thought that he spoke of two new gods of whom they had never previously heard, for they took the expression "resurrection," which in Greek is *Anastasis*, to be the name of a god! Therefore, they invited him to go up to Mars Hill, or the Areopagus, where the philosophers were accustomed to presenting their teachings, and there tell them what the new doctrine was of which he had been speaking. There was no evidence of a working in the consciences of these men. It was characteristic of the Athenians to delight in anything new or novel. So they evidently gave Paul the opportunity of presenting his doctrine simply for their personal gratification.

Ever ready to seize any opportunity to preach the truth of God, Paul presented what is perhaps one of the finest specimens of pulpit oratory extant (Acts 17:22-31). It helps us to understand what Paul meant when he said that he was made all things to all men (1 Corinthians 9:22). We have listened to him before as he preached the gospel to the Jews, and we have seen how he based everything on the testimony of Holy Scripture. Here we are privileged to listen in as he speaks to a Gentile company who knew nothing of the Jewish Scriptures. To them he appealed to the testimony of creation as suggested in the first chapter of his letter to the Romans.

He certainly did not begin his discourse as the King James version has him saying in verse 22: "Ye men of Athens, I perceive that in all things you are too superstitious." Had he begun by calling his audience "too superstitious," he would probably have closed the door of their minds effectually against his message. The word translated "superstitious" really means "given to the worship of the gods" and is better translated "religious." That is, he began by saying, "I see that you as a people are very religious." The evidence of this was that as he moved around the city he not only saw many images of different gods, but he found an altar with the inscription, "To the Unknown God." Evidently, some pious soul, afraid that some god might be left out of the pantheon, had erected this altar. Paul took the inscription from this altar as his text, saying, "Whom therefore ye ignorantly worship, him declare I unto you."

In an eloquent and masterly way he set forth the truth of the one God by whom the world and all in it had been created. This God,

Paul said, is too great to be confined in any temples men might build. He is omnipresent, omnipotent, and omniscient. He has no need of anything that men could offer to Him. Therefore, it was absurd to think that they could purchase His favor by any of their gifts. He Himself is the great giver, bestowing all good things on the creatures He has made. He it was who had formed all the nations from one man. All the various races and tribes had sprung from the first original pair that God created, and He who knows the end from the beginning had determined their times and appointed them the lands in which they dwelt. In all these things God was giving evidence of His interest in mankind, desiring that they might seek after Him and find Him, though He be not far from us.

It is an interesting fact that the only time the word *feel* is found in the New Testament is in Acts 17:27 (KJV). It has to do with the heathen. It was the desire of God that they, though ignorant of His Word, "might feel after him." When men receive His Word, then they are not dependent on their feelings, but are asked to believe. Nor was it suggested by Paul that God was far from anyone. So close is He to all of us that it can be truly said, "In him we live, and move, and have our being."

Paul quoted an expression found in the writings of two Greek poets, Aratus and Cleanthes, "For we are also his offspring." This he fully accepted and he appealed to these men as the offspring of God. He showed how foolish it is that those who have been created by this omnipresent God should ever liken Him to images made of metal or stone by art or man's device. This was not the same appeal as that some teachers proclaim today, namely the fatherhood of God and the brotherhood of man. By this teaching they mean that men are already God's children and hence brothers in Christ apart from regeneration. God is the Father of spirits, and in that sense we are all His offspring, but man has fallen. Sin has come in to alienate man from God; hence the need of a second birth.

Verse 30 suggests something that may be of great comfort to those who are troubled when they think of a world left for many centuries without the knowledge of the one true and living God. Paul said, "the times of this ignorance God winked at," or overlooked. God deals with men according to the light they have. He does not hold them responsible for light that has not yet been revealed. But now, since Christ has come and the gospel is being preached, God commands all men everywhere to repent; that is, to change their attitude and turn to Him for that deliverance which they can find nowhere else.

He has "appointed a day, in which he will judge the world in righteousness by that man whom he hath ordained." Paul was doubtless about to mention the name of Jesus when his address was interrupted. He was in the midst of declaring that the resurrection of Christ from the dead was the pledge both of God's grace and His judgment. That resurrection assures all men that salvation has been provided for them. It also gives assurance that He who died and rose again will some day judge the living and the dead.

What a pity his hearers did not permit Paul to finish this magnificent discourse! On the contrary, we are told that when they heard of the resurrection of the dead, which to them seemed utterly absurd, some mocked and others said, "We will hear thee again of this matter. So Paul departed from among them."

At first sight it may have seemed as though his effort to interest these philosophers in the great message he had for the world was in vain. On the other hand, we learn from the closing verse that there were a few who profited by it. "Howbeit certain men clave unto him, and believed: among the which was Dionysius the Areopagite, and a woman named Damaris, and others with them."

CHAPTER EIGHTEEN

PAUL CONTINUES HIS SECOND JOURNEY

Having moved on from Athens, Paul traveled to Corinth. The story of the triumphs of the gospel in that city is one of the outstanding miracles of missions. When Paul entered Corinth there was not a Christian in it; moreover, it was one of the most debased of all the cities of the ancient Greek-speaking world. When he left it, there were literally hundreds of Christians—earnest, devoted, faithful men and women delivered from the sins that once bound them. These new Christians sought to glorify the Lord Jesus Christ, as they walked in purity and righteousness.

In Corinth (Acts 18:1-11)

The reputation of Corinth from a moral standpoint was so bad at the time the apostle Paul visited it that if a woman was conspicuously immoral, it was said of her, "She is a Corinthian." If a man was unusually vile, it was said, "He corinthianizes." That in itself is enough to show what a wicked, ungodly city Corinth was. But the gospel wins its greatest triumphs where the outward circumstances seem to be the very worst, for God delights to take great sinners and turn them into great saints.

Paul had no thought of trying to wheedle people into a confession of Christianity by preaching beautiful and profound sermons that might appeal to their delight in oratory. Neither did he desire to fill them with wonder and amazement because of the extent of his wisdom. We read, "The Greeks seek after wisdom," but Paul wrote in 1 Corinthians 2:2: "I determined not to know anything among you, save Jesus Christ, and him crucified." And he found this was enough.

Just as the message of Jesus Christ and Him crucified was enough in that ungodly city to turn many from sin to righteousness, so that is the message today that God is using to break down hard hearts. With that message He turns men and women from wicked, wayward and unhappy lives and gives them the joy and victory of God's salvation.

Paul's entrance into Corinth was in a very humble way. He was not heralded as a great preacher. There was no blowing of trumpets. There was no welcome committee to meet him at the station when he arrived, but he came in quietly and unannounced. In Corinth he found a certain Jew named Aquila, who was born in Pontus but had lately been banished from Italy because of an antisemitic stir when Claudius had commanded all Jews to depart from Rome. Paul found Aquila and his wife in the tentmaking business. He went into partnership with them because as a young man he had learned that trade and at present had no other means of support—no great church behind him, no missionary society to guarantee his salary. The three of them worked together, while Paul, as God gave him opportunity, preached the gospel and thereby won many precious souls to the Lord Jesus.

Paul was not what we would call today a "clergyman." He was not afraid to "dishonor" the cloth by soiling his hands at hard work. He was always ready, when God did not provide for him otherwise, to engage in temporal employment and make the money needed for his own support and often that of his companions, while he continued ministering Christ.

Because of the liberty in the Jewish synagogues in those days, it was customary to invite a visitor who was a gifted preacher or teacher to address the audience. There Paul testified to the Jews that Jesus was Christ; that is, that Jesus was the Messiah whom they as a people had been expecting so long. But in Corinth he had a different reception from the one he found in Berea. You will remember that we read of the Bereans, "These were more noble than those in Thessalonica, in that they received the word with all readiness of mind, and searched the scriptures daily, whether those things were so. Therefore many of them believed." They were ready to hear, and when they searched their own Scriptures they found corroboration of the message that Paul preached. But at Corinth it was different. He came up against intense prejudice so that eventually he had to turn away from the synagogue altogether.

In condemning the unbelieving Jews Paul alluded to the book of Ezekiel. God said there that when He chose a man to be a watchman for His people and the watchman was on guard and saw the sword coming upon the land, if he blew the trumpet and warned the people and they refused to heed it and the enemy came to destroy them, they would die in their sins, but the watchman had delivered his own soul. On the other hand, if the watchman saw the sword coming and did not blow the trumpet or warn the people, they would die in their sins, but their blood would God require at the watchman's hand (Ezekiel 33:1-6). Paul was God's watchman, and he faithfully warned his Jewish brethren of judgment to come if they refused Christ. Since they had rejected the warning God had sent them, he said, "You have had your opportunity. I am not guilty of your blood; now I turn to the Gentiles." So he began ministering to the degraded, ungodly Corinthians whom the Jews despised.

He went to the home of Justus, a Greek who heard, undoubtedly from the Jews, of the one true and living God, and had begun to worship Him. No longer an idolater, he was glad now of an opportunity to get further light and help through the apostle Paul and his companions. So he opened his house to them, and there they remained to minister Christ in Corinth.

Although the great multitude of Jews spurned the gospel, one of the first outstanding converts was Crispus, the chief ruler of the synagogue. Evidently the Word had already found lodgment in this man's heart. When Paul took his stand so openly in connection with the opposition that he had met, Crispus came out with a definite acknowledgment of his faith and believed on the Lord with all his house.

As Paul continued to preach the Word, "many of the Corinthians hearing believed, and were baptized" (18:8). Notice the divine order there, because it is just the same today wherever God's Word is literally carried out. The Corinthians heard the message of the gospel. When Paul preached Jesus Christ and Him crucified, they listened earnestly. They believed the Word; they received it in their hearts; and then they said, "Now, Paul, we are ready to confess Christ openly in baptism." They were not baptized in order that they might become Christians; but having become Christians, they were baptized to confess their allegiance to the Savior in whom they had put their trust.

By this time perhaps Paul was becoming a little restless, and might have been ready to move on, but we are told that the Lord spoke to him in the night in a vision and said, "Be not afraid, but speak, and hold not thy peace: For I am with thee, and no man shall set on thee to hurt thee: for I have much people in this city." God often speaks of the things that have not yet occurred as though they have. When He said, "I have much people in this city," He was referring to hundreds of people who were living still in all the corruption of idolatry but would soon hear and believe the gospel message. They were still living in the wickedness that pertained to the worship of the goddess of lust who was the chief deity in the city of Corinth. But God looked on that which He was about to do, and He saw those people cleansed from their sins, made new creatures in Christ. So He said in effect, "Go on, Paul. Do not let anybody turn you aside. I have much people in this city, and they are to be separated to me by the preaching of the gospel."

Writing to these Corinthians afterwards, Paul depicted the awful condition of those who were living in sin and who will not have any part in the kingdom of God, and he said in 1 Corinthians 6:9, "Know ye not that the unrighteous shall not inherit the kingdom of God?" Then he continued by describing the very kind of people that he had labored among for eighteen months: "Be not deceived: neither fornicators, nor idolaters, nor adulterers, nor effeminate, nor abusers of themselves with mankind, Nor thieves, nor covetous, nor drunkards, nor revilers, nor extortioners, shall inherit the kingdom of God."

In this awful list he was depicting the type of men and women who made up a great part of the city of Corinth; but he could add in the next verse (11): "And such were some of you: but ye are washed,

but ye are sanctified, but ye are justified in the name of the Lord
Jesus and by the Spirit of our God."

What a wonderful triumph it was for this dear servant of Christ
to go into that wicked city and, as he lifted up Jesus, find these
corrupt, evil-loving people looking to Him! And when they looked
to Him, it was as when those smitten Israelites in the wilderness
looked to the brazen serpent, they were healed, they were changed.
They never lived again as they had lived before.

People say, "I do not believe in this idea of salvation by faith
alone. I think something more is required than that." But many forget that when the sinner looks in faith to Christ, a change takes
place. The sinner receives eternal life, which means he has been
born again—he has a new nature. He learns to hate the sins in which
he lived, and he learns to love the things that once he hated—holiness, goodness, purity, and truth. This is the result of looking in
faith to the Lord Jesus Christ. This was what accompanied the
preaching of the gospel in Corinth. It is what accompanies it everywhere in the world when men believe it and receive it in their hearts
in the simplicity of faith.

So Paul went on in Corinth for a year and a half, teaching the
Word of God among them. If you want a full understanding of what
took place there, read very carefully the two letters to the Corinthians. You will see how a strong church grew up in that vile, corrupt
city, a church that came behind in no gift. God gave to the Corinthian
Christians a great testimony and they went out to help and bless
others. It is true that later Paul had to rebuke them for certain evils
that had been allowed to creep in among them. There will always
be danger of this kind when a church of God is established in a
wicked, ungodly location. But it is the delight of God to plant a
church in such a place, because His purpose is that every true Christian church should be a light shining in darkness so that poor, weary,
wandering souls seeing that light may find life everlasting.

The same gospel that brought such miracles in Corinth long years
ago is the gospel that works today. Men talk of the need of a new
gospel for a new age, but our Lord Jesus Christ, in commissioning
His apostles, charged them to go out into all the world and disciple
the nations, baptizing them in the name of the Father, and of the

Son, and of the Holy Ghost; and He added, "Lo, I am with you alway, even unto the [consummation of the age]." Until a new Savior is needed, we do not need a new gospel. We need no new Savior, for Jesus is the same yesterday, today, and forever, and He is still changing men and women from sinners into saints. He is still giving life to those who are dead in trespasses and sins. He is still bringing peace to troubled hearts. He is still releasing men from the bondage of sin.

If these words come to any who are oppressed by any burden and who realize something of the bondage of iniquity, who feel that they are slaves and cannot free themselves, let me bid you look away to Jesus. On the cross He gave Himself for you. There He was wounded for our transgressions, bruised for our iniquities; there the chastisement of our peace was laid upon Him that with His stripes we may be healed. Millions have looked to Him. Untold myriads have trusted Him. They know the miracle of salvation, and you may know it today if you will only turn to Him.

Gallio the Indifferent (Acts 18:12-17)

In this section we have Paul's hearing before Gallio. History tells us that his full name was Anneas Junius Gallio, and interestingly enough he was the half brother of the philosopher Seneca, who was Nero's tutor. The two brothers were separated when they were very young and were adopted into different families and did not see each other for years. When Seneca finally did meet his brother Gallio again he was greatly impressed by the graciousness of his demeanor. He used an expression in describing him that we do not ordinarily apply to men. We would be more likely to apply it to a gracious lady. He called him "Most sweet Gallio," and said of him, "Few men are so amiable about anything as my brother Gallio is about everything." That was a great tribute for one brother to say of another, was it not? And as we read this account in Acts we can see how this accolade runs true to form.

"When Gallio was the deputy of Achaia, the Jews made insurrection with one accord against Paul." Paul had already spent a year and a half in Corinth, and God had used him in a mighty way in the conversion of a great number who had turned from idolatry to the Lord Jesus Christ. These were delivered from the corruption in which they had been living and brought into lives of holiness and righteousness. Now God allowed Paul's ministry to be interrupted by this persecution. "The Jews made insurrection with one accord against Paul, and brought him to the judgment seat"—dragged him before Gallio.

Their charge against him was rather peculiar for men who were themselves monotheists and who did not believe in the idols generally worshiped by the people of Corinth. They said, "This fellow persuadeth men to worship God contrary to the law." It is remarkable how those who are opposed to the gospel of God can often seem to fit in with others with whom ordinarily they would have very little in common! These men, who had a revelation from God as given in the Old Testament and knew He was the one living and true God, were yet so prejudiced against the apostle Paul they did not even allow themselves to become thoroughly familiar with the message that he preached. So they charged him with persuading men to worship God contrary to the law.

Just as Paul was preparing to explain himself and his message Gallio interrupted: "If it were a matter of wrong or wicked lewdness, O ye Jews, reason would that I should bear with you: But if it be a question of words and names, and of your law, look ye to it; for I will be no judge of such matters." It was as if he said, "If you had evidence that this man was doing anything corrupt or that he was actually breaking the law of the country, then it would be reasonable that I should hear the charge that you have against him. But if it is simply a quarrel about religion, then it is too insignificant for me to pay any attention to it." Gallio was not interested in Paul's message. It seemed such a puerile matter that Paul went about the country giving people a little different slant on religion than that to which they were accustomed! To him it meant little whether what the man preached might contain a modicum of truth or not.

Yet Paul proclaimed the only message that could prevail for the salvation of a lost world! He wrote in his letter to the Corinthians what that message was: "I determined not to know anything among you, save Jesus Christ, and him crucified." He recognized, of course, that ungodly, worldly men did not understand until the Spirit of God had opened their hearts and exercised their consciences, so he said "The preaching of the cross is to them that perish foolishness; but unto us which are saved it is the power of God...and the wisdom of God" (1 Corinthians 1:18-24).

But Gallio did not think it even worth his while to give the apostle Paul an opportunity to declare his message. How much he lost; how different his after-history might have been if on that day, though he silenced Paul's accusers, he had turned to him and said, "Now, Paul, tell me what it is you are preaching! What is this message about a crucified God that you are carrying throughout the world? I understand you are telling men that you have the only message of life for lost sinners. Tell me about it."

If Gallio had only been concerned enough to hear Paul's message, patient enough to listen to it thoughtfully and carefully! For as we trace his history in secular volumes we find that at last he became a thoroughly disillusioned man, who found that the world could not satisfy, and who possibly committed suicide. It seems sad indeed that this well-meaning, amiable man, this gracious and kindly philosophical Roman governor, should have no interest in the gospel of God!

Are there not a great many like him today—people scattered throughout the world who are amiable and kind, who have a certain interest in the welfare of others, and yet do not think the gospel of God worthy of their consideration? If this be true of you, will you not give for once in your life serious consideration to the gospel message? Face the matter honestly. This gospel has been used of God down through the centuries to transform millions of human lives. There must be something in it worth investigating. There must be something about it worth considering.

Thousands of intelligent, well-read, cultured, and refined people have found in the gospel that which has brought peace and blessing and joy to their lives. It has given them deliverance from the power of sin and altogether given life a wholly new meaning. Gallio missed his opportunity. He drove away the Jews who accused Paul from the judgment seat, but he turned away from Paul also.

Then we read that "all the Greeks took Sosthenes, the chief ruler

of the synagogue, and beat him before the judgment seat." These
Greek idolaters were only too glad to vent their contempt for the
Jews who had accused Paul, and so they began to beat them. Gallio
apparently did not interfere. He turned superciliously away. Let them
fight out their religious quarrels between themselves if they would.
These things were of no interest to him.

Gallio stands out on the page of Holy Scripture as a man utterly
indifferent to the claims of the Lord Jesus Christ. He "cared for
none of those things." And so he passes off the page of Scripture.
But we may be sure that if we could follow him out into that eternity into which he has gone, we would find that Gallio cares now.
We do not know whether or not before he left this world he had his
eyes opened to the importance of spiritual realities. The inference
would seem to be that he had not, but only God and he know what
passed between them at the last before his soul and body separated.
But one moment after he reached the other side he became thoroughly aware of the vital importance of the message that once
seemed of so little account to him.

Though men turn away now from the voice of God as His servants proclaim it, we can be certain that the day will come when
that message will be to them the most important message in all the
universe. For many it will then be too late to accept the gospel invitation and know the cleansing that the blood of Christ brings. "Gallio
cared for none of those things."

Paul Begins His Third Missionary Journey (Acts 18:18-23)

Now we pass on to the record of Paul's activities as he concludes
his second missionary journey. "And Paul after this tarried there
yet a good while, and then took his leave of the brethren, and sailed
thence into Syria, and with him Priscilla and Aquila."

Then we have a statement that has puzzled many commentators:
"Having shorn his head in Cenchrea: for he had a vow." Does that
indicate that Paul, though an apostle of the Lord Jesus Christ, had
put himself under the bondage of a legalistic vow? I think it rather
indicates this: That Paul, when he was converted on the Damascus
road, was a Nazarite; some time before his conversion he had taken

the vow of one separated to God. The Nazarite devoted himself to the Lord for a given time. It might be a certain number of months or many years, or possibly for life. As long as he was under the vow of a Nazarite, he was not to cut his hair, no razor was to come upon his head; he was to eat no fruit of the vine, whether moist grapes or dried, whether wine or fresh grape juice; and he was to come near no dead body, no matter how close of kin. All this had a spiritual significance. The Nazarite was a picture of one separated to God, one who turned from the pleasures of this world and sought to walk in holiness before God, undefiled by the dead. By sin came death. That was why the Nazarite was not to come near a dead body.

If Paul were a Nazarite at the time of his conversion, which seems to me most likely, he would not feel free to break that Nazarite vow even after he was converted. He would feel that he must go on and fill out his time. He had taken a vow to be a Nazarite for a certain number of years, and now, long after his conversion, those years had at last run out. If he had been unfaithful in his pledge, he would have lost the confidence of Jews to whom he sought to present Christ, and so he kept that vow conscientiously. The time had now elapsed and Paul was free to wear his hair as other men do. So he had the long locks of Nazariteship shorn.

There is one thing you will notice he did not do. He did not take an offering up to Jerusalem, which the law commanded when one had fulfilled the days of his separation. You see, he himself was under no such bondage.

> And he came to Ephesus, and left them there: but he himself entered into the synagogue, and reasoned with the Jews. When they desired him to tarry longer time with them, he consented not; But bade them farewell, saying, I must by all means keep this feast that cometh in Jerusalem: but I will return again unto you, if God will. And he sailed from Ephesus. And when he had landed at Caesarea, and gone up, and saluted the church, he went down to Antioch (Acts 18:19-22).

Paul had begun both his first and second missionary journeys from Antioch. He often returned to that church to give an account

of the marvelous things that God had done among those who heard
the message of the gospel. And now, after laboring in various places,
Paul returned once more to Antioch to tell the church of the wonders he had seen of the grace of God working not only among the
Jews, but among the heathen. To them the message had come, and
tens of thousands of them had turned from idols to serve the living
and true God and to wait for His Son from Heaven. We can imagine
something of the welcome that Paul received, and how the brethren
there rejoiced over the evidences of God's grace which he related
to them!

Notice in verse 23 that after spending some time there he started
out on his third missionary journey. He was getting to be an old
man, but there was such a desire in his heart to carry the gospel to
distant places and to help and encourage those who had already
believed, that he could not be content in Antioch. He must go into
the regions beyond. So "he departed, and went over all the country
of Galatia and Phrygia in order, strengthening all the disciples."

How we would like to see today an awakening all over our own
beloved land! In these dark and difficult days in which we live,
should we not as Christian people be calling on God to make bare
His mighty arm that men and women would realize their need of
Him and fall to their knees before our Lord Jesus Christ?

Apollos Learns of the New Creation (Acts 18:24-28)

The author of Acts now returns our attention back to Ephesus
where Paul had left his good friends Aquila and Priscilla. The interesting story of Apollos recorded in these verses of chapter 18 serves
as an introduction to the events recorded in chapter 19. "A certain
Jew named Apollos, born at Alexandria, an eloquent man, and
mighty in the scriptures, came to Ephesus."

Alexandria, at this time one of the great cities of the ancient world,
had a very large Jewish population. It was there that the renowned
Philo had taught—a man whose system was a strange mixture of
Judaism and Greek philosophy. It is possible that Apollos was first
of all a disciple of his and then, as we shall see later on, of John the
Baptist.

Apollos is described as an eloquent man. God does not have a great many eloquent men, even in the ministry of the gospel. It is just here and there that He lays His hand on a man who can so speak as to stir men's hearts. Such men are rare. Apollos was perhaps the outstanding pulpit orator of the first century in the Christian church.

He is also described as "mighty in the scriptures." That is, he was familiar with the Old Testament. Remember, the Scriptures that were in the hands of all the early Christians were the Old Testament books. They did not as yet have the books of the New Testament. But Apollos had studied the Old Testament and knew it well. He knew the promises and the prophecies. He knew something perhaps of the types and shadows, and was looking for the full manifestation of the Messiah of Israel as promised therein.

"And being fervent in the spirit." I like that. The word *fervent* means "boiling hot." It is a great thing to find people who have received a message from God that so moves their own hearts that it fires them up and sends them out to proclaim it with great earnestness of purpose. You remember the apostle in writing to the believers in Rome, said we should be "Not slothful in business; fervent in spirit; serving the Lord."

I think a great many of us are fervent in business, slothful in spirit, serving ourselves! Of course we are not to be remiss in temporal things, but we are to see to it that we are fervent in spirit, that spiritual things grip our hearts and consciences and move us to earnest devotion to Christ. Well, this man was fervent in spirit, and "he spake and taught diligently the things of the Lord."

But we are also told of his limitations: "Knowing only the baptism of John." Evidently he had heard of John the Baptist preaching in the wilderness of Judea. Whether he made a special journey to Judea or not we are not told, but he probably heard John preach and was baptized by him. Being fervent in spirit, he started out to visit the Jews in distant places and to carry to them the message that John was preaching, calling on men to repent and be baptized in preparation for the coming of the Messiah. Apollos doubtless felt that if Messiah's advent was so near, the Jews of the dispersion as well as those in Palestine should hear of it.

Now a good many years had gone by, but evidently Apollos had not returned to Jerusalem and he did not know that Messiah had come. We need not be surprised that this man, traveling and living among the scattered Jews, had not learned that Messiah had appeared, been crucified, raised from the dead, and ascended to God's right hand. These things had not been made known to him. So he went out preaching John's baptism of repentance for the remission of sins. "He began to speak boldly in the synagogue."

In the city of Ephesus Paul's two good friends, Aquila and Priscilla, were living. These, you remember, were the folk who were tentmakers and Paul had labored with them in Corinth. Now they had moved to Ephesus, and when Priscilla and Aquila heard of this eloquent Bible teacher who was giving out the Word of God in the synagogue, they went to hear him. There was no prejudice on their part that would keep them from entering the synagogue. And they were stirred as they listened to the messages of this man Apollos. But we can well imagine what they said one to another as they walked home: "It's wonderful; everything that he says is true, but the fact is he doesn't go far enough. He is telling the people to get ready for the coming of Messiah. Evidently he doesn't know that Messiah has already come, that He died and arose and ascended into Heaven. He must not have heard of the Holy Spirit that has come down from Heaven to baptize all believers into one body and to bring in the blessed and glorious truth of the new creation—a new creation in which all saints on earth are united to the glorious Head." So they decided that they must try to help this man.

You will notice that they didn't go at him in a carping, critical way. We sometimes hear somebody giving out a measure of truth, and we approach them in a harsh, unkind manner. We find fault with them because they do not know more, and often we frighten them off instead of helping them. We Christians who love the Lord Jesus need to pray for a spirit of grace. We need to present the fundamental truths of Christianity with the winsomeness that characterized our Lord Jesus!

We meet people who have come just so far, and we find fault with them because they do not see more clearly. We forget that perhaps they have not been instructed. Many modernists are modernists only because they do not know any better. If we who know the truth would pray for them and would try in a gracious, kindly way to give them the truth of God, either by speaking to them personally or by putting into their hands some upbuilding literature, many of them might be won to a full, clear knowledge of Christ.

I think I have told before of a dear young man who came to me in a nearby city. He said, "Do you recognize me?" I looked at him and said, "I'm afraid I don't. Your face looks somewhat familiar (he had two eyes and a nose and a mouth, you know), but I can't recall your name." "Well," he said, "I couldn't forget you because God used you to help me when I needed it, oh so badly. I had gone as a young man to a certain seminary. I went in as an earnest, flaming evangelist, and after four years in cold storage there I came out practically an agnostic. They had filled me with doubt and perplexity. They told me the Bible was not the inspired Word of God. They told me that blood atonement was not the way sinners were saved, and I came out of there with nothing to preach. I did not know where I myself stood. I thought I would go into business or take up some other profession. I was passing through Chicago, and my train connection left me some hours to look around. I had heard of the Moody Church, so I thought I would go up there. I inquired how to get there and I went up and met you and you took me through the building and then up into your study. I told you how confused I was and you sought to help me, and prayed with me. Just as I was leaving you handed me your book on the Epistle to the Romans. I read it on the train. By the time I got home, all my doubts were gone, and I had a gospel to preach again. That book changed my life, and for eight years I have been preaching the gospel in a Methodist church and winning many souls to Christ."

I felt so unworthy. But it did me good because it made me feel more than ever the importance of trying to help those who really want to give out the Word of God but some way or other they do not understand. The full revelation of God's mind has not been opened up to them.

Priscilla and Aquila were wise! They did not find fault with Apollos. I think they went up to him after the meeting and said, "Brother Apollos, we certainly enjoyed your message this morning. We would love to have you come home and have dinner with us." So they took him to their home and then when they got him fed and he was feeling rested and happy, "they expounded unto him the way of God more perfectly." I think they would say something like this: "My, we enjoyed your preaching, Apollos! That was a wonderful message, but did you not hear that Messiah did come and that He was crucified and raised again? He has gone up to glory, and He has sent the Holy Ghost down." Why, I can imagine Apollos saying, "What proof have you of these things?" And then they would begin to tell him of all the wonderful things they had received through the apostle Paul and other Christians; and as they opened up the Word, Apollos just drank it in. Oh, how grateful he was for these friends who so graciously and so kindly took him into their home and taught him. And as he learned these things, he felt, *Well, I am not fit to go on preaching here, but if I could get to a Christian assembly somewhere, maybe I could learn more and extend my ministry to other places.*

"And when he was disposed to pass into Achaia, the brethren wrote, exhorting the disciples to receive him: who, when he was come, helped them much which had believed through grace" (Acts 18:27). He went to them expecting to get help from them, and undoubtedly he did. On the other hand, this fine, fervent, Bible-taught young preacher, standing up among them giving out the truth, was a means of real encouragement to them. I don't know anyone who does a staid, old Christian so much good as a young convert in the full flush of his first love for Christ and the truth! It was thus with Apollos. And so he helped the local assembly there and became one of the outstanding messengers of the early church. "For he mightily convinced the Jews, and that publicly, showing by the scriptures that Jesus was Christ."

CHAPTER NINETEEN
MAGNIFYING THE NAME OF JESUS

In this chapter of Acts some most interesting things are brought out in connection with the marvelous ministry of the apostle Paul. The theme of Acts 19 is found in the last part of verse 17: "The name of the Lord Jesus was magnified." So we will trace the record through and notice what it is that magnifies His name. What are the events as here recorded that glorified that name so long ago? What similar things would glorify and magnify His name today?

The New Baptism (Acts 19:1-7)

As Paul continued his third missionary journey he came again to Ephesus where Apollos had received the message of the new creation through the Holy Spirit. We note from the first verse of Acts 19 that Apollos had moved on to Corinth. We read that when Paul arrived in Ephesus he found "certain disciples." Who were these disciples? They were Jewish converts who had been instructed by Apollos. He had been preaching in the synagogue regarding the baptism of John, and teaching them all that he knew. Now he had gone on, and as Paul arrived, Priscilla and Aquila no doubt asked him to come and preach to these people in the synagogue. And Paul, always ready to communicate to others what God had made so precious to his own soul, went with them and found these disciples.

Paul wanted to help them, so he asked: "Have ye received the Holy Ghost since ye believed?" Actually what he asked was this: "Did you, upon your believing, receive the Holy Spirit?" In other

233

words, "When you listened to Apollos and heard his messages about the coming Christ and you believed it, did you receive the Holy Spirit?"

This was not a question asked of Christians. It was a question put to disciples of John the Baptist—those in, what we might call, the halfway house between Judaism and Christianity. Their answer was, "We have not so much as heard whether there be any Holy Ghost." Of course, as Jews they had heard of the Holy Spirit. But what is actually meant here is: "We have not so much as heard whether the Holy Ghost is come." You see John had said: "I indeed baptize you with water; but one mightier than I cometh, the latchet of whose shoes I am not worthy to unloose: he shall baptize you with the Holy Ghost and with fire" (Luke 3:16). Apollos had told them about that, but they had not heard of the arrival of the Holy Ghost and His work in the believer's life.

Paul inquired, "Unto what then were ye baptized?" Notice the implications of this question. Why did he ask them that question? What did this question have to do with whether or not the Holy Spirit had come? Our Lord Jesus, before He went away, gave His last commission to the apostles: "Go ye therefore and [disciple] all nations, baptizing them in the name of the Father, and of the Son, and of the Holy Ghost." They were to go out and carry His message everywhere in the world, and baptize the converts in the name of the Father, and of the Son, and of the Holy Ghost. That is Christian baptism.

If these Ephesians had received Christian baptism, they should have known the Holy Spirit had come. So Paul asked in effect, "Into whose name were you baptized?" They answered, "Unto John's baptism." That was a different baptism. It was a baptism of repentance, a preparatory baptism, looking forward to the coming of the King. Christian baptism looks back to His death, looks up to His throne at the Father's right hand, and on to the end of the dispensation when He will come again. The age has not ended yet. Therefore, we are responsible still to baptize believers in the name of the Father, and of the Son, and of the Holy Spirit. So when Paul heard their answer, he explained, "John verily baptized with the baptism of repentance, saying unto the people, that they should believe on him which should come after him, that is, on Christ Jesus."

And so Paul, we have no doubt (everything is not recorded here in a few verses), preached the gospel to them. He told them the wonderful story of how Jesus came and died at Calvary, bearing our sins in His own body on the tree. He told how His precious body was laid away in the tomb then arose in triumph, and before He went home He commissioned His apostles to go into all the world preaching the gospel and baptizing men in the name of the Father, and of the Son, and of the Holy Ghost. He taught them how some day He is coming back again to set up His glorious kingdom. And we read, "When they heard this"—that is, the unfolding of the truth concerning our Lord Jesus Christ—"they were baptized in the name of the Lord Jesus."

Someone may say, "Why, you see, they were not baptized in the name of the trinity. They were baptized only in the name of the Lord Jesus." People who reason this way fail to take into account what is involved in that expression. "In the name" speaks of authority. Why do I preach? It is because I have been commissioned by the Lord Jesus to carry His gospel into all the world, and I preach in the name of the Lord Jesus—by His authority. So these men were baptized in the name of the Lord Jesus, that is by His authority, which implies baptism unto the name of the holy trinity. Whether Paul baptized them himself we know not—but he saw that they were baptized when they confessed Christ as their Savior. And now, having been baptized with Christian baptism, Paul laid his hands on them and as at Pentecost, as in Samaria, as in Cornelius's house, immediately the Holy Spirit came on them and there were the same wonderful signs as at Pentecost: "They spake with tongues, and prophesied."

You see, this little group was living in a transition stage. They were neither Jews as such, still on legal ground, nor were they on full New Testament ground. They were Jews who were looking forward to the coming of Messiah, and had been baptized with the baptism of John. In order that there might be definite evidence that they were brought into the body of Christ, the Spirit fell upon them, thus baptizing them into the body of believers and giving them special gifts as He had given to the Jews at Pentecost. There were not many of them. "All the men were about twelve."

This was the last group brought in to complete the various companies to whom the gospel message was to go. First, Peter began at Pentecost and preached mainly to the Jews with some Gentiles present. Then later on Philip went down to Samaria and carried the gospel message to that group who were of a mixed religion of Judaism and paganism, and they were brought to faith in Christ. Next Peter went to the Gentiles, preaching the gospel to Cornelius's household, and as he preached they believed, and the Holy Spirit fell on them and brought them into the body of Christ. Finally, the Spirit of God led Paul to this little company who had accepted John's baptism but had not yet heard the further message. They believed and were baptized by the authority of the Lord Jesus, and the Holy Spirit fell on them. There are no other groups to be found in the book of Acts. Everywhere else that the message is carried it will go to Jews, Samaritans, John's disciples, or Gentiles.

And so God has given us a sampling of some people taken out of each of these groups and brought into the body of Christ. The coming of the Holy Spirit is the great, outstanding witness that God is satisfied with the finished work of His beloved Son, and His Spirit now dwells in every believer and baptizes every believer into the body of Christ.

Today there are but three classes of people in the world—Jews, Gentiles, and the church of God. And when Jews and Gentiles accept the gospel message, they are no longer seen by God as such but are new members of the new creation, the church, of which Christ is the exalted Head.

The Power of the Name (Acts 19:8-20)

Paul continued at Ephesus for a long time. While the synagogue was open to him, he availed himself of the opportunity given to go there and preach the message of the new covenant.

"And he went into the synagogue, and spake boldly for the space of three months, disputing and persuading the things concerning the kingdom of God." Some well-meaning but uninstructed people interpret this to mean that during the ministry and journeys of the apostle Paul, he preached the gospel of the kingdom, and that after he got to Rome he received a fuller revelation of the unity of Jews and Gentiles in one body, and therefore no longer preached the gospel of the kingdom.

That, of course, is an utter mistake for when we turn to the very last verse of the book of Acts, we read that during Paul's imprisonment, after he had supposedly received this special revelation, he was still preaching the kingdom message:

> And Paul dwelt two whole years in his own hired house, and received all that came in unto him, Preaching the kingdom of God, and teaching those things which concern the Lord Jesus Christ, with all confidence, no man forbidding him (Acts 28:30-31).

Up to the very last, Paul preached the kingdom of God, and with that he proclaimed the truth of the church, the one body. The believer in the Lord Jesus is both a member of Christ's body and a subject of the kingdom of God. He would be a poor Christian indeed who did not recognize the divine authority over his life. Being a Christian is more than receiving a creed, more than subscribing to a system of doctrine, more than agreeing to certain church rules and regulations. Being a Christian implies submission in all things to God our Father, who is Sovereign of the universe.

Paul continued preaching the things concerning the kingdom of God. But opposition broke out. The name of the Lord Jesus always provokes the opposition of wicked, ungodly men who are determined not to submit to the will of God. In the synagogue he saw that he was only going to produce strife and division because of the opposition of those who hated the name of Christ Jesus. Paul therefore concluded that it would be useless to continue under such conditions, and he said to the Christians—those who had already received the testimony—"We will have to separate ourselves from all this."

So they evidently rented a public schoolroom. How often the

schoolroom has been used for the proclamation of the gospel! How often our home missionaries found no other place but the school-room open to them, as they went about from place to place in the rural areas. Well, they had a good precedent to follow in Paul's experience in Ephesus.

In the school of Tyrannus he continued to preach for two more years, so that we are told, "All they which dwelt in Asia heard the word of the Lord Jesus, both Jews and Greeks."

In this we see how wonderfully God carries out His own plans. You remember on the second missionary journey when Paul wanted to go into the province of Asia, the Spirit suffered him not. But now, on this third journey, the door had not only been opened to Asia, but God had so arranged that Paul would stay here long enough for the whole district to be permeated with the message. When we read that all they which dwelt in Asia heard the word of the Lord, it does not necessarily mean that all of them came to hear the apostle Paul, but it does mean that many of those who did hear the apostle preach believed the message and in turn carried it to those around them.

We have seen something like that in our own country when there has been a great spiritual awakening. I can remember, for instance, when Dwight L. Moody was in the city of Toronto, Canada, when I was only a little lad. The whole country talked about it, all the news-papers carried reports of his sermons, and everywhere one went throughout the province he would hear of the messages that Moody had brought to the city of Toronto. Even today I can remember the hymns they used to sing as they went to and from the great gather-ings. I can remember how people were stirred. All in the province of Ontario heard the Word. So it was with Paul. The converts car-ried Paul's message throughout the district called Asia and many heard about the wonderful name of Jesus, the sinner's Savior.

"And God wrought special miracles by the hands of Paul: So that from his body were brought unto the sick handkerchiefs or aprons, and the diseases departed from them, and the evil spirits went out of them." We are not told exactly that God commanded this, but it is very evident that the people in their enthusiasm, in their recognition of the fact that God was working in a mighty way through Paul, came to him and said, "Let us just press this handkerchief against your body in order that it may carry healing to our sick friends." I have known people who have tried to do that today, but they are very poor imitations. Here in this special way God authenticated the message of His servant. Sometimes it is said that it is only when the Word was being ministered to the Jews did we have any miracles, but here the apostle Paul is ministering in the great Gentile center where there were comparatively few Jews.

Next we find in verses 13-16 an effort to imitate the work of the Lord. If Satan cannot hinder that work by direct opposition, he will try to spoil it by patronage or imitation. You remember how in Philippi he used this method with a poor, demon-possessed woman (Acts 16:16-18).

"Then certain of the vagabond Jews, exorcists, took upon them to call over them which had evil spirits the name of the Lord Jesus, saying, We adjure you by Jesus whom Paul preacheth." These vagabond Jews were untrue to their own religion, for God's holy law sternly forbade communication with evil spirits of any kind. God condemns spiritism in no uncertain terms in the writings of Moses and of the prophet Isaiah. But these renegade Jews had given themselves over to this evil practice. They professed to cast out evil spirits by some system of incantation, and they even attempted to use the name of the Lord Jesus as a kind of charm in order to exorcise these demons.

Well, they tried it once too often. "There were seven sons of one Sceva, a Jew, and chief of the priests, which did so. And the evil spirit answered and said [that is, a voice came from within the man who was raving in the characteristic manner of one who was demon controlled], Jesus I know, and Paul I know, but who are ye?" And energized by Satanic power the possessed man leaped on them and would have torn them to pieces if they had not run out of the house in dismay. It was the false confronted with the true. They had dared to use the true, the holy name of Jesus in this wicked way to authenticate their own pretensions to power, and God would not permit it.

This incident became known throughout the whole country, and people began to realize that there was power in the name of Jesus. Oh, that lovely name! What does it mean? "Thou shalt call his name

Jesus, for he shall save his people from their sins." "Jehovah, the Savior" is the meaning of the name *Jesus*. And oh, how precious that name is to every believer! "And this was known to all the Jews and Greeks also dwelling at Ephesus; and fear fell on them all, and the name of the Lord Jesus was magnified."

Even unsaved people recognized the fact that there was something marvelous, something stupendous about the name of Jesus, something well worth their attention in the gospel message, which is the story of the Lord Jesus. The result of this preaching of the Word and the miracles accompanying it was that many believed.

Their belief was not simply an intellectual acceptance of certain truths, but they truly and definitely opened their hearts to Christ. They trusted Him as their own personal Savior, and they stepped out boldly before the world, and, as we read, "confessed". What did they confess? Well, of course, they confessed the name of the Lord Jesus for one thing; but they also confessed their sins, and openly repudiated them. It is written: "That if thou shalt confess with thy mouth the Lord Jesus, and shalt believe in thine heart that God hath raised him from the dead, thou shalt be saved" (Romans 10:9). The Lord Himself has said: "Whosoever therefore shall confess me before men, him will I confess also before my Father which is in heaven" (Matthew 10:32). They confessed that wonderful name, but that was not all. There was another confession they made. "And many that believed came, and confessed, and showed their deeds."

These people had been linked with the evil one. Their lives had been marked by sins of the vilest character. Many of them were what were called magicians and witches. They probably had been actually indwelt and controlled by evil spirits who performed lying wonders in order to deceive the people. Such charlatans as these were found all over the ancient world of that time. We have many among us even today.

A certain spiritist medium named Helen Templeton once sent me a long communication that she declared D. L. Moody had given through her. While in a cataleptic condition she wrote what was supposedly a direct message from some disembodied spirit. The letter she sent me was of five or six pages, professedly from D. L. Moody. He had come to her and wanted to give a message to the pastor of his old church. I was interested in reading this message that went something like this: He said he was so sorry that when he was here on earth he did not understand. He had preached as well as he knew, but he did not know the glorious truth of spiritism. Now that he was dead, he had discovered he was all wrong. Now he knew the blessedness of spiritism, but he was far behind others, and it would take him centuries to make up what he missed by wrong instruction on earth. In the letter he said this: "You know, the whole trouble was my father. He followed in the old paths, and he brought me up in the old ideas. Of course, when I became of age I was responsible and I should have refused, and accepted the truths of spiritism, but not knowing any better I followed his teaching."

I wrote to her and replied, "Evidently the spirit that controlled you was not very well up on his history. He did not know that D. L. Moody had no father after he grew up. His father died when Moody was a little baby; and certainly his mother never taught him the old truths, because she was a Unitarian, and was converted through Moody himself years afterward." Evidently some impersonating demon put one over on Helen!

But, oh, how people can be deceived by these things; how they will follow all these wretched efforts to talk with the dead, and work signs and wonders! In all our cities we have clairvoyants, astrologers, dream interpreters, spiritist mediums, and such as those.

Well, many of these Ephesians had been involved with this kind of wickedness. But see what happened. They that believed, confessed and showed their deeds. "Many of them also which used curious arts [that is, magicians' arts] brought their books together, and burned them before all men: and they counted the price of them, and found it fifty thousand pieces of silver." Here was real repentance! Those books cost alot of money. They brought all their books containing magical charms and had a great public bonfire. My, if you could get all the astrological texts and magicians' books today, what a bonfire you would have! How readily people are taken up with every kind of superstition. People can believe the most outlandish fables yet tell you they cannot believe the glorious truths of the gospel.

But the gospel did its work there in Ephesus. The light of the truth delivered them from the darkness of error. They were set free. And they said, "We do not want our books any more." Someone might suggest that they should have taken them down to the second-hand bookstore and realized a little profit on them, but they would have replied: "If they are not good for us, they are not good for anybody else. We are not going to pass poison on to the other people. We are not going to make money on them." These people were so earnest, that they wanted to be right with God at whatever cost. So we read, "Mightily grew the word of God and prevailed."

Today we would like to see revival; we would like to see marked blessing; we would like to see a great awakening. It will only come when the people of God put eternal things above all else. How many of God's beloved saints are trifling with things that hinder their spiritual lives! How many tampering with unholy things! How many giving their time to reading and pondering over books of a wicked character! (The presses of our day are literally teeming with the filthiest literature that one could possibly see.) What a cleaning out there would be in many Christian homes if they brought out these vile books and periodicals and burned them, and said, "By the grace of God, from now on we will read only what is pure and upbuilding." Give God's own Word the first place in your life and then surround it with the books that help you to enjoy that Word more, books that tend to give you a deeper understanding of the ways of God with men, and you will find real edification.

May I ask you who profess to have accepted the Lord Jesus as your Savior, What have you ever given up for Him? Have you given up anything for Him? Face that challenge honestly in the light of God's Word, and remember that He who has redeemed you now claims you as His own. We read:

> I beseech you therefore, brethren, by the mercies of God, that ye present your bodies a living sacrifice, holy, acceptable unto God, which is your reasonable [intelligent] service. And be not conformed to this world: but be ye transformed by the renewing of your mind, that ye may prove what is that good, and acceptable, and perfect, will of God (Romans 12:1-2).

When God's people put Christ first, when they make everything else subject to Him in their lives, then there will be revival; then there will be blessing; then our prayer meetings will be thronged, and our gatherings for the ministry of the Word will become centers of warm Christian testimony. God give us to be as real today as those Ephesian believers were so long ago!

Christ Challenging Idolatry (Acts 19:21-41)

This somewhat lengthy section of the book of Acts is a narrative that requires little explanation. It describes a very striking instance of the beginning of a great conflict between Christ and idolatry. Some perhaps do not realize that at the beginning of the first century A.D. the great bulk of the world lay in the darkness of paganism. Except for the Jewish nation itself and an occasional few among the more philosophically minded Greeks, idols were worshiped everywhere. Throughout the entire Roman empire the people generally were devotees of false gods. The beginning of the end of pagan worship came with the preaching of the eleven apostles on the day of Pentecost. And in the three hundred years that followed that event idolatry had been practically banished from the civilized parts of the world. It is not entirely banished from the world today, but wherever the gospel of grace goes and men open their hearts to receive it, idolatry is destroyed. But this has always been through conflict, and so one of the first of these conflicts is pictured for us in Acts 19.

Paul had made up his mind, after visiting Macedonia and Achaia, that he would return to Jerusalem, and thus complete his third missionary journey. Then he said in his heart, "After I have been there, I must also see Rome." He had little idea how he would get there. You remember, in writing to the Romans he said he often prayed, "making request, if by any means now at length I might have a prosperous journey by the will of God to come unto you" (1:10). God answered that prayer, but not in the way that Paul expected. He went to Rome as a prisoner, and was shipwrecked on the way. I think Paul could have said:

> I asked the Lord that I might grow
> In faith and love and every grace,
> Might more of His salvation know,
> And seek more earnestly His face.
>
> 'Twas He who taught me thus to pray,
> And He I trust has answered prayer;
> But it has been in such a way
> As almost drove me to despair.

What God considers prosperity may often seem to our shortsightedness to be adversity.

Paul then sent into Macedonia Timothy and Erastus, two of his fellow workers, but he continued for a little longer, laboring in the city of Ephesus in Asia where he had already been preaching for about two years. And now, because of the great inroads that Christianity had made in the conflict with idolatry, a riot broke out.

Demetrius, a silversmith who made silver shrines for Diana—a lucrative business to the craftsmen—called together his fellows. Appealing to their cupidity, he said to them as it were, "Now brethren, you know that it is through making these idols that we get our living, and this man Paul has come among us and is persuading people that there are no gods which are made with hands, and the result is depression in the idol business. Our business is falling off. People are not buying silver shrines as they did in the past; and unless something is done to stop this new propaganda, our craft will lose its place among the people." He saw the danger and so mentioned it, simply from the standpoint of a worldly minded, selfish man.

It was said that the image of Diana that was enshrined in the temple, and accounted one of the seven wonders of the ancient world, had fallen down from heaven—a gift from Jupiter, the supreme God. Actually what was enshrined in that temple was a great meteorite, which was shaped, very roughly, after the figure of a woman. The people said, "This is an image of the goddess Diana, and she sent it down from heaven that it might be worshiped, and that our city may become the center of her cult." On the site of a marsh outside the city they built a gorgeous temple in which was enshrined this black meteorite, and the people thronged there by the thousands to worship Diana. And those who desired to carry back to their homes replicas of the image purchased the silver shrines that they might worship them in their own cities.

So by appealing in this way to the greed of these shrine manufacturers, Demetrius stirred them up to indignation. We read: "And when they heard these sayings, they were full of wrath, and cried out, saying, Great is Diana of the Ephesians." Very often, the less that certain people know about something, the more they shout about it and try to convince themselves as to its truth by the noise they make. It was so on this occasion.

"And the whole city was filled with confusion: and having caught Gaius and Aristarchus, men of Macedonia, Paul's companions in travel, they rushed with one accord into the theatre." There was a great theater in Ephesus, the ruins of which are still to be seen.

Finally the mob lit upon a prominent Jew, a man by the name of Alexander, and they drew him, "out of the multitude, the Jews putting him forward. And Alexander beckoned with the hand, and would have made his defence unto the people." Evidently he was to show that as a Jew he had no part in this Christian worship, though both Jew and Christian worshiped the one true and living God, and both of their systems therefore were opposed to idolatry. But no one would listen to him.

If Diana had never been great before, all that shouting ought to have made her great, but it didn't! She was soon utterly defeated and fell before the advance of the cross of Christ.

The town clerk was a stickler for law and order, and he realized that a mob was simply an unruly group liable to go to any excess, and so he sought to quiet them. Notice how sure he was of the greatness of Diana. Yet today there is no man living on the face of the earth who worships the goddess Diana!

Finally the town clerk was able to dismiss the mob. In closing we notice that the word translated "assembly" in the final verse of Acts 19 is the Greek word *ecclesia*. This word is used throughout the

New Testament to indicate the people of the new creation, the church of the living God. The *ecclesia* is really a called-out company, and it might be used of a crowd like this as well as an orderly Christian group.

CHAPTER TWENTY
PAUL BEGINS HIS FAREWELLS

A s we read of the continuation of Paul's journey we note the use of the pronoun *us* indicating that Luke remained with Paul. He was the author of this record and the apostle's intimate companion. Paul's other traveling companions appear to have waited for him at Troas, the city almost on the site of ancient Troy, celebrated by Homer.

Breaking of Bread at Troas (Acts 20:1-12)

In verse 7 Luke proceeded to record something to which the Holy Spirit evidently desires to draw our attention in a special way. We read that he and Paul arrived in Troas and remained there seven days until the first day of the week rolled around. And what is the first day of the week? The day that we call Sunday. On this day, not on the Jewish Sabbath, but on the first day of the week, apparently it had already become customary for the disciples of the Lord Jesus Christ to gather together for a specific purpose. That purpose was "to break bread."

This refers, of course, to that simple yet beautiful feast that our Lord Jesus instituted before He left this world. When He gathered His disciples about Him in the upper room and after they had observed the Jewish feast of the Passover, He took bread (one of the Passover flat cakes) and broke it and gave it to His disciples saying, "This is my body which is given for you; this do in remembrance of me" (Luke 22:19). He also took the cup after supper. There was a cup on the Passover table of which ordinarily no one partook. It was called "the cup of blessing," and if the members of a household asked, "Why is this cup on the table?" the Jewish father would answer, "It is the cup of blessing for Messiah when He comes." Jesus, celebrating the Passover with His disciples, took the cup of blessing for He was the Messiah, and He said, "Drink ye all of it; For this is my blood of the new testament. which is shed for many for the remission of sins" (Matthew 26:27-28). Thus He instituted the Lord's supper.

Now we find that after some twenty years had elapsed it seems to have become a customary thing for the disciples to meet together frequently to observe this feast of love. On this occasion in Acts 20 we read that they gathered on the first day of the week. It may not always have been so, but I am sure that where love is warm, people delight to observe this as often as they can.

They came together on the first day of the week, not to hear a preacher, though the greatest of preachers was there, the apostle Paul; not to hear a teacher, though the greatest of teachers was there, for there has never been another teacher as great as the apostle Paul; they did not come together just to sing hymns, though we know they did sing, as we are told in 1 Corinthians 14:26. They did not come for any of these purposes, and they certainly did not come to be entertained or amused; but "they came together to break bread." They gathered together to remember the Lord Jesus Christ. Whether there was a preacher or not made little difference, or whether there was a teacher or not did not matter; whether there was beautiful singing or not, they were not concerned about that; but they *were* concerned about remembering the Lord Jesus in the breaking of bread.

And so Paul and his companions took advantage of this opportunity to meet with the disciples. Notice that it was in the evening. Most of the disciples were slaves. They had to work all day, but when evening came they were able to slip away and gather together in some quiet place and show the Lord's death in view of His coming again. Paul, led by the Spirit of God, preached to them, and he "continued his speech until midnight." You see, they did not have many opportunities to listen to the expounding of the Word, and even fewer opportunities to hear the apostle Paul. Although the meeting went on and on, hour after hour, we do not read that there was any complaint. But we do read of one poor man who was completely overcome.

"There were many lights in the upper chamber" (they were in an upper room somewhere), "and there sat in a window a certain young man named Eutychus, being fallen into a deep sleep." This dear fellow wasn't the last man to be overpowered by drowsiness in a meeting! But Eutychus was seated in a rather dangerous place—in the window. "And as Paul was long preaching, he sunk down with sleep, and fell down from the third loft, and was taken up dead." But "Paul went down, and fell on him, and embracing him said, Trouble not yourselves; for his life is in him"; that is, he was apparently in a state of coma. So Paul was used of God for his restoration. Every preacher does not have that power. It is too bad perhaps that we do not; so if you endanger yourselves by going to sleep under our sermons, you will yourselves have to endure whatever results. But in this episode Paul was able to overcome the bad consequences.

We can just imagine what a wonderful occasion it was to that little group at Troas. Brought out, some from paganism and some from Judaism, and now together as representing one body, they had come to remember the Lord in the breaking of bread. I think I see them wending their way from their different places to the third story of that building, and when they got there, what a delightful surprise! Who are these visitors? Why, the apostle Paul and Dr. Luke and their friends! And they are all there to break bread with them and to have happy Christian fellowship together. But now they say, "We must not lose this opportunity. Paul is here; we are ready to give attention to any word he has for us from God." So, for some hours Paul went on opening up the precious Word of God, and even after the serious accident to Eutychus and his restoration they continued to listen to Paul. They were still conferring together about the things of the Lord when the morning sun began to rise.

What a delightful picture of the genuine Christian fellowship that existed among believers in those early days. And is it not a standing miracle that although centuries have passed since then—almost two millennia—still all over the world, wherever the gospel has been carried, you will find people coming together for the breaking of bread in tender, loving memory of the Lord Jesus Christ.

Someone may ask, Of what value is the communion service? Does it save the soul? We say, No. The communion is for those whose souls are saved. Well, of what real worth is it? Do we have to do this thing? Oh, no. If we had to do it, it would lose its preciousness, but our Lord Jesus has requested us to do it. He has said: "This do in remembrance of me." And its value is this: That as we obey that word, it brings Christ Himself more preciously before our hearts; we meditate on His love, we think of His passion, we consider His cross, His bitter sorrows. We say in our hearts, "The Son of God loved me and gave Himself for me," and we express on our part our love for Him who has thus redeemed us to Himself.

Paul's Farewell Testimony to the Ephesian Elders (Acts 20:13-27)

After preaching the Word at Troas Paul prepared to go on toward Jerusalem with the intention of stopping by Ephesus on the way. His companions, including Luke, left him at Troas and went by ship, sailing along the coast to a place called Assos. There they intended to take Paul in, for he had walked from Troas to Assos. After meeting him, they sailed on to Mitylene, and then, as Luke said, "We sailed thence, and came the next day over against Chios; and the next day we arrived at Samos [an island in the Aegean sea], and tarried at Trogyllium; and the next day we came to Miletus." Miletus was the port for the city of Ephesus, a few miles inland.

"Paul had determined to sail by Ephesus." He was anxious to be at Jerusalem on the day of Pentecost if possible. You remember the marvelous events that had happened on Pentecost nearly thirty years before! From all parts of the Roman world the Jewish people gathered together annually for the feast, and Paul undoubtedly realized this would be a good opportunity to meet and present Christ to many of them. So, stopping near Ephesus, he asked the elders of the church to come to him. As they gathered together, Paul gave them his final testimony.

He said, "Ye know, from the first day that I came into Asia, after what manner I have been with you at all seasons, Serving the Lord with all humility of mind, and with many tears, and temptations [trials], which befell me." His tribulations were chiefly because of the hatred of some of his own nation who did not understand. They thought he had turned away from the faith of their fathers to teach something that was utterly false. Yet Paul went on earnestly, devotedly ministering Christ.

He described what should characterize every true minister of Christ: "Serving the Lord with all humility [lowliness] of mind." If there is any position, any calling where pride should have no place, it is in connection with the ministry of the Word of God. To begin with, the minister of Christ is one who was just a poor, lost, needy sinner, but who has been saved by grace and entrusted with a message to the world and to the people of God. He does not receive this because of any merit of his own. It is all because of the goodness of the Lord. Certainly therefore he has nothing to be proud of.

When people used to crowd around George Whitefield and praise him because of his marvelous preaching, he would stop them like this: "The devil told me that just before I came down from the pulpit." Then he would add, "There are many who can preach the gospel better than I can, but none can preach a *better* gospel." It is the message that counts. The servant is really nothing, and the more we realize this and are willing to take the place of nothingness, the more God delights to come in and work through His servants.

We see in Paul the ideal minister of Christ, characterized by lowliness of mind and tenderness of heart. That comes out in this testimony. He had served the Lord with all humility of mind, and he was not ashamed to weep with them that weep. We who try to minister Christ may well pray for tender, compassionate hearts. Men and women on every hand are in grief and sorrow. We can well understand the instruction given to a group of ministerial students: "Young gentlemen, always preach to broken hearts, and you will never lack for an audience."

Oh, the sorrowing people in the world today, the broken hearts all about us! How men need that tender message of comfort that the gospel brings! But unless it comes from a heart that is really softened by divine grace, it is powerless to help and bless others. And so Paul said, "I served the Lord with many tears." They were not sham tears: they were not crocodile tears.

I heard of a clergyman who had all kinds of instructions written in the margins of his typewritten sermons. When some of his hearers found one of these sermons that had been left on the pulpit, they were surprised to read the following instructions: Smile here; Raise the voice here; Lower the voice here; Weep here, and so on! It was all made-to-order emotion. That does not glorify God. But one who is in touch with the tender, sympathetic heart of the Lord Jesus, who really feels for those to whom he ministers, will be able to bring a message of consolation to those who are troubled. Such an one was the apostle Paul. His own trials also never turned him aside. He pressed forward in spite of them.

And then he was so true to his commission. He said, "I kept back nothing that was profitable unto you, but have showed you, and have taught you publicly, and from house to house." He was not simply a man of the pulpit. As he stood on the platform he was faithful in giving out the Word of God; he sought to be just as faithful when he visited the people in their homes.

It is pitiable, I think, that to a great extent the good old fashioned custom of pastoral visitation has almost died out. A strange thing occurred to me once. While speaking in a certain city, I learned of a dear soul who was very ill and longed to come to our meetings but was greatly disappointed because she could not come. So I thought, *I will look her up.* I found her address and went to see her. I had a most delightful visit, and then I asked, "Shall we read a little from God's Word?" "Oh," she replied, "how I wish you would!" So I read a portion of Scripture, then bowed with her in prayer. And our hearts were moved. But this was the strange part: when I was leaving, she said, "This is the first time in twenty years that I have ever had a minister read God's Word or pray with me when he visited me." "Well," I said, "perhaps you haven't been visited often." "Oh, yes," she answered; "our minister comes about once a month, and he usually tells me the latest good story and tries to cheer me up a bit." Isn't it pitiable? I do not know any more precious ministry than that of going into the homes of God's dear people and opening up the Word and then lifting up the heart to God in prayer. This is true apostolic service.

What was the burden of Paul's ministry? "Testifying both to the

Jews, and also to the Greeks, repentance toward God, and faith toward our Lord Jesus Christ." Notice the two classes—the Jews that God had set apart for Himself, who had been instructed by prophets and teachers throughout the centuries; and the Greeks. Here, *Greeks* is an all-inclusive term for the different Gentile peoples. Greek was the language spoken almost universally in the Roman world at that time. Paul's testimony was the same in character whether it was to the Jew or to the Greek.

What was the character of that message? "Repentance toward God, and faith toward our Lord Jesus Christ." I am afraid the preaching of repentance is largely missing in many places today. I believe there are many who profess to be fundamental preachers who seldom call men to repentance. And yet if you will go through the book of Acts and on into the Epistles you will see what a large place repentance had in apostolic ministry. The apostle Peter went from place to place calling men to repentance. Paul himself insisted on it wherever he went, and he could say to these Ephesian elders, "During all the time I was with you, and wherever else I have gone, I have called men to repentance." In a preceding chapter we saw that God "commanded all men every where to repent: Because he hath appointed a day, in the which he will judge the world in righteousness by that man whom he hath ordained" (Acts 17:30-31).

I suppose the reason some of my dear brethren are so afraid of the word *repentance* is that they imagine people will think of it as a meritorious act. Repentance is just the sick man's acknowledgment of his illness. It is simply the sinner recognizing his guilt and confessing his need of deliverance. Do not confuse repentance with penitence. Penitence is sorrow for sin, and "godly sorrow worketh repentance to salvation not to be repented of." Do not confuse repentance with remorse. Remorse generally consists in grieving because you are found out. How many a man in prison is filled with remorse, because he got caught! Remorse is not real repentance. Judas was deeply remorseful when he saw how things were going with Jesus, and he brought the thirty pieces of silver and threw them down in the office of the high priest, but he was not truly repentant before God. The words translated, "Judas repented," more properly should be "Judas was remorseful," and he went out and hanged himself. That is the sorrow of the world that results in death, but godly sorrow leads to repentance.

Repentance is not penance. It is not trying in some way or other to make up for the wrong things of the past. Repentance is far more than that. It is judging oneself in the presence of God; turning rightabout-face, turning to God with a sincere, earnest desire to be completely delivered from sin. And when a man takes that attitude toward God and puts his faith in the Lord Jesus Christ, he finds salvation. Faith will never be real apart from repentance. The two things go together—repentance toward God and faith toward our Lord Jesus Christ.

May I ask you who read this: Have you ever faced your sins in the presence of God? Go back into the Old Testament and you find that God has given us an entire book to show us the importance of repentance. That book is Job. It is the record of the best man that God could find in the ancient world, and he demonstrated even to Satan himself that his outward life was absolutely flawless. Yet before God finished with that good man, he cried out from the depths of a broken heart: "I have heard of thee by the hearing of the ear: but now mine eye seeth thee. Wherefore I abhor myself, and repent in dust and ashes" (Job 42:5-6).

My friend, if a good man like Job needed to make a confession like that, surely you and I need it. We may well come before God and take the place of lowliness and repentance. If you are grieving over the sins of the past, recognizing your guilt and longing for deliverance, then I would point you to the Lord Jesus Christ. In infinite grace He bore your sins on the cross in order that you might be forever delivered from the judgment due to sin. Paul linked up faith toward our Lord Jesus Christ with repentance toward God. Put your trust in Him. Look to Him. He has said, "Look unto me, and be ye saved...for I am God, and there is none else." When you look up in faith to Him, then He takes you up in grace, puts away all sins of the past, gives you a new life and a new standing before Him.

Paul continued his farewell by looking forward into the future. He said, "Now, behold, I go bound in the spirit unto Jerusalem, not knowing the things that shall befall me there." He felt that he must go. There are certain things that we read later on in Acts that might make us wonder if he was right in that decision. Even the best of men err in judgment, and it may be that Paul was wrong in going up to Jerusalem.

We are told in Acts 21 that certain disciples said to him "through the Spirit" that he should not go to Jerusalem. But he did not recognize this as the voice of God. He felt that he must go. One reason that he wanted to go was because of his intense love for his Jewish brethren. He was a Christian, but a Hebrew Christian, and he could say, "My heart's desire and prayer to God for Israel is, that they might be saved. For I bear them record that they have a zeal of God, but not according to knowledge" (Romans 10:1-2). He desired to help them; and he felt that to go to Jerusalem at Pentecost and meet them and witness to them might mean the salvation of many. Yet he said, "Wherever I go, I am told that bonds and afflictions await me." Doubtless the Spirit of God spoke through various brethren who said, "Paul, we are afraid you are making a tremendous mistake. Your mission is specially to the Gentiles, not to Israel."

But somehow he could not recognize that as the voice of the Lord to turn him aside. He took it rather as the voice of the tempter seeking to dissuade him. "But," he added, "none of these things move me, neither count I my life dear unto myself, so that I might finish my course with joy, and the ministry, which I have received of the Lord Jesus, to testify the gospel of the grace of God." In other words, he is saying, "After all, my life is of no account except as it is used for the glory of God, except as I have the privilege of ministering Christ to others. I am not afraid of bonds and imprisonment, but I am afraid of dishonoring my Lord, and so my great concern is to finish my course with joy."

It is very interesting to notice in connection with this, the apostle's last Epistle—Second Timothy. There we find him writing from a dungeon death cell, "I have finished my course, I have kept the faith." That which he longed for actually came true. Notice the great assignment he had received from the Lord Jesus was to testify to the gospel of the grace of God. And there can be no higher calling than to be a preacher of the gospel.

I sometimes feel that some of us who minister the Word are inclined to undervalue the work of the evangelist and to think that teaching believers is a more important work. But there is no greater ministry than that of going to poor, lost, needy sinners with the gospel of the grace of God.

I have been told of Duncan Matheson who, on one occasion, was asked to address a meeting. Over a thousand Christians had gathered to hear the Word. He read a portion of Scripture that had a wonderful message for Christians, then expounded upon it for their edification. But as he thought of poor, needy sinners he turned to them instead and went on to fill the whole hour with a gospel message. At the close of the meeting one of the conveners came up to him and said, "Brother Matheson, it was really too bad. Here were a thousand Christians who came for some spiritual food, and you spent the entire hour preaching the gospel." "Oh," said he, "were no unsaved ones there?" "There might have been a half-dozen or so." With a twinkle in his eye, the old man replied in his Scottish way, "Oh well, ye ken, Christians, if they are Christians, will manage to wiggle awa' to Heaven some way, if they never learn any more truth, but poor sinners have got to be saved or be in Hell!" We never want to forget that, and that is why the most important message God ever gave to man was the message of the gospel of the grace of God.

A friend of mine inquired of an older minister about a young preacher he had known. The other replied, "I am afraid he is not doing very well. He has fallen from being a gospel preacher to becoming a prophetic lecturer." Some people would think that was going up, but it might really be going down. Of course it is perfectly right and proper to minister on prophesy if the Lord so leads, but not to the neglect of the gospel of the grace of God.

Paul continued his farewell message by saying, "And now, behold, I know that ye all, among whom I have gone preaching the kingdom of God, shall see my face no more. Wherefore I take you to record this day, that I am pure from the blood of all men." I know that his heart was sad when he said this. What did he mean by it? In effect Paul was saying, "I have delivered my soul. I have not ceased to warn you day and night. I have not shunned to declare unto you all the counsel of God." He was thinking doubtless of that passage in Ezekiel 33 where God speaks of the watchman's responsibility for the safety of the city.

Paul's Charge to the Ephesian Elders (Acts 20:28-38)

An elder, according to the Word of God, is a man approved in life and doctrine; one who, because of mature years and consistent Christian living, is selected by the Holy Spirit to have oversight of the spiritual affairs of the church of God. It is a very serious thing to be called to assume such responsibility. It is not something that any man should ever seek as a matter of personal advancement. It is not an honor that the church should bestow on a man simply in recognition of his spiritual gifts or his fine personality, or because he happens to have a standing in society that would make him an outstanding representative of the church. Nothing like that. But it is a divine calling to serve the people of God. The elder is to be known by his earnestness, his devotedness, his tender compassion for others, his faithfulness in living and proclaiming the truth. God holds him responsible to a very great extent for the spiritual welfare of the believers who recognize him as called by God to this office. Understand, when I am speaking of an elder, I am not simply speaking of a pastor or a teacher, but of an overseer in the church of God. Scripture says that elders are to give an account as those that watch for the souls of believers committed to their charge; so they have a very, very responsible place indeed (Hebrews 13:17).

We who are members of the church of God should ever be ready to recognize our elders and to give to them the honor that belongs to them. Scripture says the elders that rule well should be accounted worthy of double reverence (1 Timothy 5:17). I sometimes think that the church of God is about the only place left today where age really counts. You cannot jump over twenty years of Christian experience.

So often dear young Christians are impatient of restraint and impatient of the kind and fatherly care of God-appointed elders. On the contrary, they should recognize the fact that these men of God have been over the path ahead of them, and have experienced the struggles, temptations, and the trials that the young are now facing. There was a time when they too had to combat the world as young people do now, but through grace they were enabled to overcome. Now with the experience they have attained they are able to guide and direct younger men. In the world outside the church when a man reaches even middle age he is often thrown to one side as one no longer fit to take a responsible position. In the church no man is ready for a responsible position until he has become a mature servant of God.

Paul sent for the Ephesian elders and told them first of his ministry and then he gave them a very definite charge. "Take heed," he said, "therefore unto yourselves and to all the flock." Notice the order. Yourselves first, then the flock. It is possible that even an elder who has known the Lord for many years may be tripped up by some snare of the enemy. Therefore the elder needs to be careful of his own walk, of his own spiritual fellowship with God, and then he is to have care for the flock of God.

You will notice that twice in this passage (verses 28 and 29) the apostle used that term, *the flock*. It is a very lovely expression. It suggests, as our Lord Jesus has told us in John 10, that the people of God are His sheep. You remember He said that He came as the Good Shepherd to call His own sheep out of the fold of Judaism. Then He added, "Other sheep I have which are not of this fold; them also I must bring," referring to the Gentiles, "and there shall be one [flock] and one shepherd." Judaism was a fold without a center. Christianity is a flock; there is a center without a circumference. There is no fold built around the flock of God. Its safety is in keeping close to the Shepherd. There are various similes used for God's people. This is one of the most beautiful. As members of the flock of God, how careful we should be to keep close to our Shepherd, to walk in His steps!

Paul said to these Ephesian elders, "The Holy Ghost hath made you overseers, to feed the church of God." The word translated "overseers" is our word *bishops*. Some of us have come to think of a bishop as a man set over a great many churches, but here the apostle speaks of a number of bishops in one local church, for a bishop is an overseer. They have the spiritual oversight in the church of God, and he commands them, "to feed the church of God." The same company he spoke of as a flock he now speaks of as a church, a called-out company, which is the literal meaning of the Greek word *ecclesia.*

What a wonderful thing it is to belong to that company! Paul once persecuted that company! God forgave him, but he could never forgive himself (see 1 Corinthians 15:9). I imagine many a night he lay awake thinking of the affliction that he had brought on God's dear children in years gone by. "But," he said, "I obtained mercy because I did it ignorantly in unbelief" (1 Timothy 1:13). Notice the company that he persecuted is the same company to which he joined himself after he was converted. The church at Ephesus was the church of God. The church of God was the object of his persecution.

"Purchased with his own blood." "Purchased with the blood of His own," would be a better rendering of this. Fundamentally, you could not speak of the blood of God, because God is a Spirit without physical form, and therefore to speak of the blood of God would be incongruous. If you turn the phrase around, you get the exact meaning of what Paul said to these men: "Feed the church of God, which He hath purchased with the blood of His own," that is, the blood of His own dear Son. The Lord Jesus Christ was God; but in order that He might shed His blood for our redemption, He became man. He who was God and man in one person went to the cross and poured out His precious blood to make propitiation for our sins. Now we who believe in Him constitute the church of God and the flock of God, and as such we need food.

It is the business of the elders to feed the flock of God. How do they do this? By ministering the truth to them—the truth about Christ. As the Word of God is opened up and brought home in power to the flock, they feed on Christ Himself. That is one reason why we are warned against "forsaking the assembling of ourselves together, as the manner of some is" (Hebrews 10:25).

Many Christians today shrug their shoulders and say, "Oh, I am not interested in going to church. I don't need to go; I can worship God just as well at home." But in so acting they deliberately rob their own souls of the food that they need for their spiritual upbuilding. We need the Word of God, and He has appointed that as His people gather together, the truth should be presented that the saints may be nourished on the words of sound doctrine.

Then the apostle brought in a warning to the elders. He looked with prophetic eye down through the centuries and there he saw what has now become history. As the centuries progressed, unconverted men came into the outer circle of the church. Professing to be Christians, many of them pushed forward into places of leadership, and the history of the professing church is a very sad history indeed. Many unrighteous, unconverted men seek to hold positions of authority over God's people. They are like "grievous wolves" entering in from the outside, not sparing the flock! But then, not only did they come in from the outside, for the apostle added, "Also of your own selves shall men arise, speaking perverse things, to draw away disciples after them."

One of Satan's favorite methods of disrupting the peace among the saints is to raise up in their midst men who in large measure are self-seeking, although perhaps truly converted. These men endeavor to pressure the saints of God to accept certain teachings in order to create division in God's house. Then they gather a group around themselves with the object of attaining personal recognition and support. Just as though he were living today and could see what is going on in so many places, the apostle predicted this very thing!

What is the Christian's confidence? What is his safety in view of such circumstances as these? Paul said, "Therefore watch, and remember, that by the space of three years" (the three years in which he had labored at Ephesus) "I ceased not to warn every one night and day with tears." The apostle was not ashamed of tears. To him eternal things were so real that when he saw people turning coldly away from them it almost broke his heart, and he wept over them. And then as he entered into the homes of God's saints and saw the sorrows that many of them had to endure—bereavement, sickness, poverty, and persecution—he was no unsympathetic onlooker. He could weep with those who wept and rejoice with those who rejoiced. This expresses the heart of the true pastor. "I serve with tears, and I cease not to warn you with tears."

Paul next said, "I commend you to God and to the Word of his grace, which is able to build you up." In other words, "But now I am going away from you. I am never going to see you on earth again, but here is your resource in the day of difficulty." What is this resource? God and His blessed, infallible, and inspired book, the Bible. This shall abide when His servants pass on.

Why is it that many Christians today make such slow progress in the Christian life and are so weak when they ought to be strong? It is because they give so little time to the reading of the Word of God. I would like to ask you, dear friends, How much time do you really give to the Bible day by day? Do you study the Word? Do you take time to meditate on the Word?

I was in Glasgow, Scotland when a missionary from India, returned home on furlough, took part in the meeting. He read us a letter that he had received from an Indian elder in the church which the missionary had left behind. This is what he read: "Dear brother, we have missed you greatly while you have been gone, but we are trying to carry on. We are all studying the Word more faithfully than ever, and God has already been at work and we are having a great rebible." He meant "revival." And you know, that dear missionary reading the letter said, "Brethren, I do not think there was any mistake in that letter because whenever there is a re-Bible movement, there will be a revival."

And that is what we need—to get back to the Bible, to give more attention to the Bible. There are professing Christians who rarely open their Bibles from one Sunday to the next unless perhaps to read the Sunday school lesson. There are many Christian homes that no longer have a family altar, where husband and wife and children never sit down to read the Word together and lift up their hearts to God in prayer. Is it any wonder that the church of God is so weak? Is it any wonder that worldliness is coming in like a flood? Is it any wonder that false doctrines are so readily accepted when God's own beloved people are not acquainted with His holy Word?

Our resources in the day of evil are God and the Word of His grace, "which is able to build you up, and to give you an inheritance among all them which are sanctified." What is it to be sanctified? It

is to be set apart to God, and every believer is set apart through
God's grace. As we study the Word our sanctification goes on practically, resulting in lives and hearts that are separated to the Lord
alone.

Paul continued his charge to the Ephesian elders by referring to
his own attitude as he ministered among them. He who would seek
to help and bless others need not expect to lift them any higher than
he is himself. Water does not rise above its own level. The minister
of the gospel must be very careful to walk with God in his private
life as well as publicly, and so Paul said, "I have coveted no man's
silver, or gold or apparel." In other words, "I have not been among
you for what I could get from you." "Yea, ye yourselves know, that
these hands have ministered unto my necessities, and to them that
were with me."

Whenever his funds ran out, you never saw Paul trying to stir up
the people to give him anything. I was rather shocked to read in the
newspaper of a minister who was suing the church for not having
been given all his salary. Paul never did anything like that. He never
appealed for anything for himself. He was not afraid to solicit for
others, however, such as when he asked funds for the poor saints at
Jerusalem. When his own money ran out, he went around and got a
job. He was not afraid of degrading the "cloth" or of getting his
hands dirty. He found a job at tentmaking, and he not only supported himself, but he supported those who were with him. "I have
showed you all things, how that so laboring ye ought to support the
weak, and to remember the words of the Lord Jesus, how he said, It
is more blessed to give than to receive."

When did Jesus say this? Where is it recorded? You search the
four Gospels and you will never find these words, "It is more blessed
to give than to receive." And yet Paul, speaking to these Ephesian
elders, Gentiles far away from Palestine where Jesus had lived and
preached, records them. It is evident that these words fell frequently
from the lips of the Lord Jesus. They are not actually recorded elsewhere, but the saints spoke of them as they moved from place to
place. Different ones remembered they had often heard Jesus say
them. He was probably in the habit of saying, "It is more blessed to
give than to receive."

It makes one so happy to be at the giving end rather than the receiving end. Folks who are always going around with an open hand, hoping you will give them something, are not happy people. The happy ones are those who give to others. I do admire Mrs. Wiggs of the Cabbage Patch. No matter how many came in to dinner, she said "It's all right, we can just add another ladle of water to the soup." She found it was more blessed to give than to receive; and so it is with the consistent Christian who is living in fellowship with his Lord.

Well, Paul's address is concluded. Luke's words help us to visualize this little company: "When he had thus spoken, he kneeled down, and prayed with them all." We see Paul on the seashore, and the Ephesian elders are all kneeling around him. What a hallowed little prayer meeting that must have been!

They were sad because the one who had led them to Christ was going away, and they feared some dreadful thing was about to happen to him. They did not understand it all, but they bowed reverently before God while Paul prayed with them. Wouldn't you like to know what he said? If only there had been a record made of his prayer so that we could hear it today! How I would love to enter into that prayer! Oh, I know that he must have poured out his heart for these elders that they might be given all needed grace and wisdom to guide the saints aright. It affected them very deeply, for we read: "And they all wept sore, and fell on Paul's neck, and kissed him." Strong men they were, and yet they were not ashamed in this way to express their deep love for the man of God who had won them for Christ when they were strangers to grace.

But they sorrowed "most of all for the words which he spake, that they should see his face no more." And they never did. It was Paul's farewell. He went on to Jerusalem, was arrested, incarcerated at Caesarea, and taken on to Rome. Although after two years of imprisonment in Rome he was set free for a little time, evidently he never reached Ephesus again. His work with them was done, but oh, done so well! Surely he had no regrets as he looked back. He had served faithfully. God grant that when you and I finish our work we may be able to rejoice in what God has done and not have our consciences troubling us because of unfaithful service.

CHAPTER TWENTY-ONE
PAUL'S FINAL VISIT TO JERUSALEM

In our study of Acts we have followed Paul from the days when he was a bitter persecutor of the church of God, through his conversion and dedication to the work of the Lord. We have accompanied him on his three missionary journeys as he carried the gospel throughout the Near East, and finally we saw him leaving Ephesus for the last time to continue his journey to Jerusalem.

The early verses of Acts 21 are very interesting if you read them with a map before you. You can trace Paul's journey from Miletus right on to Jerusalem. In verse 4 we read that Paul and those traveling with him arrived in Tyre where they remained for seven days. While they were there a most unusual incident occurred in the life of Paul. There they found disciples who said to Paul—now observe this—"through the Spirit, that he should not go up to Jerusalem." Now was this simply a test of his readiness to suffer, or was it really a warning word forbidding him to go? It may be a little difficult for us to decide, but the statement is plain. These disciples said to Paul through the Holy Spirit that he should not go up to Jerusalem.

Already the Spirit of God had intimated through various servants of His that this journey would not be as successful as Paul had hoped. As we previously noted, it is very evident that it was his deep love for his own people, the Jews, that led him to go to Jerusalem. He was bringing them alms that had been collected by the Christians in the Gentile churches to assist those in Judea who were suffering because of famine. He felt that this opportunity to minister in a temporal way to his people—both converted and uncoverted Jews—

would enable him to show them how truly he loved them. Also he hoped that this outpouring of love would be used of God to break down the bigotry and the bitter opposition in the hearts of so many of them.

Paul knew exactly how his Jewish brethren felt. He himself had felt as they did. There was a time when he thought of Jesus as a deceiver, as one who was misleading the people, and he bound himself to do everything he could to hinder the work of the gospel. But the Lord had won his heart, and now he hoped by special kindness to his own people to be able to win them.

But we need to remember this. When God saved him, He especially commissioned him to preach the gospel to the Gentiles. Although wherever Paul went he invariably entered the synagogue and preached to the Jews first, yet it was always among the Gentiles that he found the most fruit.

With the apostle Peter it was different. The Lord seemed to have given Peter a special gift and ministry for the Jews. When Paul, James, Peter, John, and others met together in Jerusalem years before, they agreed among themselves that evidently Peter's special mission was to the Jews and Paul's to the Gentiles (Galatians 2:1-9). But he could not forget the blood ties that held him fast to his Jewish brethren, and he still hoped to be God's special messenger to them. So he was determined to pursue his way toward Jerusalem.

Did he make a mistake in so doing? Did Paul really disobey the voice of the Lord? It is hard for us to say. We may be sure of this, that if he did make a mistake, he made it from the best of motives. If he blundered here, he blundered out of an overpowering love for the Jewish people. I am afraid that some of us cannot say of our mistakes that they have always been motivated by love.

If Paul was mistaken here, it should be a great encouragement to some of us. You see, we are apt to think of the apostles of our Lord Jesus Christ as though they were men of a much higher caliber than ourselves, and therefore there is no possibility of our being used as they were. But we learn as we study the book of Acts that these men were of like passions with ourselves. They had the same fallible judgment that we have. They could be misled as we are misled. The apostle Peter was clearly misled at Antioch when he withdrew himself from the Gentiles and refused to eat with them when Jewish brethren came down from Jerusalem (Galatians 2:11-13). We have already seen how Paul and Barnabas misunderstood one another and had a bitter quarrel over the case of young John Mark. All these things impress on us the fact that these were men like ourselves who needed daily to seek guidance from the Lord that they might be directed aright, and who had to confess their own sins and their failures. This is a great encouragement to me and I cannot help thinking it ought to be to others also. I realize that one blunders so frequently; one errs in so many ways. Even when one has attempted to do the very best thing, he often feels in looking back that he has made a mistake by going too far to the right or the left.

It is such an encouragement to know that all the work God has accomplished through His servants in this world He has done through imperfect instruments. He has never had a perfect instrument. The Lord Jesus of course was perfect, but He was more than an instrument. He was God Himself manifest in the flesh. But all the merely human servants that God has ever had have blundered somewhere.

Go back into the Old Testament. Noah failed terribly after the flood when he came under the power of wine. Abraham denied his wife. Isaac failed because of fleshly appetite. Jacob's record was one of blundering and failure! Moses' spirit was provoked at the waters of Meribah, as a result he was not permitted to enter into the land of Canaan. David had a great blot on his record, though he bitterly repented of his sin.

So one might go on through all the Old Testament, and find that even when we come to the New Testament the same thing is true. We think of John as the gentlest and most loving of the Lord's disciples, and yet John and James would have called down fire from heaven and burned up the city of the Samaritans because they refused the testimony of the Lord Jesus Christ. Peter denied his Lord. Thomas doubted. Over all of them *Failure* could be written. And yet God used these men in spite of their failures and lack of good judgment. He brought them to repentance and cleansed them from all unrighteousness, and gave them opportunity after opportunity to magnify His grace. So we are not surprised to read a record like the one found in Acts 21.

It is very evident that if this was a positive command given to Paul not to go to Jerusalem, he did not recognize it as such. He rather took it as a test of his readiness to endure, and so he went on. Luke, who was with him, said, "When we had accomplished those days, we departed and went our way; and they all brought us on our way, with wives and children, till we were out of the city: and we kneeled down on the shore, and prayed." We had something similar to that in the previous chapter. There Paul kneeled down on the shore and prayed with the Ephesian elders, and now here is this little group. It is gratifying to notice the women and the little children all knelt together and prayed as they commended Paul to the Lord, and as he commended them to the grace of God.

Then Luke wrote, "When we had taken our leave one of another, we took ship...and came to Ptolemais...And the next day...came unto Caesarea." There another interesting incident occurred. "We entered into the house of Philip the evangelist, which was one of the seven; and abode with him." This is the Philip who years earlier was chosen to be a deacon and was called by the Spirit of God to go down to Samaria and preach Christ to the Samaritans. Many of the Samaritans believed and were saved. Then the Spirit of God took Philip out of what we might consider a great spiritual awakening and revival and told him to go toward the south to the road that leads from Jerusalem to Gaza. Without any question he obeyed and finding a man from Ethiopia reading from the prophecy of Isaiah, Philip took the opportunity to preach to him of Jesus Christ.

Now this was the Philip who was living at Caesarea. We are told that he had four daughters, and these young women, anointed servants of God, all had the gift of prophecy. But God did not use these young women to admonish Paul.

We read, "As we tarried there many days, there came down from Judaea a certain prophet, named Agabus. And when he was come unto us," he did a most striking thing. He unloosed Paul's girdle. The Easterners wore long, flowing robes, held together at the waist by a girdle. With Paul's girdle Agabus bound his own hands and feet and solemnly declared, "Thus saith the Holy Ghost, So shall the Jews at Jerusalem bind the man that owneth this girdle, and shall deliver him into the hands of the Gentiles."

Was that another warning, telling Paul not to go, or was it simply another test of his faith? We don't know, but it will all come out clearly at the judgment seat of Christ. Certainly Paul's companions took it as a warning not to go on, but he himself interpreted it otherwise. Luke wrote, "When we heard these things, both we, and they of that place, besought him not to go up to Jerusalem." They felt he was making a mistake. He was putting himself in unnecessary jeopardy, which might result in the cutting short of his great ministry, and so they pleaded with him not to go.

But Paul, unable to view it from their standpoint and moved by his great love for his Jewish people, answered, "What mean ye to weep and to break mine heart? for I am ready not to be bound only, but also to die at Jerusalem for the name of the Lord Jesus." In other words, Paul said, "Bonds and afflictions do not terrify me; the thought of persecution and trial does not trouble me. I am ready to endure all these things for Christ's sake." Truly he did not take this as an intimation that he should not go to Jerusalem, though it may have been that. So when the others heard what he had to say, they simply added, "The will of the Lord be done."

It is not incumbent on us to judge the apostle Paul. It looks as though he missed the mind of God here. Yet if he did, we realize that we too have often missed His mind. Still He has been so wonderfully patient and kind. Our hearts can only go out to Him in deep thanksgiving.

We need also to remember that there is not only God's directive will, but His permissive will, and if Paul misunderstood the former he was in line with the latter. God was going to work out some special purpose in the experiences that His servant would have to undergo at Jerusalem.

In Acts 21:15(KJV) we have a curious instance of how a word may completely change its meaning in the course of time. The word translated "carriage" is better translated today "baggage," that is, "We took up our baggage and went up to Jerusalem."

"There went with us also certain of the disciples of Caesarea, and brought with them one Mnason of Cyprus, an old disciple, with whom we should lodge. And when we were come to Jerusalem, the brethren received us gladly." When Paul had gone to Jerusalem some years before to have the apostles there decide whether or not Gentile believers must be subjected to the law of circumcision there had been some feelings of discord. Now Paul and his fellow travelers were received gladly, and apparently with true brotherly confidence.

But on the day following, something took place that fills us with perplexity. How could it be that the incident which is next recorded could ever have had Paul's approval? After Paul recounted his ministry among the Gentiles, the elders rejoiced in what God had done. But something was troubling their minds in regard to Paul's attitude toward Jewish Christians. James said unto him, "Thou seest, brother, how many thousands of Jews there are which believe; and they are all zealous of the law." The apostle Paul had written the Epistles to the Galatians and to the Romans long before this, and he had told believers that they were not under law but under grace. To Jewish believers he wrote: "The law was our [child-leader] to bring us unto Christ"-our *paidagogos* (Galatians 3:24-25). The word translated "schoolmaster" in the King James version can be literally translated "child-leader." In other words, the law directed Israel in the days of their minority; but, Paul said, after Christ came, "we are no longer under a schoolmaster." But these Jewish Christians at Jerusalem had never learned this. They were still carrying out the various commandments given in connection with the Old Testament ritual.

James said to Paul, "And they are informed of thee, that thou teachest all the Jews which are among the Gentiles to forsake Moses, saying that they ought not to circumcise their children, neither to walk after the customs" (that is, the Jewish customs). He did not refer to what Paul taught the Gentiles because they were never under Moses, and Paul did not seek to put them under him. He gave them the truth of grace.

Then James devised a little plan that would put Paul right with his Jewish brethren at Jerusalem. It was what you might call an example of religious politics, and here again we see how easily a great man of God may fail and be misled, for James was certainly an outstanding servant of our Lord Jesus Christ. He was intimately related to Christ after the flesh, and he had the full confidence of the Christians in Jerusalem. And yet he put this plan up to Paul.

James told Paul of four men who had taken the Nazarite vows. In the book of Numbers we read that if a Jew took the vow of a Nazarite, he was to devote himself wholly to the things of God for a certain period of time. It might be a few days or a number of weeks, months, or years. A Nazarite had to let his hair grow, but at the end of the period of his vow he was to shave it off and bring certain sacrifices to present to God.

Paul himself was a Nazarite when he was converted (see commentary on Acts 18:18). But when Paul had concluded his vow, he did not bring a sacrifice. Why? He knew that Christ, by offering Himself, had perfected forever them that are sanctified, and he knew that the sacrifices under the law had no more place in the Christian economy.

But these Jewish Christians had not learned this. They were concluding their Nazariteship and were going to the temple to present their sacrifices. Sometimes men were poor and unable to buy proper offerings. Certain well-to-do Jews would purchase the lambs for the sacrifice, and so meet the need of their poorer brethren. That was considered a very meritorious thing.

James saw this as an opportunity for Paul to square himself with his Jewish brethren. He said, "Them take, and purify thyself with them, and be at charges with them," (that is, You pay for the sacrifices) "that they may shave their heads: and all may know that those things, whereof they were informed concerning thee, are nothing; but that thou thyself also walkest orderly, and keepest the law. As touching the Gentiles which believe, we have written and concluded that they observe no such thing." You see, they were making a difference between Christian Jews and Christian Gentiles. But Paul himself had emphatically declared that there was no such difference before God.

Now what would you have expected of Paul in circumstances like these? What would you have supposed would be the attitude of the man who wrote Galatians and Romans? Surely you would have expected him to say, "I cannot do that. For me to go with those men to the altar in the temple and pay for their sacrifices would be the denial of what I have preached during all the years of my ministry." But again I say that if Paul failed here, he failed because of his intense love for his Jewish brethren. He wanted to do something to win them, and so he agreed, for we read: "Then Paul took the men, and the next day purifying himself with them entered into the temple, to signify the accomplishment of the days of purification, until that an offering should be offered for every one of them."

Just imagine if that rite had been consummated, what it would have meant! It would have nullified to a large extent the testimony of the apostle Paul in the years to come. Imagine him stepping up with them to the altar and offering animal sacrifices—a virtual denial of the one sacrifice of our Lord Jesus Christ.

But God did not permit it. He so overruled that the very Jewish people that Paul wanted to reach misunderstood him entirely and took steps that led to his arrest. "When the seven days were almost ended, the Jews which were of Asia, when they saw him in the temple, stirred up all the people, and laid hands on him." They accused Paul of polluting the temple by bringing in Gentiles. That was not true. He had not brought Greeks into the temple, but the next verse explains why they said that: "For they had seen before with him in the city Trophimus an Ephesian, whom they supposed that Paul had brought into the temple." How easy it is to get excited over suppositions and to go to extremes because of imaginary things without seeking to find out the truth!

As the mob prepared to kill Paul God intervened to take care of His dear servant. There may have been mistakes; he may have failed to ascertain the mind of God; but the loving heart of the Savior goes out to him still, and He is going to protect him. And so He does it through the Roman chief captain who, we read, "immediately took soldiers and centurions, and ran down unto them: and when they saw the chief captain and the soldiers, they left beating of Paul. Then the chief captain came near, and took him, and commanded him to be bound with two chains; and demanded who he was, and what he had done" (Acts 21:32-33).

It was absurd on the face of it. There was a mob in an uproar and instead of first inquiring the reason for the clamor, the chief captain took it for granted that Paul must be to blame. So he had him bound and then inquired what he had been doing.

"And some cried one thing, some another, among the multitude: and when he could not know the certainty for the tumult, he commanded him to be carried into the castle"—that is, the castle of Antonia that overlooked the temple court.

It is easy to stir up a mob. Half of them did not even know what the trouble was about, but mob spirit is infectious, and so this great host shouted for the death of the apostle Paul. As he was about to be led into the castle, he said to the chief captain, "May I speak unto thee?" He spoke in Greek, and the captain asked in amazement, "Canst thou speak Greek? Art not thou that Egyptian, which before these days made an uproar, and leddest out into the wilderness four thousand men that were murderers?" There had been an uprising against the Romans some time before, and the chief captain supposed that Paul was the guilty man who headed that rebellion.

But Paul said, I am a man which am a Jew of Tarsus, a city in Cilicia, a citizen of no mean city: and, I beseech thee, suffer me to speak unto the people. And when he had given him license, Paul stood on the stairs, and beckoned with the hand unto the people. And when there was made a great silence, he spake unto them in the Hebrew tongue (Acts 21:39-40).

Acts 22 records his speech to the crowd in Jerusalem in which he gave the testimony of his wonderful conversion.

Let us gather up a few thoughts in closing this chapter. How often you and I in our very effort to do the will of God are likely to miss His leading, sometimes through prejudice, sometimes through wrong information, sometimes through not being wholly surrendered to do His will. But oh, how wonderful the mercy of God that, even if we blunder, He never gives up on us. He is still looking after us in His lovingkindness. While we may have failed, God is going to see us safely through to the end. And when at last we reach glory land, we will look back over the path we have come and we will be able to praise Him for it all.

> Oh, Lord, whate'er my path may be,
> If only I may walk with Thee,
> And talk with Thee along the way,
> I'll praise Thee for it all some day.

CHAPTER TWENTY-TWO
PAUL'S PERSONAL TESTIMONY

There is tremendous power in personal testimony. It is a great thing to proclaim Christ and Him crucified. "The preaching of the cross is to them that perish foolishness; but unto us which are saved it is the power of God" (1 Corinthians 1:18). We are commanded to go into all the world and preach the gospel to every creature. When "the world by wisdom knew not God, it pleased God by the foolishness [or the simplicity] of preaching to save them that believe" (21). But I am afraid the mere proclamation of the gospel would avail very little unless there were men and women to support the preacher and his message and say, "I believed the message and my whole life was transformed. I came in my sin and my guilt and I trusted the Lord Jesus, and He has cleansed me from my sins. When I heard the gospel message, I was under the power of evil and wicked habits. They bound my soul like fetters, but He snapped the chains that bound me, and set me free. My whole being was diseased with sin, but Jesus healed me. I was blind to eternal realities, but whereas once I was blind, now I see." This kind of testimony confirms to men the power that is in the gospel of our Lord Jesus Christ.

It is a very interesting fact that five times in Scripture we have the story of Paul's conversion. I have sometimes heard people object to men frequently relating the account of God's dealing with them. They think that they should just preach the doctrinal message, but in the Word of God we read Paul's testimony five times. In Acts 9 we have the historical account of his conversion as related by Luke. In

275

this twenty-second chapter of Acts we have what we might call Paul's Hebrew account of his conversion as, standing on the stairs of the tower of Antonia that overlooked the temple court, he told his Jewish brethren how God had saved him. He presented the story in such a way that it would have appealed particularly to their hearts.

Then in Acts 26 we have what might be called the Gentile account of his conversion. Standing before Festus, the Roman governor, and King Agrippa, he again related at length God's dealing with him. That account was given in such a way that it would have been of special interest to that cynical, unbelieving ruler, Festus, as well as to Agrippa.

Then in Philippians 3 we have the whole wonderful story told again. Paul described his religion, his hope, and in what he had trusted before he knew the Lord Jesus. Then he spoke of the wonderful revelation of the righteousness of God in Christ, which led him to put away all confidence in any righteousness of his own.

In 1 Timothy he wrote once more what he had been—a blasphemer, a persecutor of the church—in his ignorance and unbelief. Then he told how God in infinite mercy reached out to him, saved his guilty soul and made him His messenger to those still in their sins.

You remember, as we saw in the last chapter of Acts, the people took Paul and were about to kill him. The Roman chief captain, not knowing what was going on, came down and arrested Paul, but gave him an opportunity to speak for himself. So Paul stood on the stairs and related the story of his conversion to the great Jewish multitude gathered below in the court of the temple.

"Men, brethren, and fathers, hear ye my defense which I make now unto you." Paul was a Jew by birth. He was speaking to his Jewish brethren, and he addressed them in an appropriate manner. He had long since learned to make himself all things to all men, declaring, "Unto the Jews I became as a Jew, that I might gain the Jews...To the weak became I as weak, that I might gain the weak" (1 Corinthians 9:20, 22). And so he addressed them here in what they themselves would recognize was a proper way to speak to his own Hebrew people.

"And when they heard that he spake in the Hebrew tongue to

them, they kept the more silence." Oh, the appeal there is in the tongue that one has been accustomed to from childhood! There is something about your own native idiom that especially grips your attention.

Paul recognized the intense bigotry in their hearts, and religious bigotry is the worst kind to overcome. He began his story in a very simple way. Since they considered him a hater of their nation who wanted to tear down the things that they loved, he reminded them that there was a time when he was just as zealous as any of them in maintaining the institutions of Judaism.

Although there are people in the world who despise the Jews, no one should ever be ashamed of being a Jew. None need be ashamed to be known as a member of that chosen race—that race to whom God committed the divine oracles and which, through the millennia, has maintained the truth of the one God.

When Disraeli was speaking in the British Parliament, a certain lord rose to his feet and cried out in most contemptuous tones, "You, sir, are a Jew." Disraeli drew himself up to his full height, which was not very much, and replied: "My lord, you accuse me of being a Jew. I am proud to answer to the name, and I would remind you, sir, that one-half of Christendom worships a Jew and the other half a Jewess. And I would also remind you that my forefathers were worshiping the one true and living God while yours were naked savages in the woods of Britain."

We Gentiles will never be able to thank God enough for what the Jews have meant to us in preserving the Holy Scriptures and giving us our Savior, the Lord Jesus Christ, who declared: "Salvation is of the Jews" (John 4:22).

Paul began his testimony by saying that he was a Jew—one of those dispersed among the Gentiles. He was educated in Jerusalem, a student of Gamaliel, a well-known rabbi, whose reputation for righteousness is revered among the Jews to this day. He continued, I was "taught according to the perfect manner of the law of the fathers, and was zealous toward God, as ye all are this day."

It is possible to have a zeal for God and yet not have it according to knowledge. Paul said of his own kinsmen after the flesh in another place:

Brethren, my heart's desire and prayer to God for Israel is, that they might be saved. For I bear them record that they have a zeal of God, but not according to knowledge. For they being ignorant of God's righteousness, and going about to establish their own righteousness, have not submitted themselves unto the righteousness of God (Romans 10:1-3).

That was the state of Paul himself for years. Ignorant of how righteous God really is, he imagined he could work out a satisfactory righteousness of his own. He was endeavoring to do that very thing until he was brought into contact with the living Christ and found in Him a righteousness in which he could stand perfect before God. But in the former days, he had "persecuted this way unto the death." It is interesting to note that *the way* is frequently used in the book of Acts as the term for Christianity. Christianity is *the way* to God, to life, to Heaven.

Then he said, "The high priest" (perhaps the high priest was standing there as he spoke) "doth bear me witness, and all the estate of the elders: from whom also I received letters unto the brethren, and went to Damascus, to bring them which were there bound unto Jerusalem, for to be punished." And there those elders stood, waiting to bring their accusations against him.

But as he drew near Damascus, the great event that transformed his life had taken place. The most remarkable thing about the story of Paul's conversion is that he had a conversion to tell of. I know a great many professing Christians who can tell scarcely anything about their conversion. Of course, we recognize the fact that many have come to know the Lord Jesus Christ in early childhood. It is not necessary, nor may it be possible for them, to retain the memory of the time when they first came to Christ. These things fade from the child's mind. But others who have gone on to adult years before they came to know the Lord ought to be able to give some account of what took place when they turned from darkness to light and from death to life.

A parishioner once asked his minister, "Would you mind if I suggested a subject that you should use on some occasion?" The minister said, "I am very pleased to have you show that much interest.

What is it you would like me to speak on?" "Well," the man replied, "I would like very much if you would give us a sermon on the
text, 'Except ye be converted, and become as little children, ye shall
not enter into the kingdom of heaven.'" "I shall be delighted to do
that, and I will notify you in advance when I am going to speak on
that subject."

The time came when he was to speak on the text, and he thought,
*Let me see, how will I divide it? Conversion—what? Conversion—
how? Conversion—when? Conversion—where?* He thought a little
on conversion—what? Well, conversion must be the turning of the
heart to God; and he elaborated on that. And then he came to conversion—how? How is a man converted? A little perplexed, he
thought, *Well, let me see, how was I converted? Why, I don't know.
I think I'll pass over that just now.*

He came to the next point: conversion—when? Well, one may
be converted as a child; one may be converted in youth; or one may
be converted in mature years. But then the thought came to him,
*When was I converted? Was I converted when I was a child? I can't
remember. Well, was I converted when I was a youth? No, I am
sure I was not, for I got far away from God out in the world. No, not
as a youth. Was I converted when I came to more mature years? I
do not recall.*

So he passed on to the next point: conversion—where? It might
take place in the home, in the church, in the Sunday school, or out
in the open. God is ready to meet men wherever they may be. Then
the thought came to him, *Where did it take place with me? Was I
converted at home? Was I converted in church? Have I ever been
converted?* And suddenly it came to him in tremendous power, *I am
preaching to other people and I have never been converted myself.
I don't know when, how, or where I was converted. I have never
been converted at all!*

He preached his own sermon to himself, and got down before
God and told the Lord Jesus that he would trust Him as his Savior,
and that was the beginning of a new life and a new ministry. When
he came into the pulpit on Sunday to preach on conversion, his words
had tremendous power for he was a new man.

Do you know anything about conversion? You may be a church

member, but that is not conversion. You may have been baptized, but that is not conversion. You may take the sacrament of the Lord's Supper, and be interested in missions, but these are not conversion. You like to help the cause of Christ perhaps, but that is not conversion. Conversion is a turning to God from self. It is taking the place of repentance toward God and faith in the Lord Jesus Christ. Do you know anything of the experience that Paul knew of trusting Christ?

Paul continued: "And it came to pass, that, as I made my journey, and was come nigh unto Damascus about noon, suddenly there shone from heaven a great light round about me." Paul saw an actual light shining from Heaven—the light of the glory of God reflected from the face of Jesus Christ. Seeing the light is always the beginning of real conversion. Men go on in darkness until light from Heaven shines into their hearts as they come under the convicting power of the Word in the energy of the Holy Spirit. That Word causes the light to shine in and shows man what he really is—a poor, lost sinner in the sight of God—and then reveals the Savior that He has provided.

Paul continued, "And I fell unto the ground, and heard a voice saying unto me, Saul, Saul, why persecutest thou me?" He was amazed, and said: "Who art thou, Lord? And he said unto me, I am Jesus of Nazareth, whom thou persecutest." The men with Paul heard a strange noise but could not discern actual words. They thought perhaps it was thunder or something like that, but he could hear every word distinctly. And he asked, "What shall I do, Lord?" And the Lord said to him, "Arise, and go into Damascus; and there it shall be told thee of all things which are appointed for thee to do."

Then we read, "And when I could not see for the glory of that light, being led by the hand of them that were with me, I came into Damascus." I think we may take a spiritual meaning out of those words, "I could not see for the glory of that light." The glory that shone from the face of Jesus blinded Saul of Tarsus forever to all the glories of earth and to all thought of self-righteousness. When his eyes were opened again, he saw things in a new light. Everything was different.

But he entered Damascus a blind man, and was led by the hand to the home of a friend with whom he was to lodge. There he remained in deep soul exercise until Ananias came to him with the message, "Brother Saul, receive thy sight."

What a wonderful thing! Ananias was a Christian Jew. Saul had been a persecutor of the Christians, and Ananias was one of the very men that Saul had come to arrest, but now he says to him, "Saul, my brother." Grace had made them brothers. And Paul said,

> The same hour I looked up upon him. And he said, The God of our fathers hath chosen thee, that thou shouldest know his will, and see that Just One, and shouldest hear the voice of his mouth. For thou shalt be his witness unto all men of what thou hast seen and heard. And now why tarriest thou? arise, and be baptized, and wash away thy sins, calling on the name of the Lord (Acts 22:13-16).

Do not link the expression "wash away thy sins" simply with baptism. Even though baptism is a picture of the washing away of sin, no sin can be purged by water. Sin is only purged by the precious blood of Christ. But there is a sense in which when Paul was baptized, his past was all washed away. He had been a bitter hater of the name of the Lord Jesus, but when he went down into the water of baptism, all that disappeared. He came forth not to be a persecutor but a preacher of the gospel of the grace of God. The past was gone. Henceforth he walked in newness of life.

Then Paul skipped over a number of years, and explained why he had to give himself to the work among the Gentiles. He was told to leave Jerusalem because the Jews would not believe his testimony. However Paul thought, *Surely, Lord, they will believe; they will see the wonderful change that has taken place.* But when men have made up their minds, they are hard to change: "A man convinced against his will is of the same opinion still." And so the Lord said in essence, "No, Paul, you are not the one to make them believe. I have another work for you among the Gentiles."

As soon as that hated word *Gentiles* came from his lips, there was a riot and that Jewish crowd began to throw dust into the air and to cast off their clothes. They cried: "Away with such a fellow from the earth: for it is not fit that he should live." The chief captain had to come down and rescue him again and take him into the castle to get him out of their hands. What a terrible thing religious prejudice is, and what a wonderful thing it is for a man or woman to have an open mind and be ready to examine themselves and be taught of God!

As they were leading Paul away, the captain commanded the soldiers to scourge him, which was a common practice in those days. But Paul turned to the centurion and said, "Is it lawful for you to scourge a man that is a Roman, and uncondemned?" It was the practice of the Roman government to permit one method of dealing with those who did not have full Roman citizenship, and another for those who did. Among those rights guaranteed to a free-born Roman citizen, or one who had paid a certain sum of money to purchase his citizenship, was the right to be tried in court without scourging. So as they were about to scourge the apostle Paul, he stood on his right as a Roman citizen.

I believe there is a lesson for us in that. Sometimes we are told that because Christians are heavenly citizens, they have no responsibility whatever as to citizenship here on earth. We have even heard it said that inasmuch as one cannot be a citizen of two countries at the same time here on earth, so one cannot be a citizen of Heaven and a citizen of earth at the same time. But this certainly does not follow. Since it *was* right for Paul to claim Roman citizenship in order not to suffer scourging, then it was also incumbent on him to fulfill the responsibilities of that citizenship. And this is true of any citizen of any country in this world. In other words, if I am to have certain protection as a citizen, I owe it to my country to act accordingly when it comes to fulfilling my responsibilities. It is true I am primarily a citizen of Heaven, but I am also a citizen of whatever country to which I belong on earth by natural relationship. So I am to be loyal to my government, pay my taxes, and to accept even military responsibilities if I am subject to them. It would be unthinkable that one would be entitled to claim protection from a country if he did not loyally respond to the rightful demands of its government.

So when the centurion heard that Paul was a Roman citizen, he went and told the chief captain saying, "Take heed what thou doest: for this man is a Roman." Then the chief captain came and asked him, "Tell me, art thou a Roman?" He had not suspected anything of the kind. Paul said, "Yea." The chief captain answered in effect, "Well, it cost me a great deal to obtain this freedom." Paul answered, "But I was free born." That is, Paul's father was a Roman citizen, and so although Paul was a Jew of Tarsus, he himself was born a Roman citizen, and as such had all a citizen's rights and liberties. So those that would have examined Paul withdrew from him. However the chief captain, anxious to know just what crime Paul was supposed to have committed, "loosed him from his bands, and commanded the chief priests and all their council to appear, and brought Paul down and set him before them."

CHAPTER TWENTY-THREE
PAUL BEFORE THE SANHEDRIN

As this chapter of Acts opens we are reminded that Paul was standing before the Jewish Sanhedrin. There they were, all these religious leaders, the seventy elders of the people of Israel waiting to pass judgment on him. "And Paul, earnestly beholding the council, said, Men and brethren, I have lived in all good conscience before God until this day." That was a tremendous claim to make. Observe, he did not say, "since I became a Christian," but he looked back over his whole life—his life as a Jew before he knew Christ, as well as his life as a Christian since he came to know Him.

"Why," you say, "surely that could not be. How could he have persecuted the church of God with a good conscience?" His conscience lacked instruction. There was a time when Paul thought it was the right thing to do to try to destroy Christianity. He said in another place, "I verily thought with myself, that I ought to do many things contrary to the name of Jesus of Nazareth" (Acts 26:9).

People sometimes say, "If we follow our consciences, everything will be all right. There are many different ways, but they all lead to Heaven. We can each take our own way as our conscience leads us." But conscience uninstructed by the Word of God may lead people to do the most unscriptural and even evil things. For example, a poor Hindu mother makes her way to the filthy Ganges river. She holds in her arms a darling child. She waits a minute or two, mumbles a prayer and then hurls that little baby into those foul waters. She does that in all good conscience, for she has been told that it is the way to appease her vile gods and to find peace. And so people, led by an uninstructed conscience, may do a great many things that are thoroughly wrong.

The important thing is that we come to God's own Word and ask "What saith the Lord?" Find out what the mind of God is, and then act accordingly. You say, "I endeavor to keep the ten commandments and to live up to the sermon on the mount, and I think if I do these things it will be all right with me." Have you always kept the ten commandments and have you always lived up to the sermon on the mount? Is it not a fact that you have broken those commandments over and over again? Is it not true that often you fail to fulfill the injunctions of the sermon on the mount? Why then talk about being saved by trying to keep the law or live up to the golden rule or something like that? Where is your good conscience? Already you have violated the law of God; and if you are honest before Him, you will have to confess that you have a bad conscience and it needs to be purged by the blood of the Lord Jesus Christ.

So far as Paul knew, he was doing the right thing in persecuting the church of Christ, until he learned the truth, and he learned it in the presence of the Son of God that day on the Damascus road. So he could make this declaration: "I have lived in all good conscience before God until this day."

We read then that the high priest, Ananias, forgetting the responsibility that rested on him as the leader of the people to be perfectly just and maintain the law in that high court of the Jews, in his indignation "commanded them that stood by him to smite him on the mouth." Then Paul lost his temper. You say, "Paul, that holy man of God?" Yes, Paul got thoroughly stirred up that day. Paul was filled with anger, and he turned to the high priest and said, "God shall smite thee, thou whited wall: for sittest thou to judge me after the law, and commandest me to be smitten contrary to the law?" This was pretty strong language for him to use, and immediately somebody spoke up and said, "Revilest thou God's high priest?" In other words, "Do you turn to God's high priest and call him a whited sepulcher? Do you dare use language like that in addressing the high priest?"

Oh, how I love the spirit that Paul exhibited next! He did flare up

a little and say something he should not have said, yet when it was
called to his attention, he immediately condemned himself: "I wist
not, brethren, that he was the high priest: for it is written, Thou
shalt not speak evil of the ruler of thy people." And so he used
God's own Word to condemn himself. The next best thing to never
having failed at all is to confess it the moment you find out you
have done wrong and not to try to justify yourself. So Paul immediately acknowledged that he should not have spoken in that manner
to the high priest.

Why did he not know that he was addressing the high priest?
Well, you may consider me a bit imaginative about this, but I think
Paul had defective vision. Several things in Scripture have led me
to that conclusion, and I believe that as he stood there before the
council he was not able to recognize those at some distance from
him. The high priest may have been standing at the other end of the
long room or in the galleries. Therefore he did not realize it was the
high priest who had spoken. I think that this visual difficulty is suggested in the letter to the Galatians, "Ye see how large a letter I
have written unto you with mine own hand" (6:11). But as we see,
the moment Paul found out his mistake, he calmed himself and was
ready to apologize for what he had said.

The Hope of the Resurrection (Acts 23:6-11)

> But when Paul perceived that the one part were Sadducees, and
> the other Pharisees, he cried out in the council, Men and
> brethren, I am a Pharisee, the son of a Pharisee: of the hope and
> resurrection of the dead I am called in question. And when he
> had so said, there arose a dissension between the Pharisees and
> the Sadducees: and the multitude was divided. For the Sadducees
> say that there is no resurrection, neither angel, nor spirit: but the
> Pharisees confess both (Acts 23:6-8).

There were two rival sects in Judaism nineteen hundred years
ago. The Sadducees were materialists. They did not believe that
man existed in another world after death. The Pharisees, on the other
hand, were entirely Scriptural and orthodox and believed in the

resurrection of the dead. They believed in the conscious existence of the spirit of man between death and resurrection. They also believed in angels created by God and sent forth to be ministers to men.

Paul, seeing that there were men of both parties in that group sitting in judgment on him, took advantage of the situation to get the help of the Pharisees. You might ask, "Well, is that fair?" I think I may have done the same thing, and so I am not going to condemn him. He knew that the Pharisees confidently believed in the resurrection of the dead, and this gave him an opportunity to testify regarding the hope of the resurrection.

Is there a resurrection from the dead or does death end all? Paul, if they had given him an opportunity to reply, would have said this: "I have met the One who died and rose again. I have looked into His face; I saw Him in the Glory; I heard His voice; and I received from Him, the risen Christ, the commission to go out into the world and proclaim the gospel to needy men and women. Everything for me rests on the truth that you Sadducees refuse to believe—the truth of the resurrection of the dead. I stand with the Pharisees today for the hope of the resurrection."

Every Christian can take his stand with the apostle Paul. We believe in the hope of the resurrection, and we rejoice today to know that Christ who died lives again. Has He not said, "Because I live, ye shall live also"? That is why we join with all Christendom in commemorating the resurrection of our Lord Jesus Christ every Easter Sunday.

Alas, there are tens of thousands of people who observe Easter yet know nothing of the risen Christ as their own personal Savior. These Pharisees believed in the resurrection of the dead, but they denied the resurrection of the Son of God. You may believe in your mind all the things we have been speaking of, but perhaps you have never rested your soul on the fact that Jesus died and rose again. Remember, that is the fundamental Christian confession, "If thou shalt confess with thy mouth the Lord Jesus, and shalt believe in thine heart that God hath raised him from the dead, thou shalt be saved. For with the heart man believeth unto righteousness; and with the mouth confession is made unto salvation" (Romans 10:9-10).

I have often called attention to the fact that Romans 10:9 commences with uncertainty—that little word *If*—and ends with glorious certainty—*saved*. What a wonderful thing it is to be able to say, "Thank God, I am sure that my soul is saved." This verse can be best illustrated by the fingers of one hand, thus making it easy to remember. *If*—there is the thumb. In between the thumb and fourth finger there are three *shalts*: "If thou *shalt* confess with thy mouth the Lord Jesus"—there is the first finger; "and *shalt* believe in thine heart that God hath raised him from the dead"—there is the second finger; "thou *shalt*"—the third finger; and now the fourth finger—"*be saved*." Now you have the gospel at your very fingertips! Think of it! It is not enough to believe in resurrection; it is not enough to believe in Christ's resurrection. What we need to know is that we have trusted the risen Christ as our personal Savior.

When Paul insisted that the reason he was called in question was because of his faith in the hope and resurrection of the dead, "there arose a great cry, and the scribes that were of the Pharisees' part arose, and strove, saying, We find no evil in this man: but if a spirit or an angel hath spoken to him, let us not fight against God." You see, these Pharisees realized that it was best for them not to be too insistent now in persecuting a man who was such a strong defender of the very truth they believed—the truth of resurrection.

> And when there arose a great dissension, the chief captain, fearing lest Paul should have been pulled in pieces of them, commanded the soldiers to go down and to take him by force from among them, and to bring him into the castle. And the night following the Lord stood by him, and said, Be of good cheer, Paul: for as thou hast testified of me in Jerusalem, so must thou bear witness also at Rome.

The blessed, living, loving Savior appeared to His poor, tried, discouraged, imprisoned messenger to encourage his heart as he continued proclaiming the hope of the resurrection!

God's Overruling Providence (Acts 23:12-35)

It is important to remember that "All scripture is given by inspiration of God, and is profitable for doctrine, for reproof, for correction, for instruction in righteousness: That the man of God may be perfect, throughly furnished unto all good works." I would emphasize that truth when reading a portion such as this one in Acts. For in this particular instance we have absolutely no mention of God or of the Lord Jesus Christ or of the way of salvation, of redemption by His blood, or of any other great truth of Scripture. We simply have a historical incident, and we might well ask, "Of what profit is it to us?" But it is part of Holy Scripture, and God by the Spirit caused Luke to write it and preserve it for a definite purpose. I think it brings before us in a very special way God's providential care of His people.

God is never nearer to His people than when they cannot see His face; He is never closer than when they do not hear His voice; he is never undertaking for them more definitely than at the very times when His own name is not even mentioned. We see this truth in the Old Testament in one little book that is distinctly the record of God's providential care, the book of Esther. It is a book that brings before us some of the most thrilling experiences in the history of God's earthly people, the Jews. And yet in that little book we do not have the name of God or any pronoun referring to God; we do not have any reference to any Bible doctrine. We do not even read anything of prayer even though it records a time of tremendous stress. Yet God worked providentially for the deliverance of His people.

Somebody has well said that God is often behind the scenes, but He moves all the scenes that He is behind. It is well for us to remember that. There are times in all our lives when we seem to be forgotten by God. We find it difficult to pray, so we grope in the darkness and we can't understand God's way with us. But He is always near at hand. He is waiting to undertake for us, and He is watching over us, even when we are so weak and sick that we cannot remember His promises. In the book of Psalms we read, "He remembered *for* them his covenant" (106:45, italics added). That is a wonderful thought. When His people forgot, He remembered still and remembered it for them.

Here we find the apostle Paul in a very precarious situation. There is no outward evidence of any manifestation of divine power, and yet God is watching over him through it all. When his enemies demanded his death, the Roman chief captain took him in custody and put him in prison. Now in the opening verses of the section before us we read of a conspiracy entered into by over forty desperate men who evidently hated the gospel of God above everything else in the world. They thought they would be doing God service if they could put Paul to death. We read that they had bound themselves with an oath to carry out this mission. This in itself is suggestive. What a wicked thing it is for men to enter into a curse like this, to bind themselves with an oath to do anything, whether good or evil!

Our Lord Jesus Christ has distinctly forbidden His followers to take oaths of any kind, and yet how recklessly people talk today and how even ungodly men call God to witness as to what they intend to do. I am not speaking merely of profanity, awful as it is. I never can understand how even self-respecting men, not to speak of professing Christians, can stoop to profanity. Yet I fear there are many who actually think it is an evidence of an independent spirit and of manliness to dare to use oaths and profane language. Unconverted men sometimes do it so often that they are not even conscious of it as oath after oath comes from their lips. God's Word says, "Swear not at all"; and in the Law we read, "Thou shalt not take the name of the Lord thy God in vain." This refers not only to profanity but also to taking such an oath as these men took, for doubtless they bound themselves in the name of God that they would not eat or drink until they had taken Paul's life.

One wonders what became of the poor wretches when they were not able to carry out their oath. They must have had a terrible time until at last, I suppose, they simply broke down and violated their oath. It generally ends up that way.

Is it necessary to say a word to real Christians as to the wickedness of taking God's name in vain? One shudders sometimes to hear the language that professing Christians use. The Lord Jesus told us, "Swear not at all; neither by heaven, for it is God's throne: Nor by the earth, for it is his footstool." And yet what a common thing it is today to hear people use the word *heaven* in a careless, profane way. Do you ever use it that way? How often you will hear a Christian exclaim, "Oh heavens!" or "Good heavens!" or something like that. Do you realize that this is just as profane, just as wicked in the sight of God, as if we were to use other vile expressions that ungodly men use? Because you are taking in vain that which speaks of the throne of the Majesty of the universe. You are doing something expressly forbidden by our Lord Jesus who said, "Let your communication be Yea, yea; Nay, nay: for whatsoever is more than these cometh of evil." When you feel it necessary to add any kind of oath or give strong expression to any statement you make, you are simply departing from the simplicity of speech that should characterize believers. For we read, "That every idle word that men shall speak, they shall give account thereof in the day of judgment."

These men had bound themselves with an oath that they would kill Paul. I take it they believed it was their religious duty to get rid of him. When you can get a man to believe that it is his religious duty to do something, he will go to any length to carry it out. Saul of Tarsus must have remembered those days when, under the guise of loyalty to God and church, he sought the lives of those who trusted in the Lord Jesus Christ. So we can be sure that he now would not have any hateful feelings toward these men who were avidly seeking his life.

We find these conspirators coming to the priests and elders of the people in order to have their scheme sanctioned by these religious leaders. They told them of the oath that they had taken, and said in effect, "Now won't you act as if you wish to inquire something further concerning him? And we will be waiting nearby, and when they bring him, we will kill him." It was a diabolical plot and one might have thought of Paul as totally helpless. He knew nothing of it, and there seemed to be no way by which he could learn of it, imprisoned as he was. But there was One who knew all about it, and although unseen, He was watching over His servant all the time.

When we speak of God's providential care, we mean God's unseen interference in the affairs of men.

These men did not realize it, but knowledge of their plot came to Paul in a most interesting way. Paul had a sister living nearby (we might never have known it except for this incident) who had a son, and her son became aware of this plot. Perhaps the conspirators did not think that it was necessary to keep the thing so secret since Paul was shut up in prison. At any rate this lad heard of it, and he went to the prison and asked the guard to take him to see his uncle Paul. When he told Paul what he had learned, the apostle immediately called one of the officials, the centurion, and said, "Will you take this man in to see the chief captain? He has something to tell him."

Notice the level-headed way in which Paul acted. He did not say, "I am afraid of this, but God is able to protect me. He is still able to work miracles." God does not use miracles when it is not necessary. He would have us use good common sense and not count on His interfering or intervening in some miraculous way.

I remember years ago when I was a Salvation Army officer, we used to say that there were three things that should characterize every saint of God: "Now abideth these three: grit, grace, and gumption; but the greatest of these is gumption." Gumption is just good, common, ordinary sense, and I know many Christians who do not use good sense. Some way or other they have an idea they are God's favored people and it is not necessary to use good judgment and wisdom in regard to the affairs of life; the Lord will undertake for them. If you are hungry and a good dinner is put before you, God is not going to put the food in your mouth in some miraculous way. And so God isn't turning upside down the universe in order to please people who happen to be in difficult circumstances. He expects us to use common sense.

So Paul used his head, and he sent the young man in to the chief captain. When the lad came in to him and gave him his message, "The chief captain then let the young man depart, and charged him, See thou tell no man that thou hast showed these things to me."

The captain must have thought he had a very important prisoner, for see what he did! He called two centurions and said, "Make ready two hundred soldiers to go to Caesarea, and horsemen threescore and ten, and spearmen two hundred." That is seventy cavalrymen, two hundred infantrymen, and two hundred spearmen. Just think of it! Four hundred and seventy Roman soldiers, all to protect this Christian servant of God and keep him from his foes who were seeking his life! God saw that he was protected. Did He need the Roman soldiers? No, He could have sent several legions of angels; but God doesn't work in miracles unless it is necessary, and so He used soldiers instead.

The chief captain thought he had a good opportunity to get into the favor of the Governor down at Caesarea, so he wrote a letter which was partly true and partly false. He said, "Claudius Lysias unto the most excellent governor Felix sendeth greeting. This man was taken of the Jews, and should have been killed of them: then came I with an army, and rescued him." Well, that is all true, but the next part of the letter was absolutely false: "Having understood that he was a Roman." He did not understand anything of the kind. He thought he was an Egyptian. He told Paul that. He said, "Art not thou that Egyptian, which before these days madest an uproar, and leddest out into the wilderness four thousand men that were murderers?" (21:38) And it was not until they were about to scourge Paul, and Paul said, "Is it lawful for you to scourge a man that is a Roman, and uncondemned?" that the chief captain came to his rescue and said, "Are you a Roman?" And Paul said, "Yea."

You see, Claudius Lysias was in a tight fix, for if that lash had come down on the back of Paul, a Roman, and word of it got to the ears of the governor, Claudius Lysias himself would have been arrested for violating the law of the empire. So now he wants to make it appear that it was his zeal for the Roman government that led him to save Paul's life. That was what some people would call a "white" lie, but every white lie is absolutely black in the sight of God, and "all liars shall have their part in the lake which burneth with fire and brimstone." All lies are lies in God's sight.

Claudius continued, "When I would have known the cause wherefore they accused him, I brought him forth into their council" (which was quite true), "Whom I perceived to be accused of questions of their law, but to have nothing laid to his charge worthy of death or of bonds. And when it was told me how that the Jews laid wait for the man, I sent straightway to thee, and gave commandment to his accusers also to say before thee what they had against him. Farewell." So much for the letter.

And so the soldiers went on with Paul, taking him away at once to be sure that these conspirators did not hurt him. They took him by night as far as Antipatris, and then on the following day the infantrymen returned, but the cavalrymen went on to Caesarea, which was the seat of Roman government for that district. They delivered the epistle to the governor. "And when the governor had read the letter, he asked of what province he was. And when he understood that he was of Cilicia" (Tarsus, where Paul was born, was the chief city in Cilicia), "I will hear thee, said he, when thine accusers are also come." So now Paul was in the hands of the Roman government, in prison at Caesarea, waiting for his accusers to come down from Jerusalem and plead against him. "And he commanded him to be kept in Herod's judgment hall."

Now notice the position in which Paul was found. He had gone up to Jerusalem because he loved his Jewish brethren so tenderly, though they did not understand him, and he hoped that God would use him to bring them a knowledge of the grace of the Lord Jesus Christ. Instead they rejected his message and wanted to put him to death. Now he finds himself in a Roman prison, first in Jerusalem and then in Caesarea. Later we read that from there he was sent over land and sea, still a prisoner, to Rome. We remember that he had written some time before to the church of Rome that he hoped to visit them and he asked them to pray that he might have a prosperous journey. He attains his objective at last, but he reaches Rome in chains.

In all this God was overruling. In all this He was having His own way. It is a wonderful thing to realize that in spite of our mistakes and our blunders we have a blessed Father in Heaven who is working everything out for good. Paul could write, "All things work together for good to them that love God, to them who are the called according to his purpose."

Surely these experiences of God's gracious overruling providence ought to speak comfort to the troubled hearts of many of us. We are conscious, perhaps, of sin and failure in our own lives, or we realize that in our ignorance and shortsightedness we have missed our path. The natural tendency in such instances is to conclude that we can no longer count on God's loving care, that we have forfeited all right to His fatherly consideration. But it is not so. He loves us still, and He is ever ready to undertake for us when we put all in His hands. He will overrule even our sins and blunders for our blessing and His glory.

He is never more concerned about us than at the very time that all seems to be darkness and confusion. Let us not doubt His love because perplexities abound on every hand. Be it ours to look up in faith and say with Isaiah, "I will trust and not be afraid"; or with David, "What time I am afraid I will trust in thee." He has given a promise that can never be broken: "I will never leave thee, nor forsake thee."

Let us then ever remember that His is a love unfailing, a love that no mistakes of ours can alter. And He is working all things according to the counsel of His own will, ever having our blessing in view.

CHAPTER TWENTY-FOUR
PAUL'S DEFENSE BEFORE FELIX

S aved from the ferocity of the Jewish elders who hated him, Paul was sent down to Caesarea and there in due time he appeared in the courtroom before Felix, the Roman governor. His accusers sent a deputation to Caesarea, headed by Ananias, the Jewish high priest. A man whose name indicates that he was perhaps a Gentile by birth, Tertullus, an orator or really a lawyer, came with them. He was one of those very wordy lawyers who can paint a picture to suit himself; who call good evil and evil good, and make white black and black white.

When he was called forth, Tertullus began to accuse Paul, but first he praised Felix, a man whom the Jews themselves bitterly hated. With the fawning words of one seeking to curry favor, he said, "Seeing that by thee we enjoy great quietness, and that very worthy deeds are done unto this nation by thy providence, We accept it always, and in all places, most noble Felix, with all thankfulness."

I think Felix must have put his tongue in his cheek when he heard Tertullus speaking like this on behalf of these Jews from Jerusalem, for he knew pretty well how much they detested him. He must have known too that they were thoroughly aware of his own wicked, godless life, so that even to address him as "most noble Felix" was in itself a misnomer. He was anything but noble. This governor was a most ungodly man, one whose whole life was a reproach to the high office he held.

Tertullus proceeded to accuse Paul, and brought four charges against him, one of which was true, the other three absolutely false.

He said, "We have found this man a pestilent fellow." He used the word *pestilent* in the sense of a disrupter of the peace. Paul was not that. Then he accused Paul of being "a mover of sedition among all the Jews throughout the world." That, of course, was totally untrue. Thirdly, he declared him to be "a ringleader of the sect of the Nazarenes." That was a fact, for Paul was a Christian and Christians were called Nazarenes, after Christ their Savior who was so designated. But the fourth charge is again false: "Who also hath gone about to profane the temple"—something that Paul never even thought of doing.

Let us review these charges brought against Paul. First, they insisted that he was a pestilent fellow, a disturber of the peace. Yet this man had lived a devoted, faithful life for nearly thirty years, seeking in all his ways to glorify the Lord Jesus Christ. He labored with his own hands whenever there was a temporal need to be met, never depending on the church at home to support him. If they did not send what might be required to sustain him and his companions, he would simply work as a tentmaker in order to provide for the needs of himself and those working with him. But he went everywhere, witnessing, ministering Christ, and told both Jew and Gentile of the wonderful change that had come over his own life.

Paul was anything but a pestilent fellow, a disturber of the peace; unless one is speaking of the false peace in which men exist who are strangers to the grace of our Lord Jesus Christ. These Paul tried to arouse to see their danger and to show them that they were lost and needed a Savior. The world has always been quick to say that people who preach against its ways and expose its sins and its faults are disturbers of the peace. You remember how they said before of Paul and his companions, "These that have turned the world upside down are come hither also." There was a sense in which that was true, because through sin the world had been turned wrong side up. So Paul and his companions preached the message that turned the world right side up, and of course the devil and his followers consider that as disrupting the peace.

Satan has held men captive so long that I think none of us should be concerned about disturbing his peace. Indeed, if we are able to do something that *will* disrupt his peace and deliver captives from his snare, whatever charges the world may bring against us, we shall feel we have done something worthwhile and we can thank God for the privilege of doing it.

Then they charged Paul with being "a mover of sedition among all the Jews throughout the world," and that was very far from the truth. He never moved anybody to sedition. He always insisted, when addressing Christians, that they must be subject to the powers that be, that they must always pray "for kings, and for all that are in authority; that we may lead a quiet and peaceable life in all godliness and honesty" (1 Timothy 2:2).

We may see in the governments of this world things that are contrary to the mind of God, but we seek to overcome them by methods that are in accordance with the spirit of the gospel. The remarkable thing is that the preaching of the Word throughout the Roman empire was used by God to overturn many things that oppressed men and brought distress on the world. In fact, practically all of the great reforms that have occurred throughout the centuries owe their existence to the proclamation of the liberty-giving message of the gospel of the grace of God.

Paul was not a mover of sedition but, on the other hand, he was indeed well known as a "ringleader of the sect [or heresy] of the Nazarenes." That word translated "sect," which is also rendered "heresy" later in the chapter, really means a "school of opinions." The followers of the Lord Jesus Christ were considered just another little, peculiar school of opinions. So the Nazarenes were contemptuously called a sect because they followed Him who was called a Nazarene.

There was a time when Paul was bitterly opposed to this group, when he as Saul of Tarsus sought to destroy everyone who preached the way of Christianity. He never forgave himself for that (1 Corinthians 15:9). But what caused the change in this man? The wonderful fact that he had a glimpse of Christ in glory. He was never the same afterward. From the very moment he was brought to know Him, he was commissioned to proclaim the faith that once he had sought to destroy. Indeed he became an outstanding leader and follower of the Lord Jesus Christ, the rejected Messiah. He faithfully proclaimed the One who came in lowly grace to Israel, was refused by His own people, died on the cross for their sins, and ascended to God's right hand.

Paul had proved the reality of the gospel message in his own life so he declared to others the saving power of the Lord Jesus Christ. But when they charged him with going about to "profane the temple," that was untrue. For although he had been separated from that temple by the revelation of Jesus Christ, he always had the greatest respect for everything connected with the religion of his youth. The temple in this sense was still the house that God had established in Israel, and Paul knew that many who worshiped there had a zeal of God though not according to knowledge. He would never have thought of profaning it. In fact, at the very time he was arrested he had gone almost beyond what you might have expected of him. Knowing the high standing of the temple in Jewish thinking, he had entered the temple with several men who were just completing their days of Nazariteship. He had arranged to pay for the sacrifices that they were to offer, and he would have done so had not God Himself, I believe, intervened by causing the riot and his arrest (see Acts 21).

No, he was not a profaner of the temple. He revered and honored the God of the temple too much for that. But they did not understand. They were so bound by the shackles of legality that, when Paul came preaching salvation by the free grace of God, they could not comprehend it. They thought of him as an enemy of the old religion and an enemy of their people. Actually he was simply bringing a message that was the fulfillment of all the forms and ceremonies of the legal dispensation. He was there as the personal representative of the One who is pictured in every sacrifice ever offered on Jewish altars, our blessed Lord Jesus Christ.

Finally, the Jews declared that Tertullus had presented the case fairly, so Felix gave Paul an opportunity to defend himself. Notice how Paul began. He did not descend to flattering words, but said, "Forasmuch as I know that thou hast been of many years a judge unto this nation, I do the more cheerfully answer for myself." In other words, he realized that Felix knew the people who were accusing him, and the strong prejudices and bigotry that characterized them; therefore Paul felt all the more ready to state his own case in the presence of this Roman judge.

He told him that just twelve days had elapsed since he went to Jerusalem, not to cause a riot or stir people up, but to worship God. No one had found him in the temple disputing with anybody, or inciting the people, nor did they find him misbehaving in the synagogues or in the city. He went about continually ministering in grace to any who were willing to listen to him. "Neither can they prove," he said, "the things whereof they now accuse me." But on the other hand, he acknowledged the third charge, declaring: "This I confess unto thee, that after the way which they call heresy, so worship I the God of my fathers, believing all things which are written in the law and in the prophets."

I like to think of Paul standing there before that august assemblage, hiding nothing, covering nothing, majestic as he proclaimed himself a follower of the crucified Lord Jesus Christ. *The Way* was the term used generally in those days for Christianity, simply because the following of Jesus was taught as the way to life and blessing. And, thank God, it is, for He is the Way, the Truth, and the Life. The Lord Jesus added, "No man cometh unto the Father, but by me."

So Paul went everywhere proclaiming the Way, and we today have the same blessed privilege. We are here to tell men there is only one way to God. Men do not like that. They say something like this: "We are all trying to get to the same place. There are many different ways, but they all end up at the same place." Who says so? Our Lord Jesus declared, "I am the way. No man cometh unto the Father, but by me." The apostle Peter said, "Neither is there salvation in any other: for there is none other name under heaven given among men, whereby we must be saved" (Acts 4:12). You say, "But there are so many ways." Yes, the Old Testament tells us in the book of Proverbs, "There is a way which seemeth right unto a man, but the end thereof are the ways of death" (14:12). People say, "But I have my religion and you have yours, and my religion is good enough for me: it satisfies me." Oh, but that is hardly the question. Is it good enough for God? Does it satisfy God? It is God who has declared that there is no other name under heaven whereby we must be saved but the name of Jesus. Do you know Him? Have you trusted Him? He is the Way.

Paul was not ashamed to declare that he recognized no other way to God, no other way to Heaven, than through the Lord Jesus Christ. Further he said that in the truth revealed in Christianity we have the completion of all that was set forth in type and shadow in the Old Testament: "After the way which they call heresy, so worship I the God of my fathers, believing all things which are written in the law and in the prophets."

Do you believe all things that are written in the law and the prophets? Sometimes I tell my Jewish friends that I am a better Jew than they are! Because I find that many Jews doubt much of the Holy Scriptures, and take almost a modernistic attitude toward the whole Bible. They question whether the prophecies will ever be fulfilled.

I believe it all. I believe that all things written in the law and the prophets and the Psalms are true. I believe that the Old Testament, from the book of Genesis to the book of Malachi, is the very Word of the living God. And in that I stand with the apostle Paul who was a Hebrew of the Hebrews. But I also believe this, that all the ritual service, all that was written concerning the tabernacle and the temple in the Old Testament, pointed forward to the redemptive work of our Lord Jesus Christ. His cross is the true altar; He Himself is the true sacrifice. He is the Light of the world; He is the Bread of Life on the table in the holy place. He is the Ark of the Covenant. On His heart was written the law. He has offered Himself without spot unto God and it is through His blood alone that we approach God. And it seems to me, the more one studies the Old Testament and considers not only its types and shadows but its prophecies, the more one must come to see that the Lord Jesus Christ is the fulfillment of them all.

That was the stand Paul took. That is what made him a Christian. That was why he became from the time of his conversion such a remarkable exponent of the grace of God. Here was a man who believed for years in the Old Testament economy. When he got the fuller revelation, he believed that. He said, "I believe, therefore have I spoken." God pity the men who stand in pulpits today ministering to people, yet have not themselves real faith in the truth revealed in God's Word.

I am not ashamed of the gospel of Christ: for it is the [dynamics] of God unto salvation to every one that believeth; to the Jew first, and also to the Greek. For therein is the righteousness of God revealed from faith to faith: as it is written [in the Old Testament], The just shall live by faith (Romans 1:16-17).

This was Paul's declaration: I believe "all things which are written in the law and in the prophets: And have hope toward God, which they themselves also allow, that there shall be a resurrection of the dead, both of the just and unjust." He used the word *hope* with the sense of full assurance. And he recognized the close link between Judaism and Christianity, so that Christianity is the full flower of which Judaism was the bud.

You see, the charge they brought against him was this: He is preaching that Jesus who died has risen again. Paul replied in essence, "But I am not preaching anything that my Jewish brethren ought to think impossible. They profess to believe in resurrection, unless they are of the Sadducean sect. They believe there will be a resurrection of the just and unjust. So do I." The future for man is based on this great fact. Does this truth of the resurrection bring real joy to your heart?

Notice the two kinds of people who are going to be raised—the just and the unjust. As surely as there are two ways to live and two ways to die, so are there to be two resurrections. Our Lord Jesus Christ Himself has said,

Marvel not at this: for the hour is coming, in which all that are in the grave shall hear his voice, And shall come forth; they that have done good, unto the resurrection of life; and they that have done evil, unto the resurrection of damnation [or condemnation] (John 5:28-29).

A resurrection of the just and of the unjust! And who are the just? "The just shall live by faith." They are those who have believed God even as Abraham believed God and it was counted to him for righteousness or justice. And so when men put their trust in the Lord Jesus, receive Him as Savior, they are numbered among the just. Those who refuse Him and go on in their sinful way are numbered among the unjust; but whether just or unjust, after they leave this world they must rise in resurrection. If they leave this world in their sins, they will rise among the unjust unto condemnation. But if they leave this world cleansed by the precious blood of the Lord Jesus, they rise among the just to have part in eternal bliss.

Do not forget that there are two resurrections. We would like to believe that there is something about death so purifying and so ennobling that in the very hour of death, no matter what manner of lives men have lived, they are suddenly changed so that they pass out into eternity clean and pure and fit for the presence of God. But our Bibles forbid us to believe that. Our Lord Jesus said, "I go my way, and ye shall seek me, and shall die in your sins: [and if you die in your sins] whither I go, ye cannot come" (John 8:21).

If men die in their sins, they will be raised in their sins, and in their sins they will stand before the great white throne and be judged for their sins and condemned throughout eternity. But, on the other hand, we read, "Blessed are the dead which die in the Lord from henceforth: Yea, saith the Spirit, that they may rest from their labours; and their works do follow them" (Revelation 14:13). It is possible to die in the Lord, and those who die in the Lord enter into rest.

Who are they who die in the Lord? They are those who trust the Lord, those who receive the Lord as their own Savior. They reveal by devoted, godly lives that they have really been born from above. These die in the Lord, and these are raised in the Lord, and spend eternity with the Lord; for of these it is written, "They shall not come into condemnation, but [are] passed from death unto life."

Paul continued his defense by saying, "And herein do I exercise myself, to have always a conscience void of offence toward God, and toward men." In other words, these truths that meant so much to him had gripped his conscience and made him concerned about his manner of life. He sought so to behave that none could accuse him honestly of any ill-doing, and that God might ever be glorified in him. People say sometimes that we Christians are interested in only one thing and that is that men accept Christ as Savior. But that is because we believe that if men definitely put their faith in the truth that God has revealed in His Word, it is going to work a miracle within them. They will receive a new life and nature, and will be concerned about living a holy way. A love for holiness always follows new birth.

Then Paul told Felix what it was that brought him to Jerusalem: "Now after many years I came to bring alms to my nation, and offerings." He had not gone to create trouble, or even to proselyte them to his doctrines or peculiar views. Famine prevailed, and he came to bring gifts that Christian people had given to him for those in need. "Whereupon certain Jews from Asia found me purified in the temple, neither with multitude, nor with tumult, Who ought to have been here before thee, if they had ought against me"; but they were not there. When Paul stood before the Jewish council, they could not find any evil in him unless it was this, that he had interrupted the peace by crying out, "Touching the resurrection of the dead I am called in question." The whole matter of whether Christ is Messiah or not is linked with the question of whether resurrection is possible. Every orthodox Jew said it is possible. Paul said it was not only possible but it had taken place, for Jesus had risen from the dead. And this was the message that he carried throughout the world.

"When Felix heard these things, having more perfect knowledge of that way"—he had evidently come in contact with Christians before—"he deferred them, and said, When Lysias the chief captain shall come down, I will know the uttermost of your matter." In other words, "We will wait." He should have cleared Paul, but this man Felix was given to procrastination. It characterized him throughout. He put off setting Paul free. In the meantime, "he commanded a centurion to keep Paul, and to let him have liberty, and that he should forbid none of his acquaintance to minister or come unto him."

It was very evident that Felix knew Paul was innocent of the charges brought against him. As one set to administer the law, he should have freed him. He was like Pilate, who said of Christ, "I find no fault in this man," yet allowed His accusers eventually to carry out their will against Him.

As you think back, what a record Paul has had! How he delighted to go from land to land, glorifying Christ! As we continue our study of Acts, we see that God had in store for him, although a prisoner, still greater opportunities to magnify the One who had redeemed him.

In the closing verses of Acts 24 we have a very special message for any who have not yet definitely decided for Christ yet intend to so decide some day. God's Word says, "Now is the accepted time; now is the day of salvation." But it seems so natural for us to put off the settlement of this greatest of all questions. Felix took that attitude of procrastination and, so far as we have any record, he lived and died a Christ-rejecter.

We read, "After certain days, when Felix came with his wife Drusilla, which was a Jewess, he sent for Paul, and heard him concerning the faith in Christ." Antonius Felix— to give him his full name—was appointed by Claudius Caesar to be procurator in Judea some two years before Paul was arrested and brought to stand before him. He was a most unprincipled man, an ungodly, scheming politician who stooped often to the very lowest of methods in order to bring about his own purposes.

It is recorded of him in history that when he could not accomplish his purposes, he would not hesitate to call into his service a group of assassins—a secret order bound together by an oath, who were pledged to undertake to destroy anyone for whose death they were paid. Felix in this way managed to remove a great many of his enemies and, as he fancied, to secure his own position. But he failed dismally, as men always do who stoop to cruel and wicked methods to obtain and hold power. Scarcely a few more years had passed before he was in disgrace and, so far as we know, died a suicide.

The Spirit of God mentioned his wife Drusilla, evidently in order that we might realize something of a power over this man that kept him from making a definite decision for Christ. Who was Drusilla? She was the youngest daughter of King Agrippa I. It was a sad family—three sisters, every one of whom lived a life of infamy—Bernice, Miriam, and Drusilla.

Drusilla at fourteen became the wife of Azizus, the king of Emesa, but some years afterwards Felix met her and lured her away from her husband. Then in defiance of all law, both human and divine, he took her as his own wife. And so as Paul stood before Felix there sat with him on the judgment seat this woman, the partner of his life of sin and corruption. God draws special attention to Drusilla's presence with him. Her father was of Edomite and Jewish extraction. She was brought up in the religion of Israel. Felix was a heathen; Drusilla knew better. She had been instructed in her earliest days in the knowledge of the one true and living God. She knew something of the high standards set forth in the law of God, and she must have been conscious that she was flaunting them all in the life she lived.

These two sent for Paul from time to time in order that they might discuss with him or hear him tell of the faith in Christ. Evidently Felix's interest was something like that of Herod's some years before. Herod was curious about Jesus and desired to see Him. He had heard of His wonderful miracles. But at last he was instrumental in putting Jesus to death; that is, his attitude helped in the final rejection of Jesus.

And so here Felix was interested in Paul and his message. He evidently knew a great deal about what had happened in Palestine, particularly in Judea where he was procurator. He knew about Jesus; he knew about His crucifixion. He knew that it was commonly reported that He had risen in triumph from the dead. He knew how the gospel was spreading through all that part of the world, and how it was reaching out even to distant lands. Undoubtedly deep in his heart he wondered whether Jesus was not what He professed to be—the Son of the living God. If so, Felix must have felt that he owed allegiance to this blessed One. But to step right out and accept Christ, to yield his heart to Christ, would mean facing the sin in which he was living. Drusilla, too, would have to face her sin.

I do not know of any harder test for a man or woman today than this. It is difficult for people when they know they have violated God's holy law and entered into a relationship contrary to God and are living in sin—hard for them to judge their sin and get right with God. So Felix, while interested, yet shrank from taking the step of full allegiance to the Lord Jesus Christ.

We read that as Paul "reasoned of righteousness, temperance, and judgment to come, Felix trembled." No wonder he shuddered, with another man's wife sitting there beside him on the throne! When Paul reasoned of righteousness, he must have brought before Felix the fact that he had no righteousness. I imagine that Paul used the

line of reasoning that he presented in the Epistle to the Romans—
that is, that the judgment of God is against all unrighteousness, and
that all men everywhere are sinners and in need of a Savior. And
then he would not hesitate to witness to the fact that Felix, instead
of holding his physical passions in subjection, had allowed them to
run away with him and dominate his reason; so that, instead of living in self-control, he was controlled by evil.

And Paul went on to tell of judgment to come. "It is appointed
unto men once to die, but after this the judgment" (Hebrews 9:27).
There was no sugar-coating here. There was no palliating the message; no "soft-pedaling." It took tremendous courage for this little
Christian Jew to stand there before that Roman governor and his
paramour, and press home the corruption of their lives and the wickedness of their hearts; then to insist that for all these things God was
going to bring them into judgment!

And yet we do not read that Felix responded in repentance. He
realized the truth of much of Paul's words, and he shuddered. The
memory of his sins rose up before him, and as he sat there facing
God about those sins, he was in trouble and distress, but there was
no repentance.

What folly it is to try to cover up and forget our sins! Remember,
if our sins go unconfessed, God does not forget them. He said, "I
will not forget any of their sins." They are there in His books of
record, and in His judgment day they will be revealed. We are told
that "some men's sins are open beforehand, going before them to
judgment; and some men they follow after" (1 Timothy 5:24).
Whether hidden and covered here on earth or not, they will come
out there. You say: "Well is there no way of deliverance? Is there
no way of salvation, for I have sinned? I have violated God's holy
law, but is there no forgiveness?"

Ah, yes. And as Paul reasoned of righteousness, temperance, and
judgment to come, he must have put clearly before Felix the glorious message of the gospel. It is not necessary that the sinner go on
to meet God in judgment—that is, if he is willing to judge his sins
now and come into the presence of God now and face those sins.
But men need to remember this: the first time that a man comes into
the presence of God, he must come with all his sins upon him. If he

never comes into the presence of God until the day of judgment, he will stand there with all his sins upon him, and he will hear that voice saying, "Depart from me, ye cursed, into everlasting fire, prepared for the devil and his angels."

On the other hand, if you are ready to come now into the presence of God, you must come with all your sins upon you. You can not get rid of them otherwise. You cannot cleanse your own heart. Job says, "If I wash myself with snow water, and make my hands never so clean; Yet shalt thou plunge me in the ditch, and mine own clothes shall abhor me" (9:30-31). It is absolutely impossible for you to cleanse yourself, to wash out the stains of sin. But thank God, if you are ready to come to Him in repentance—and repentance involves a complete change of attitude in regard to sin—if you are ready to come now, earnestly desiring the forgiveness of sins, there is forgiveness with Him, thank God. For "if we confess our sins, he is faithful and just to forgive us our sins, and to cleanse us from all unrighteousness."

We read in the book of Proverbs, "He that covereth his sins shall not prosper: but whoso confesseth and forsaketh them shall have mercy" (28:13). That mercy was offered to Felix. That mercy was extended to Drusilla, but this impenitent couple, doubtless putting their heads together, said in effect: "We are not ready to face this thing; we are not ready to separate one from another; we are not ready to break the tie that binds us in our unholy union." So we read that though Felix shuddered, he answered Paul, saying, "Go thy way for this time; when I have a convenient season, I will call for thee."

That is the answer that so many make. Felix, the procrastinator! We have a saying that "Procrastination is the thief of time"; and the Spaniards say, "The road of by-and-by leads to the house of never." And here is this man, realizing his lost condition, knowing that he is not right in the sight of God, knowing that he should put his trust in the Lord Jesus, yet he puts it off.

Forget Felix for a moment and let me ask you, reader, to face this question honestly. Are you saying as Felix did, "Go thy way for this time; when I have a convenient season, I will call for thee"? You fully expect to be saved sometime. Perhaps a dear father or mother has gone on to Heaven, and you promised before they left that you would meet them there later on. Perhaps they are still living, and again and again they have prayed for you and pleaded with you to come to Christ, and you have said, "Oh yes, some day, some time, but not now. When I have a more convenient season, then I will get right with God."

When do you think that more convenient season will arrive? When will you ever have a better opportunity of coming to Christ than you have today? When will it ever be easier to repent of your sins, to confess your need, to trust in the Lord Jesus Christ, than it is now? Do you think it may be a more convenient season when perhaps the health that you now enjoy is taken from you and you toss on a bed of sickness? I have ministered to hundreds on sickbeds, but I have never yet been at a sickbed of a Christian who was not glad that he had trusted Christ when he was well and strong. I have had many say to me, "I am so thankful that I do not have that matter to settle now when my body is racked with pain, when my poor mind is troubled and distressed. I am so thankful that I knew Christ as my Savior before I became ill."

Often when I have stood by the sickbed of an unsaved one, I have been stirred to indignation when some doctor or nurse has said, "Don't talk religion to him. Don't disturb him. He is too sick to be bothered by anything that might excite him." I know what they mean. They mean that we are not to tell dying men and women that it will be Christ or Hell, and that to reject the one is to choose the other. And I admit that it is hard to go into the room of one who is lying low in weakness, and faithfully present the great realities of eternity. It is only occasionally that I have seen one in such a condition ready to listen and to turn to God for salvation.

Do not be guilty of the inexcusable folly of saying, "When I have a more convenient time, I will call for you—when I am laid aside on a bed of sickness, then I will face the question of my soul's salvation."

I wonder if someone is saying, "When I can take life more leisurely, then will I consider this question. Today I am engrossed in study; I am overwhelmed with the pressure of things at school." Or, "I am out in the business world and occupied with all that I have to face day by day. Give me a better opportunity. When I have finished training, or when I have reached the place where I can retire from the activities of business and can look at things more thoughtfully, then I will call for you." Let me tell you this: The average person who spends a lifetime occupied with the things of this world will not leave all those for the things of God when it comes to what he calls a time of leisure. Oh, the elderly men and women whose spiritual sensibilities seem to be absolutely atrophied! They never seem to have interest in eternal things. They remind one of a solemn verse in the book of Revelation, which literally translated reads, "And the fruit season of thy soul's desire has gone from thee" (18:14).

Now is the time to get right with God—in the midst of study, in the midst of business, in the midst of all the various things you have to face. Take time to settle this greatest of all questions—that of your soul's salvation. People say, "When I am old it will be time enough; after I have had my fling, after I have enjoyed the things of the world, then as an old man or woman I will turn to Christ." Oh, the wretched hallucination that leads one to be so foolish as to speak like that! Think of the Lord of glory as a young man, in the very prime of life, dying for you. Yet you say to yourself "After I have drunk the cup of sin to the full, I will give the dregs of my life to Him." Could there be baser ingratitude than that? Old men seldom turn to Christ.

When I was only twelve I went into a meeting in an auditorium in Los Angeles. About ten thousand people were gathered in the building which had two galleries—a building that has since been torn down to make way for another. I went to hear D. L. Moody preach. Because I could find no other place, I crawled out on a rafter beneath the ceiling. I remember how in the course of his address he said, "I want everyone in this auditorium who is a Christian, who knows he is a Christian, to stand up. Now, remain standing until the ushers can tell me about how many are on their feet." Then he said, "There are between five and six thousand people standing. What a testimony—five to six thousand Christian people in this building! Now," he said, "I want everyone here who became a Christian before he was fifteen years of age to sit down." And over half of that company sat down. Then he said, "Now how many of those who remain standing accepted Christ before they were twenty?" More than half of those remaining sat down. And then he went on, moving up the years by tens. By the time he got to fifty, there were only about twenty left standing in that great congregation who had trusted Christ after they were fifty years of age! It was an object lesson I have never forgotten.

Youth is "the time to serve the Lord, the time to win the great reward." But if you are past your youth, thank God, He still waits for you to come. Yield to Him now. Do not say, "Go thy way for this time; when I have a convenient season, I will call for thee," lest when you call He is no longer listening to your cry. For we read in the Word that Wisdom speaks to those who refuse her voice and says, "Then shall they call upon me, but I will not answer; they shall seek me early, but they shall not find me" (Proverbs 1:28).

Felix lost his opportunity. Acts 24:26 suggests another reason why he did not decide. Not only lustful, he was a covetous man. "He hoped also that money should have been given him of Paul, that he might loose him: wherefore he sent for him the oftener, and communed with him." A judge on the bench, he was corrupt, wicked, hoping that this poor, penniless prisoner would perhaps raise money from his friends in order to bribe the judge for his deliverance! Of course Paul would not resort to that. He would rather have remained in prison for years than to buy his way out. So he stayed in jail, but Felix "sent for him the oftener, and communed with him." I imagine every time he spurned the voice of God, his conscience grew harder, his spirit more indifferent.

"After two years Porcius Festus came into Felix' room: and Felix, willing to show the Jews a pleasure, left Paul bound." So Felix passed off the page of Holy Scripture, but he did not pass out from under the eye of God. He lived and died in wickedness and corruption. Some day he will stand before a Judge who can never be bribed, and he will have to answer Him for refusing the message of grace.

What about you, dear friend? Have you been refusing to yield to the Spirit of God? Have you been waiting for a more convenient season? Oh, will you not believe God when He says, "Now is the accepted time; now is the day of salvation"?

CHAPTER TWENTY-FIVE
PAUL AND FESTUS

We have followed Paul step by step as he answered the charge of sedition, first on the temple stairs in Jerusalem, then before the chief captain himself, and later, before Felix. As Acts 25 opens he is still in the prison at Caesarea, but Felix has been displaced by Festus. Felix was a man of most immoral character, but Festus was a Roman governor of a rather different type. He was, in a sense, high-minded, a man who studied philosophy, but one who had no faith in anything beyond this world. He tested everything by human reason and was not prepared to believe in anything concerning which he could not rationalize.

This man was scarcely in office—only three days—when he went up from Caesarea to Jerusalem, and the high priest and other leaders of the people informed him of their charges against Paul. They pleaded with him that he would send for Paul to come to Jerusalem, because they secretly plotted to kill him on the way. What a corrupt thing religion is when it leaves God out! These men were the religious leaders of the people, yet they sought in this nefarious way to destroy the apostle Paul. Their own plans were flagrantly contrary to the law, yet they pretended that they wanted to judge him in accordance with the law.

However, Festus, fortunately for Paul, answered that the apostle should be kept at Caesarea and that he himself would return there shortly. Then he added, "If you have anything against the man, send your accusers down and I will hear them at my judgment seat." So we read in verse six: "And when he had tarried among them more than ten days, he went down unto Caesarea; and the next day sitting on the judgment seat commanded Paul to be brought."

One notices the energetic way in which this man Festus does things. He is the very opposite of Felix. Felix, the procrastinator, always put things off, always said: "Tomorrow, some other day, some other time; when I have a more convenient season." But Festus dealt promptly with the matters that came before him, befitting one to whom it was given to dispense Roman justice. "And when he was come, the Jews which came down from Jerusalem stood round about, and laid many and grievous complaints against Paul."

But Paul was a man who had nothing to fear. He had always made it a point to have a clear conscience before God and before men. He could stand at the judgment seat of Festus and say, "There is absolutely no charge of criminal action of any kind that can be proven against me." Not one of their charges could be sustained. But Festus in this respect was a little bit like Felix. Wanting to please the Jews, he asked Paul if he would be willing to stand trial before him in Jerusalem.

However, Paul recognized that he had certain rights as a Roman citizen, and he insisted on the recognition of those rights. An appeal to Caesar was the right of every Roman citizen, but it evidently took Festus by surprise. He hardly expected this poor missionary, this almost friendless man (from his standpoint), to insist on facing the great Caesar himself. So without realizing for the moment that he had no actual charges to prefer against him, he said, "Unto Caesar shalt thou go." Later, the incongruity of allowing a man's case to be appealed to a higher court when he had not been condemned in a lower one came home to him with power, and that leads us to the next step in this drama.

In verse 13 we read: "And after certain days King Agrippa and Bernice came unto Caesarea to salute Festus." I ask your attention to the words—*and Bernice.* You will notice that you have them a number of times in this section of the Acts. Here in verse 13 when they come before Festus; again in verse 23 when they sit on the judgment seat; and then again in Acts 26:30 as they leave the palace after hearing Paul's defense. Why does the Spirit of God three times bring in this woman's name like this? She was not sitting in judgment on Paul. She had no authority to pronounce on his case, and yet when king Agrippa is referred to, her name is also mentioned.

Who was Bernice? She was the sister of Agrippa, and lived in an incestuous relationship with her own brother. God recognized the seriousness of their sin, the wickedness of their life. She is attached to Agrippa, and when his name is mentioned God adds, "and Bernice." If Agrippa died unsaved, we may be sure God links Bernice with him still; and when Agrippa stands eventually at the judgment of the great white throne, Bernice will stand there with him! It is a terrible thing to sin against God, to trample God's truth under foot. Sin once embraced will be with you forever unless you find deliverance through the atoning blood of the Lord Jesus Christ.

When Agrippa hears the words, "Depart from me, ye cursed, into everlasting fire, prepared for the devil and his angels," Bernice will be there too. So far as we can tell, both lived and died in their sins and they will go out into everlasting fire as "Agrippa and Bernice." Surely there is an intensely solemn lesson here!

After many days had passed Festus approached the king about the problem of what to do with Paul. Festus had taken it for granted that Paul must have been guilty of some very grave crime, either against the Jews themselves or against the Roman Empire. But when he had listened to the trivial things the Jews were charging against him, he was amazed that reasonable people would expect a Roman governor to pay any attention to their foolish religious quarrels. He may have said to Agrippa: "It was one of the most absurd things you ever heard of. I thought that as they stood before my judgment seat they would charge the man with some very, very grave crime. Instead they talked of trivialities of their own Jewish faith. Then they thrust forth the silly idea that this man Paul was going through the country talking about a man named Jesus who was dead. Everybody knows he had died; everybody knows he was crucified. But their charge against Paul was that he preached that this Jesus who was dead is now alive."

I think I can see the lips curl as Festus, the rationalist, looked inquiringly into the face of Agrippa as if to add, "Did you ever hear the like? All this fuss about a man who is dead, simply because Paul imagines he is alive again, something that nobody of course believes!"

It was a very small thing to Festus—this story of one Jesus who

was dead, but whom Paul affirmed to be alive. Festus did not realize it, but the resurrection of Christ is the greatest matter that the
world has ever been called on to face. That story about the resurrection of Jesus was to be declared throughout the world. It was to
overthrow the paganism of Rome, to make men over, and eventually to bring in a new heaven and a new earth. And yet it seemed
such a trivial thing to this philosophic Roman.

Now Agrippa was one thoroughly conversant with the Jewish
religion, and doubtless he had heard a great deal about this new
Christian movement. Certainly he seemed to have a genuine desire
to hear what Paul had to say for himself. We are told that on the
morrow "Agrippa was come, and Bernice." Then Festus introduced
the subject of Paul and his dilemma.

You see, it is customary in law that if a lower court passes on a
man's case and condemns him, he may appeal to a higher court and
then all that has proceeded in the lower court is presented for the
examination of the higher court. Yet Paul had not been condemned
by any court, and in order that he might have a fair hearing he appealed to the highest court of the land—Caesar himself—and Festus
did not know what charges to bring against him. He said:

> Wherefore I have brought him forth before you, and specially
> before thee, O king Agrippa, that, after examination had, I
> might have somewhat to write. For it seemeth to me unreasonable
> to send a prisoner, and not withal to signify the crimes laid
> against him (Acts 25:26-27).

I am sure we all recognize the logic of the stand that Festus took.

As I bring this chapter to a close, I want to drive home a question
to each reader as the Spirit of God may enable me. This One, Jesus
which was dead, whom Paul affirmed to be alive, what does He
mean to you today? Do you know Him as the One who was crucified on Calvary's cross, the One who was buried, but was raised
again for our justification? Have you trusted Him for yourself? If
not, why not?

CHAPTER TWENTY-SIX
PAUL BEFORE AGRIPPA

In this chapter of Acts we are given the account of Paul's testimony before Festus and Agrippa. In Acts 22 we noted that Paul's testimony is recorded five times in Scripture. Here in Acts 26 we read the third account of his conversion. Even though he was addressing King Agrippa, who had been brought up in the Jewish religion, he had in mind the Roman governor Festus. Therefore he presented the story of his great experience in a way that ought to have appealed to a Gentile as well as to King Agrippa. Paul was following his own rule for reaching men for Christ, "I am made all things to all men, that I might by all means save some" (1 Corinthians 9:22).

The first eleven verses of Acts 26 are devoted (at least in large measure) to the time of Paul's unconverted days. We are told that Agrippa said to Paul: "Thou art permitted to speak for thyself. Then Paul stretched forth the hand, and answered for himself." Recognizing Agrippa's acquaintance with the Jewish religion, Paul felt that he would be able to understand at least in measure something of what he had gone through.

Paul recounted his life as a young man who thoroughly believed in Judaism as the final revelation from God. He declared: "My manner of life from my youth, which was at the first among mine own nation at Jerusalem, know all the Jews; Which knew me from the beginning, if they would testify, that after the most straitest sect of our religion I lived a Pharisee."

You will notice the peculiar grammatical construction of a part

317

of this sentence, "the most straitest sect of our religion." One is reminded of Mark Antony's expression as given by Shakespeare, "That was the most unkindest cut of all." Ordinarily we do not use a double superlative like this, but the apostle Paul wanted to stress the fact that no man was ever more firmly convinced that Judaism was God's final word to mankind than he was. He believed in it with all his heart. He lived it. He was not simply a Jew by profession.

Many today call themselves Jews, yet are not at all careful about observing the customs of the Jewish people or the ordinances of the Jewish religion. It was otherwise with this young man. He was most punctilious about attending to everything that the law commanded. He carried out not only what was written in the law of Moses but the additional traditions of the Pharisees in Israel.

The Pharisees were the most religious and the most conscientious of Jews. I know we Gentiles are accustomed to think of Pharisees as though they were all hypocrites, but that is not necessarily true. Many of them were hypocrites, just as there are many professing Christians today who are hypocrites. The Lord Jesus had some very stern things to say to some of the Pharisees. "Woe unto you, Pharisees, hypocrites." He condemned them for making long prayers in public just in order that they might be seen of men. He condemned them for sounding a trumpet to announce that they were giving alms. But on the other hand there were Pharisees who were sincere and intensely earnest. Saul of Tarsus was one of these. No man is a hypocrite who can say, "I live what I profess"; and Saul could say, "I lived a Pharisee."

Even as a Christian he wanted Agrippa to understand that he was not divorced from the great outstanding truths of Judaism. There is not one truth that God has revealed through Moses and the prophets that is denied by Bible-believing Christians. We believe with our Jewish brethren in the unity of the Godhead, but we also believe that God is a trinity, revealed in three glorious persons—Father, Son, and Holy Ghost. We believe in the importance of knowing God, as revealed in the Old and New Testaments, and living in obedience to His Word. We believe in the resurrection of the dead, and in the final judgment—the eternal punishment of men who die in their sins, and the everlasting blessedness of the righteous. So Paul could say to Agrippa, "The Jews who have known me could testify that I have lived a Pharisee."

And now I stand and am judged for the hope of the promise made of God unto our fathers: Unto which promise our twelve tribes, instantly serving God day and night, hope to come. For which hope's sake, King Agrippa, I am accused of the Jews (26:6-7).

What did he mean by that? He meant this: "I am standing here today in chains because I believe with all my heart what every honest Jew believes. I believe in the resurrection of the dead, but I believe that Jesus Christ has already been resurrected. I believe in the Messiah promised to Israel, and that Jesus Christ is that Messiah, and that he died for our sins, just as depicted in Isaiah 53. I believe that He was raised from the dead and taken up to the Father's right hand as described in Psalm 110; "The Lord said unto my Lord, Sit thou at my right hand, until I make thine enemies thy footstool." Paul could say, "I believe all of these things, and I stand here a fettered man because I believe with all my heart what you Jews profess to believe. I am convinced that Jesus Christ is the fulfillment of the Jewish hope."

Then he added, "Why should it be thought a thing incredible with you, that God should raise the dead?" I take it that here he was addressing Festus directly, for Festus had ridiculed the thought that Jesus Christ could be alive again. But why should one think it incredible that the same Lord who created this universe, and breathed into man the breath of life, could also be able to bring back His own blessed Son from the dead, or any others whom death has claimed?

Then Paul continued to tell Agrippa something of the circumstances of his life before he knew Christ. He said, "I thought I ought to be opposed to Jesus Christ." I have no doubt there are some people who really believe they are doing right in opposing the gospel of the grace of God. Let me stress this: Sincerity of belief does not in itself prove anything. You might, for instance, board a railroad train and be absolutely sincere in thinking that it was going to take you to Minneapolis, and yet you might later discover that it was going to

Omaha. Your sincerity of belief would not alter the facts. It would not change anything. Saul of Tarsus sincerely believed that Christianity was a delusion. He sincerely believed that Jesus of Nazareth was a deceiver. He sincerely believed that the Christians were a fanatical people who ought to be rooted out of the world. He was sincere, but he was sincerely wrong. You see, you need to test your facts by the revelation God has given. "Should not a people seek unto their God?...To the law and to the testimony: if they speak not according to this word, it is because there is no light in them" (Isaiah 8:19-20).

Sincerely believing that Christianity was wrong, Paul acted accordingly: "Which thing I also did in Jerusalem: and many of the saints did I shut up in prison, having received authority from the chief priests; and when they were put to death, I gave my voice against them." This seems to imply that Paul himself was a member of the Jewish high council, otherwise he would not have been entitled to participate in their deliberations. "And I punished them oft in every synagogue, and compelled them to blaspheme; and being exceedingly mad against them, I persecuted them even unto strange cities." In these words he covered his whole life from his childhood up to the moment of the great crisis when the Lord Jesus was revealed to him as the Son of the living God.

Next, Paul related his conversion experience. However you may try to explain the event on the Damascus road, however you may understand it, the fact remains that something happened that day which changed this man completely. He himself told us what happened. You may not want to believe him, but then how are you going to account for the marvelous change in his life and in his way of thinking and acting from that moment on? One instant he is the hater of the Lord Jesus Christ and the bitter persecutor of Christians; the next he is a humble, obedient Christian, willing to lay down his very life for the name of the Lord Jesus Christ. And for thirty years he continued in the position he took that day. What brought it about? He had seen the Christ of God. God was pleased to reveal the Lord Jesus directly to this man. He felt himself struck to the ground, a light from heaven shining round about him. He said, "I could not see for the glory of that light." He heard a voice in the language that he loved the best—the Hebrew tongue—calling him by name and pleading with him tenderly, "Saul, Saul, why persecutest thou me? it is hard for thee to kick against the pricks."

In commenting on Paul's conversion experience (Acts 9), we noted that something within Saul revolted against the bitterness of persecution. He was uneasy at heart. Perhaps he remembered the light that he had seen in the face of Stephen who, looking like an angel, cried, "Lord, lay not this sin to their charge." And he may have remembered Stephen's words, "Behold, I see the heavens opened, and the Son of man standing on the right hand of God." Perhaps Paul was conscious of the prayers of his kinsmen, to whom he referred in Romans 16 as those who "were in Christ before me." Who can question but that these kinsmen of Saul often prayed for their young relative, prayed that God might speak to him and quicken him, that he might come to see and know the Lord Jesus! So he was like a refractory ox kicking against the goad that was prodding him. When Jesus appeared, he cried out, trembling and amazed, "Who art thou, Lord?" And a voice came back, an audible voice from Heaven, "I am Jesus whom thou persecutest." The revelation of Jesus Christ changed everything! That is what conversion really is—when a man is brought for the first time in his life to look in saving faith upon the face of the Lord Jesus.

Some try to explain away the wonder of Paul's conversion. Someone in Britain years ago insisted that it was to be explained in this way: Paul was evidently an epileptic, and as he went along the Damascus road he had a fit and fell to the ground, foaming at the mouth, and thereafter was a changed man! Spurgeon said, "Oh, blessed epilepsy that made such a wonderful change in this man! Would God that all who oppose the name of Jesus Christ might become epileptics in the same sense."

Some are saying today that it was a sunstroke. A modern writer declared that as Saul traveled on the road the sun became so hot he was struck and fell to the ground, and that was his conversion! As I read it, I thought, "Would God that all modernists could be so sunstruck that they might begin to preach Christ, and so come back to the grand old gospel of redemption by the blood of Jesus!" And yet I am quite in agreement with the modernist explanation except for one letter. It was a *Son*-stroke, not a sunstroke! It was the light of the glory of God in the face of Christ Jesus the Son that struck home to the very heart of that man and opened his eyes to see the One he had been persecuting—the Savior of sinners. And so the great change took place.

The voice of the Lord continued speaking to Paul: "I have appeared unto thee for this purpose, to make thee a minister and a witness both of these things which thou hast seen, and of those things in the which I will appear unto thee." This was Paul's ordination to the ministry. No human hands had anything to do with it. Henceforth he could say:

> Christ, the Son of God, hath sent me
> Through the midnight lands;
> Mine the mighty ordination
> Of the pierced hands.

The blessed Christ of God commissioned Saul that day to be His messenger. He was to go forth as His witness. As such he would be rescued from his own people, the Jews, and the Gentiles, unto whom now he was to be sent; for this man's work was to be particularly among the Gentiles, though he never forgot his own people. Everywhere he went it was the Jew first.

What was his commission? "To open their eyes, and to turn them from darkness to light, and from the power of Satan unto God, that they may receive forgiveness of sins, and inheritance among them which are sanctified by faith that is in me." What a glorious, full commission was this! It is as though the Lord was saying, "Saul, all over the world men are sitting in darkness, and in the shadow of death. They are blind; they cannot see. But you are to go out as My servant and, as you proclaim My Word, these blinded eyes will be opened and men will be turned from darkness to light, from the awful, ruinous power of Satan to God Himself who waits in grace to save them." When they turn to Him, they will be cleared of every charge that God had against them, and they will have a glorious inheritance among those who are separated unto God in Christ Jesus through faith. This was his message, and this is the message that

God is still sending out into the world. Oh, how men's eyes need to be opened! They are open enough to the things of this world, but they are blind to the things of eternity. And God's truth alone can give enlightenment. "The entrance of thy words giveth light; it giveth understanding unto the simple" (Psalm 119:130).

Beginning with Acts 26:19, we read something of Paul's life after his conversion. He said the essence of his message to Jew and Gentile alike was "that they should repent and turn to God, and do works meet for repentance." Sometimes we are told that repentance has no place in the message for this present glorious dispensation of grace. But here is the man who is preeminently the apostle of grace saying in essence, "Wherever I have gone, this has been my message, to tell both Jews and Gentiles that they should repent and turn to God, and do works that prove their repentance."

What is repentance? It is a complete change of attitude. It is a rightabout-face. Here is a man who is living in open, flagrant sin, and he does not care anything about the things of God and is totally indifferent to the claims of righteousness. But once the Spirit of God takes hold of him, he suddenly comes face to face with his sins in the presence of God. He turns rightabout-face and comes to the God he has been spurning and to the Christ he has been rejecting and he confesses his sins and puts his trust in the Savior. All this is involved in repentance.

We look at yet another man. He is not living in open sin, but has been living a very religious life. He has been very self-righteous. He has been thoroughly satisfied that because of his own goodness and because of his punctilious attention to his religious duties, God will accept him and eventually take him to be with Himself. But suddenly he is brought to realize that all his own righteousnesses are but filthy rags, that nothing he can do will make him fit for God's presence, and he faces this honestly before God. For him too there is a change of attitude. He turns away from all confidence in self, the flesh, his religion, and cries: "In my hand no price I bring; simply to Thy cross I cling." This is repentance. It is a rightabout-face.

And so everywhere that Paul went he preached repentance toward God and faith in the Lord Jesus Christ. And today God, through

His servants still calls on "all men everywhere to repent: Because he hath appointed a day, in the which he will judge the world in righteousness by that man whom he hath ordained; whereof he hath given assurance unto all men, in that he hath raised him from the dead" (Acts 17:30-31). It is repent or perish; turn or burn! Face your sins now and find deliverance from them or face them in the day of judgment when it will be too late for deliverance.

In bringing his marvelous account to a close Paul added: "I continue unto this day, witnessing both to small and great, saying none other things than those which the prophets and Moses did say should come" (26:22). That is, there is not one thing in Christianity that is contrary to any truth revealed in the Old Testament. There is a greater fullness. We have been given additional light on many old truths, but every servant of Christ today who is really faithful to the Word can say what Paul said.

Paul himself opened up wonderful truths of grace not hitherto made known. The glorious truth of the believer's justification from all things; his union with Christ; the baptism of the Holy Spirit; the truth of the one body. In all these truths Paul shared the light revealed to him as the messenger of the risen Christ.

As Paul spoke for himself, Festus the skeptic, Festus the rationalist who would not acknowledge the miraculous, leaned forward and cried, "Paul, you are going crazy. You have been dwelling too much on religious problems, and have lost your wits; you don't know what you are talking about." Paul looked the Roman governor straight in the face, not a sign of fanaticism about him, and calmly, coolly, answered: "I am not mad, most noble Festus, but speak forth the words of truth and soberness." Turning to Agrippa for corroboration, he said: "For the king knoweth of these things, before whom also I speak freely: for I am persuaded that none of these things are hidden from him; for this thing was not done in a corner."

Then addressing Agrippa directly, he pressed the question home: "King Agrippa, believest thou the prophets?" Without waiting for an answer, he added, "I know that thou believest." And Agrippa, leaning forward, exclaimed, "Almost thou persuadest me to be a Christian." Possibly that is not an exact translation. Perhaps it was, as a more literal translation records it: "With but little persuasion would you try to make a Christian of me!" Paul answered: "I would to God, that not only thou, but also all that hear me this day, were both almost, and altogether such as I am, except these bonds." And he held up his manacled hands! "Oh, Agrippa, I wish you and Festus and Bernice and all the rest here, I wish that you had the same blessed hope that I have." And that is what we say to all who do not know Christ.

"Then said Agrippa unto Festus, This man might have been set at liberty, if he had not appealed unto Caesar." But God had permitted him so to appeal in order that he might witness in Rome.

CHAPTER TWENTY-SEVEN
GOD'S SOVEREIGNTY AND MAN'S RESPONSIBILITY

Acts 27 is one of the chapters of the Bible that we really ought to study with a map of the Mediterranean before us. Those who have carefully investigated Luke's record are amazed at the accuracy with which he refers to the various ports and to ancient shipping routes. Some people have suggested that perhaps certain portions of the Bible were written at a date later than they professed to be. The book of Acts has been particularly attacked.

Some years ago a little group of freethinkers in Scotland decided on a plan whereby they might show up the supposed inaccuracies of Scripture, and so discredit the Word of God. One member was given the task of going to Asia Minor, southern Europe, and the islands of the Mediterranean, visiting all the places mentioned by Luke in connection with Paul's journeys. It was hoped that he would be able to unearth enough information to make evident any falsity in Luke's record, so that many who had pinned their faith to the book of Acts as a part of God's inspired Word would have to give it up.

The young man chosen was Sir William Ramsay. He investigated very carefully, and after the most minute examination concluded that Luke was absolutely accurate in every particular. He himself, once a freethinker, became a Christian and wrote some splendid books in defense of the Word of God.

It would be interesting to trace the details of Paul's voyages from one place to another, but space forbids this. There are a few things though to which I would like to call particular attention. First, the use of the little pronoun *we*. It is very evident that Luke, the writer of this book, volunteered to accompany Paul after his arrest. Also the continuing use of this pronoun in the next chapter shows that Luke was with Paul to the last.

Another person of note who accompanied him was Aristarchus, one of Paul's own converts from Macedonia. We read of Aristarchus elsewhere as an outstanding witness for Christ. He was not ashamed to share the prisoner's lot in order to be a comfort to Paul (Colossians 4:10).

As we read the book of Acts we are struck by the way in which Paul the prisoner takes command. This man of God, wherever you find him, seems to be master of every situation. When they put him and Silas in jail and made their feet fast in the stocks, he and his companion put on a sacred concert. There were only two of them and they had no organ accompaniment, but they gave such a splendid performance that they brought down the house! There was an earthquake, and next thing you know the jailer and all of his household were converted.

Then when Paul was arraigned before various dignitaries, he always came out as the real master of the situation. Again and again we have seen the roles reversed—the prisoner questioning the judge! When he appeared before Felix he dared to reason with him concerning righteousness, temperance, and judgment to come. When he stood before Festus he said, "Why should it be thought a thing incredible with you that God should raise the dead?" To King Agrippa he declared, "I would to God, that not only thou, but also all that hear me this day. were both almost, and altogether such as I am, except these bonds"—a Christian.

In this present chapter, when he was a prisoner on shipboard, it was not long before all the crew, the soldiers, the master of the ship, and Julius the centurion, were taking orders from Paul. He is God's man for every occasion. There is one thing about a man who walks with God—circumstances never affect his fellowship and communion with the Lord. Paul could say, "I have learned in whatsoever state I am, therewith to be content." A brother once asked another brother in my hearing, "How are you getting on?" The other answered, "I am doing very well under the circumstances." The first brother replied, "I am very sorry to hear that you are under the circumstances. You know, if you keep your eyes on the Lord, He will keep you above the circumstances." So Paul always seemed to be above the circumstances.

As the ship sailed from one port to another, Paul gave wise advice that they refused to accept, and they soon ran into trouble. When they did accept his advice, God's blessing rested on them.

Reading from verse 14 however we find that they ran into a fierce hurricane. The winds became so violent that they almost lost the lifeboat. After securing it, they arranged to pass cords underneath and over the ship in order to hold the almost shattered timbers together. Paul, Luke, and Aristarchus pitched in with the sailors and the rest of the men, to help cast off the ship's tackling. They were not afraid to do their share.

"And when neither sun nor stars in many days appeared, and no small tempest lay on us, all hope that we should be saved was then taken away" (20). Here we find people who have come to the very end of their own ability. There they are in their ship, the cargo having been tossed overboard, the tackling gone, feeling absolutely hopeless of either the salvation of the ship or of their own lives. But it has been well said, "Man's extremity is God's opportunity," and so here God intervenes.

Verses 21-29 bring before us in a very striking way the divine sovereignty of God. "But after long abstinence Paul stood forth in the midst of them, and said, Sirs, ye should have hearkened unto me, and not have loosed from Crete, and to have gained this harm and loss." Think of that! Here is a prisoner talking to both the centurion and his guard, as well as the master of the ship and his sailors, saying, "You should have listened to me and let me run this ship. If you had listened to me, everything would have been all right." He had warned them that they ought not to leave a certain harbor, but they did not believe him. People do not believe God's messengers;

yet some day they are going to find out that as the servants of God tell of a fearful storm coming upon this poor world, they are speaking according to the Word of God.

Following his rebuke, Paul said: "And now I exhort you to be of good cheer." I like that. He did not turn to them and exclaim, "Well, it serves you right. You are getting what is coming to you." He said, "I have been praying and, when I prayed, God answered, and now I have something to tell you that will encourage you. You are going to lose the ship, but you are not going to lose your lives. I can promise you beforehand that every one of you is going to be saved."

How did Paul know that? Because God had told him so. He said, "For there stood by me this night the angel of God, whose I am, and whom I serve" (23). Oh, the dignity of that! Paul could look at these representatives of the Roman Empire who had put him in bonds, and say, "I am the servant of the most high God. I belong to Him, and I serve Him; I am in His service even now. He sent His angel to me. You couldn't see him. You had eyes only for the storm, the creaking timbers, and the treacherous rocks ahead, but I have seen the angel of the Lord." The man of God can see things that the man of the world can never see. Paul saw an angel who said to him: "Fear not, Paul; thou must be brought before Caesar [therefore you cannot be drowned]: and, lo, God hath given thee all them that sail with thee."

Here is a striking instance of the sovereignty of God. God spoke through His angel and declared His purpose. He said in effect, "I have settled it that all these men are going to be saved." Of course, He was speaking of their temporal salvation, their physical salvation, but it is God speaking, you might say, arbitrarily. He speaks in His sovereignty, just as He has chosen in Christ certain ones who are going to be saved for all eternity. Who are they? All who trust in the Lord Jesus. This is not hyper-Calvinistic fatalism. It is divine, elective love.

When God predestinates, He does it in love. Notice in Ephesians 1: "In love: Having predestinated us." But His predestination is to what? To go to Heaven? It does not say so, either there or in the eighth chapter of Romans. It says in Ephesians that He has "predestinated us unto the adoption of children by Jesus Christ to himself."

It says in Romans 8: "For whom he did foreknow, he also did pre-
destinate to be conformed to the image of his Son." Again, in
Ephesians we are told that He has chosen us in Christ before the
foundation of the world, that we should—what?...go to Heaven
while other people go to Hell? It does not say that. What does it
say? "That we should be holy and without blame before him."

I am not afraid of that kind of predestination. It tells me that,
having trusted Christ, I will some day be wholly like Him. I am
predestinated to be holy and without blame before Him. But nowhere in God's Word are we told that all this is purely arbitrary.
God insists on man's responsibility to face his sins before Him, to
turn to Him in repentance, and to put his trust in the Lord Jesus
Christ. He shows us that the invitation to salvation is as broad as the
human race. He says, "Whosoever will may come"; "Whosoever
believeth in Him should not perish but have everlasting life." "Whosoever will call upon the name of the Lord shall be saved."

Here we get one side of this great truth of the divine sovereignty.
God declared these men who sailed with Paul were all going to be
saved. That part was settled. But next we notice the source of Paul's
confidence: "Wherefore, sirs, be of good cheer: for I believe God,
that it shall be even as it was told me, Howbeit we must be cast
upon a certain island." Can you say, "I believe God"? It is a great
thing when God speaks, and you can just put your foot down and
say, "God says it, and I believe it."

When studying the Chinese language many years ago, I was struck
by the symbol for *faith*. It is partly made up of the character for
word: the lower part of that character stands for a mouth, and above
it are several lines indicating something coming out of the mouth.
After all, that is what a word is! Then to one side there is a character
of a man. And is not that what faith is—a man standing by the Word?
I wonder where the ancient Chinese got that. They composed that
symbol for *faith* thousands of years ago—long before the dawn of
our civilization.

Sometimes a poor soul comes to me in distress and says, "I have
been praying and praying for months for salvation, but I don't seem
to get it and I am miserable." I ask, "Do you believe in the Lord
Jesus Christ?" "Oh I do," is the response. "Do you believe He died

for you?" "Yes." "Do you believe He bore your sins in His own body on the tree?" "Yes I do." "Have you come to Him and told Him you are a sinner and are ready to trust Him?" "Yes, but He doesn't seem to accept me; I am not saved." "Where are you looking for assurance?" "Well, I expect to feel different when I am saved." I answer: "You might feel very happy and not be saved at all. You might be trusting in the wrong thing or the wrong person. The Lord Jesus Himself said, 'Verily, verily, I say unto you, He that heareth my word, and believeth on him that sent me, hath everlasting life, and shall not come into condemnation; but is passed from death unto life.' Notice, carefully what is said here. 'He that heareth my word.' Have you heard God's Word? 'And believeth on him that sent me.' Do you believe that God sent Jesus to be your Savior, to die for you?" "Yes, I believe that." "All right; now look at the next phrase: 'Hath everlasting life.' Have you everlasting life?" "Well, I hope so," was her response. "But it does not say that *maybe* he will have everlasting life. Can't you take your stand on the Word of God?" That poor woman's face brightened and she said, "Oh, I see it. I must just take Him at His Word. That is sufficient."

Why, I know people who say, "I know everything is all right. I have been baptized." But they were just deluded by the devil, for baptism itself saves nobody. Jesus alone saves and He does it for all who believe in Him.

I remember speaking to a woman who had just joined a certain church that teaches salvation by sacraments and legal obedience. She said, "Before I joined this church I never was at peace, but now I just trust my salvation to those in authority." That is false peace; a peace built on error.

Paul said to his frightened traveling companions, "God has spoken and I believe God." Christian, what about you? Do you believe God? Why do you then go about with your head hanging down like a bulrush, as much as to say, "Oh, if you only knew my circumstances; my health is poor, and I am afraid I shall lose my job; I don't know what I shall do when I get old"? Do you trust the One who has said, "I will never leave thee nor forsake thee"? Do you know that it is written: "My God shall supply all your need according to his riches in glory by Christ Jesus"? Do you know the Holy

Spirit has declared, "All things work together for good to them that love God"? Well then, why not brighten up and say, "I believe God; the devil is not going to get me down because circumstances seem to be against me? I believe there is a God who is above all circumstances."

"But when the fourteenth night was come, as we were driven up and down in Adria"—think of it! Fourteen awful days and nights in a dreadful storm, and all they had to rest on was the word of God that they would get safely to shore! "About midnight the shipmen deemed that they drew near to some country." They began to hear the roaring of breakers, and they "sounded, and found it twenty fathoms: and when they had gone a little further, they sounded again, and found it fifteen fathoms. Then fearing lest we should have fallen upon rocks, they cast four anchors out of the stern, and wished for the day" (28).

What a graphic picture of that little ship driven before the tempest all those days and nights! And now in the deep darkness they can't see what is ahead of them, but they can hear the water dashing against the rocks, so they cast four anchors out of the stern and wish for the day. How we Christians are like that sometimes. Things all seem to be going wrong, and it looks as if we are going to crush against the rocks, but faith's anchor holds because the Word of God can never fail.

The next verses suggest another side of the truth of faith and salvation. The sailors have had the word from God that they are all going to be saved, but it looks as if they are going to be dashed on the rocks. And so these miserable rascals say, "We will save our own lives and let the ship go to pieces." Under cover of the darkness and pretending to cast out the anchors, they seek to let down the lifeboat, planning to row away and find some cove of safety. But Paul is on the alert. He sees what they are up to, and to the centurion he says, "Except these abide in the ship, ye cannot be saved." Then see what happens. "The soldiers cut off the ropes of the boat, and let her fall off."

The captain might have said, "What difference does it make? You told us we are all to be saved anyway. It doesn't make any difference what anybody does; if God has foreordained it, that is what will happen." Then Paul might have replied: "Yes, it makes a great deal of difference." You see, human responsibility is one spoke in the great wheel of God's purpose, and divine foreordination is another. And so, though God foreordained the whole thing, He showed Paul that these men were responsible to abide in the ship. This was how He was to accomplish His purpose.

In a similar way, man might say, "If God is going to save me, He will save me; and it doesn't make any difference what I do." It makes a great deal of difference! If you do not respond, you will be lost, but if you turn to God and confess your sin and put your trust in the Lord Jesus Christ, then—thank God—you will be saved. And when you are saved, you will be able to look up in gratitude to the God of all grace and say, "Lord, I thank Thee that Thou hast chosen me in Christ before the foundation of the world." You see, there are two sides: Man's responsibility and God's sovereignty.

"And while the day was coming on, Paul besought them all to take meat, saying, This day is the fourteenth day that ye have tarried and continued fasting, having taken nothing" (33). Notice how he again took charge of the situation. He appointed himself chief steward, and said, "Come now, you are going to be saved, but you need some food. It has been fourteen days since you have had anything to eat. Wherefore I pray you to take some meat: for this is for your health. There shall not an hair fall from the head of any of you." What confidence possessed the soul of this man because he had a word from God that he dared to believe! In gratefulness he looked up to God and thanked Him for preserving their lives and providing them food to eat.

In the last section Luke wrote, "We were in all in the ship two hundred threescore and sixteen souls." Think of it! God had promised to deliver safely all 276 travelers! But notice how they were delivered. They were saved with difficulty, through great trials; but they were saved. God fulfilled His word.

In verses 38-40 Luke described in detail the sailors efforts to move the ship closer to shore. It took a real seaman to write this, and Luke certainly entered into the spirit of the sailor.

"And falling into a place where two seas met, they ran the ship aground; and the forepart stuck fast, and remained unmoveable, but the hinder part was broken with the violence of the waves" (41). And now the enemy comes in. Satan would make the plight of the seamen an excuse to destroy Paul. "And the soldiers' counsel was to kill the prisoners, lest any of them should swim out, and escape." It was the voice of the devil, though he spoke through the soldiers' lips.

But the centurion again intervened and God's word was fulfilled. All were saved, but they had to meet their own responsibility in the matter. There is surely a lesson here for every one of us. No word of God shall be void of power, but we are responsible to obey His Word and manifest our faith by our works.

CHAPTER TWENTY-EIGHT
PAUL IN ROME

In the first ten verses of Acts 28 we have the account of Paul and his companions as they were shipwrecked on the island of Melita or, as we now say, Malta. The Spirit of God has seen fit to draw our attention to the barbarous unlearned people, who lacked the culture and refinement of many in the Roman Empire, yet they showed to this weary company "no little kindness." God always recognizes every kindness done to His own, and so He has put it on record here.

We can imagine the shipwrecked company gathered about the fire trying to dry out their clothes after the terrible experience they had just gone through. Notice that Paul was not afraid to get his hands dirty. As the men gathered firewood to build the fire, Paul was out with them doing his part. As he picked up a bundle of sticks he saw what looked like a piece of firewood but when he laid it on the fire it turned out to be a viper, a serpent dormant from the cold. As it warmed up from the heat it fastened itself to Paul's hand.

And then we see how easy it is to jump to wrong conclusions. The Melitans assumed Paul to be a murderer on whom vengeance was sought. I think the editors of the King James version should have capitalized the word *vengeance* here, for the Melitans I believe were thinking of *Vengeance* as the name of a god. They were saying in essence, "This man has escaped shipwreck, but the god Vengeance, knowing that he is a murderer, is not going to allow him to live, and so this viper has fastened itself onto his hand." And they expected that any moment he would fall down dead, but "he shook off the beast into the fire, and felt no harm."

It is never safe to depend on snap judgments. People do that so

337

frequently. Half the scandal that goes around among members of the church of Christ is simply the result of jumping to conclusions.

Not long ago I read a little article in a church bulletin in which the pastor explained that he had been greatly troubled by a rumor that was circulating. The rumor was that his wife had attended a meeting of some heretical group and that he had gone there in great indignation and dragged her out by the hair of her head and brought her home and beat her. He undertook to explain that he had not dragged his wife out of that meeting, that he had never at any time dragged her about by her hair, that he had never beaten her, also that his wife had never attended such a meeting, and finally that he was a bachelor and had never had a wife! We are so ready to pick up bits of gossip and make so much out of them.

So these barbarous people said, "There is no question; it is evident that he is a murderer and Vengeance is not going to suffer him to live." But when Paul shook the serpent into the fire, they went to the other extreme, saying he was a god. That conclusion of course was just as wrong as the other. These people really did not understand the circumstances. Paul might have explained to them that when the Lord Jesus authorized His apostles to go out to preach His gospel in a hostile world, He even told them that they could pick up vipers and not be harmed. This was one instance of the fulfillment of that promise.

Then we see how Paul was able to return the kindness of those barbarians.

> In the same quarters were possessions of the chief man of the island, whose name was Publius; who received us, and lodged us three days courteously. And it came to pass, that the father of Publius lay sick of a fever and of a bloody flux: to whom Paul entered in, and prayed, and laid hands on him, and healed him.

Now observe we are not told that this man was saved. We are not even told that Paul first preached the gospel to him and brought him to Christ. But he saw the man in his deep need and he went in and prayed and laid hands on him, and the Lord graciously answered. As news of this spread, others who were sick came to be healed.

When after three months the apostle's company left they were showered with gifts.

Verses 11-16 give us the rest of the journey to Rome, part by water and part by land. We read that when the Christians in Italy heard that Paul had arrived on the Italian mainland, they came out to meet him: "whom when Paul saw, he thanked God, and took courage." One can understand something of the blessedness of that meeting and what it must have meant to the apostle after all the trials, the shipwreck, the suffering he had passed through, after all the false charges that had been lodged against him, and knowing that he was going on to be tried before Caesar's judgment throne! So it must have been a great joy to find that these Christians at Rome, hearing of his coming, cared enough to go all the way out to Appii forum, a town midway between Rome and the port where he had landed, and convey to him their expression of Christian love and fellowship. Paul was greatly encouraged.

"When we came to Rome, the centurion delivered the prisoners to the captain of the guard: but Paul was suffered to dwell by himself with a soldier that kept him." Of course he was still a prisoner, but he was not cast into the common prison. He was allowed to pay for more comfortable quarters where, although under guard, he had a certain measure of liberty and his friends were permitted to visit him.

The next section of Acts 28 (verses 17-22) tells us of Paul's first interview with the Jews in Rome. A great many of them were living there, and Paul felt it would be wise to send for their leaders first and explain something of the circumstances that had led to his arrest, of his appeal to Caesar, and of his coming to Rome for trial. If these Jews at Rome were fair-minded, they might be able to defend him, instead of persecuting him, or at least they might take a neutral position.

Notice Paul's attitude as he spoke to the Jews. He ever recognized the fact that he himself was by birth and by religion originally a Jew. Though now a Christian, his heart went out in love to his Jewish brethren; he never sought to influence anyone against them, or to hurt them in any way. "Not that I had ought to accuse my nation of. For this cause therefore have I called for you, to see you, and to speak with you; because [and I think I see him holding up his manacled hands as he speaks] for the hope of Israel I am bound with this chain." What did he mean by "the hope of Israel"? It was the coming of Messiah—that Messiah who was to be crucified and rise from the dead. As a true Jew, Paul looked for the coming Messiah. When Jesus came and was crucified and buried and rose again, Paul did not at first realize that He was the Messiah. He was a persecutor of those who followed His way, but now he had been brought to see in Christ the hope of Israel. He believed in the resurrection of the dead, toward which all his people looked forward, except the materialistic Sadducees. "It is because of this," he said, "that I stand here a prisoner before you."

Notice that they are very much more fairminded than the Jews were in Jerusalem. They seem to have been quite unprejudiced. That of course is the only right attitude when listening to one who brings a message he professes to be of God. These Jews in Rome said in essence, "Paul, we are ready to listen to you, to hear what you have to say, although we have heard certain things about this Christian sect that make us very suspicious as to its being worthy of our adherence."

We next read of Paul's controversy with the Jews. Let us consider this for a moment: "He expounded and testified the kingdom of God." We need to distinguish carefully between the two terms—the kingdom of God and the church of God. When some of our friends tell us that we are not to preach the kingdom of God in this dispensation, but only truth concerning the church of God, we point them back to a passage such as this and many others. For we find in the very beginning of this book of Acts that during the forty days of our Lord's sojourn on earth after His resurrection He instructed His disciples in things pertaining to the kingdom of God. Then throughout all the book we notice first the twelve and then the apostle Paul preaching the kingdom of God right through to this last chapter.

By expounding the kingdom of God, Paul was saying that God is the rightful ruler of the universe, but the world is in revolt against Him. Satan has become the prince of this world. Man has foolishly allowed himself to follow him. But everywhere the servants of God go, they are called on to tell men that God Himself is earth's rightful

King, then bid them repent and bow at His feet, acknowledging His divine authority. But more than that, it is our business to tell them that God has sent His own Son. Men have refused Him. They have said, "We have no king but Caesar. We will not have this man to reign over us." So the messenger of Christ is to go out and proclaim to men that God raised Jesus from the dead and has set Him at His own right hand, and that some day that blessed One is to rule in righteousness as the Father's representative down here. Men are called to give allegiance to Him, to bow at His feet in repentance, and to acknowledge His authority. We read, "If thou shalt confess with thy mouth the Lord Jesus, and shalt believe in thine heart that God hath raised him from the dead, thou shalt be saved." It is as we preach this that we are proclaiming the kingdom of God.

What a wonderful discourse Paul must have presented. How I would like to have been listening to it all, hearing the inspired apostle opening up the glorious truths of God's way with men, particularly setting forth the mystery of the gospel. I think it would have been better than any course in theology in any seminary that men have built.

Paul had a double kind of response: "And some believed the things which were spoken, and some believed not." Many of these thoughtful, openminded Jews compared scripture, listening attentively to what Paul, a Hebrew Christian had to say to them, and finally were convinced. They believed that Jesus was God their Savior and Messiah. Others, who did not believe, opposed him.

As Paul continued he was evidently divinely guided to quote the words from one of their own prophets. He referred them back to a book they revered as divinely inspired, and that rightly so. He read to them what Isaiah said concerning them (verses 26-27). If he had made such charges himself they might have been indignant. They might have asked, "Well, is this the way to accuse your brethren, the Jews?" But instead of that, Paul gave them God's own Word from one of their own prophets. And then he added: "Be it known therefore unto you, that the salvation of God is sent unto the Gentiles, and that they will hear it."

Some think this passage marks a distinct dispensational break, but it is not that at all. It is just the same thing that had occurred before when Paul was in Antioch of Pisidia, as recorded in Acts 13:46. He first preached the gospel to the Jews, and when many of them refused it he said to them, "Lo, we turn to the Gentiles." That was his method wherever he went—to the Jew first, then to the Gentile. And so it was here. Some of the Jews had received his message, but others refused. "Very well," Paul said in effect, "now I have been faithful with you. I have given you an opportunity. Now I shall turn to the Gentiles." Of course he had been preaching to the Gentiles for thirty years, but he meant those in Rome. "And when he had said these words, the Jews departed and had great reasoning among themselves."

The next two years of Paul's life are compressed into the last two verses of the book of Acts:

> And Paul dwelt two whole years in his own hired house, and received all that came in unto him, Preaching the kingdom of God, and teaching those things which concern the Lord Jesus Christ, with all confidence, no man forbidding him.

Here Luke's record closes. How we would like to have the additional account of what took place afterwards, but we will never know that until we get home to Heaven. It is true that historical records have come down to us from early days, telling us that after these two years Paul appeared before Caesar and was cleared of the charges of sedition brought against him in Jerusalem. He was set free and, for some three to five years afterward, went about ministering the Word of God, going first to Spain, and some say even as far as Britain. Then he returned to the Near East, visiting some of the assemblies where he had labored before. This is attested by his letter to Titus, which was written at that later time. After Paul had finished his final testimony, he was brought back to Rome and there martyred for the name of the Lord Jesus Christ.

What I want to emphasize in closing is this: Up to the last Paul preached exactly the same message that he had carried throughout

the world during the thirty years before. No new revelation came to
him after he got to prison. It was not then that he received the
revelation of the one body. He received that revelation on the
Damascus road when, at the very beginning, the Lord had said to
him, "I am Jesus whom thou persecutest." At that time he understood that to touch the feeblest saint on earth, was to touch the Head
in Heaven. It was there the mystery of the one body was revealed—
Christ the Head of His body. Doubtless this teaching was opened
up to him more fully when he went into retirement in Arabia. But
he did not proclaim this to the unsaved. Rather this is a message to
the church of God, members of that body on earth. That was one of
the mysteries kept secret from the foundation of the world.

We have seen as we studied this book of Acts how in the very
first chapter the Lord Jesus Himself outlined His program. He said,
"Ye shall receive power, after that the Holy Ghost is come upon
you: and ye shall be witnesses unto me both in Jerusalem, and in all
Judea, and in Samaria, and unto the uttermost part of the earth." We
have noted that in the beginning Peter and the rest of the twelve
bore witness in Jerusalem. That witness went out into Judea and
there for a time it stopped. There seemed to be a peculiar unreadiness
on the part of the apostles to continue the rest of the program. They
had no difficulty in going to their Jewish brethren, but they hung
back from carrying the message to the Gentiles. It was not an apostle, but a deacon—Philip—who finally had faith enough to go to
Samaria and witness there. When word came to the Christians of a
mighty work of God being done in Samaria, they sent Peter and
John to investigate. They continued the work begun there. But it
was some time before the message went out to the Gentiles. God
had to give Peter a special revelation—the sheet let down from
Heaven, which was full of all kinds of beasts and creeping things.
The message was, "What God hath cleansed, that call not thou common." Directed by God Peter went down to Caesarea to the house
of Cornelius, a Gentile, and preached Christ. All that heard believed,
and the Holy Spirit fell on them with the same power as on Jewish
believers at Pentecost. Thus Peter opened the door to the Gentiles
as in Jerusalem he had opened the door to the Jews.

At this point God laid His hands on Saul of Tarsus. He gave him a vision of world-wide evangelization and sent him out to carry the message to the ends of the earth. From that time on we find the river of grace ever broadening and deepening, reaching to the utmost bounds of creation. Before the apostle himself passed off the scene he could speak of the gospel that had been preached in all creation under Heaven. We know from secular history that the rest of the apostles later left Jerusalem and obeyed the Lord's command. So the gospel was carried into all the world. Today the stream of grace is still flowing on and on and on. We are to follow in the steps of the apostles and go to all men everywhere, warning them to repent, to believe on the Lord Jesus Christ, for "whosoever believeth in him should not perish, but have everlasting life."

From a merely literary standpoint, the book of Acts seems to be unfinished. Doubtless this is intended to teach us that until the fulfillment of the angels' prophecy that "this same Jesus" shall return even as He went away, the work of evangelization for this age will not be completed. We are to heed the injunction—"Occupy till I come."

AUTHOR BIOGRAPHY

HENRY ALLAN IRONSIDE, one of the twentieth greatest preachers, was born in Toronto, Canada, on October 14, 1876. He lived his life by faith; his needs at crucial moments were met in the most remarkable ways.

Though his classes stopped with grammar school, his fondness for reading and an incredibly retentive memory put learning to use. His scholarship was well recognized in academic circles with Wheaton College awarding an honorary Litt.D. in 1930 and Bob Jones University an honorary D.D. in 1942. Dr. Ironside was also appointed to the boards of numerous Bible institutes, seminaries, and Christian organizations.

"HAI" lived to preach and he did so widely throughout the United States and abroad. E. Schuyler English, in his biography of Ironside, revealed that during 1948, the year HAI was 72, and in spite of failing eyesight, he "gave 569 addresses, besides participating in many other ways." In his eighteen years at Chicago's Moody Memorial Church, his only pastorate, every Sunday but two had at least one profession of faith in Christ.

H. A. Ironside went to be with the Lord on January 15, 1951. Throughout his ministry, he authored expositions on 51 books of the Bible and through the great clarity of his messages led hundreds of thousands, worldwide, to a knowledge of God's Word. His words are as fresh and meaningful today as when first preached.

The official biography of Dr. Ironside, *H. A. Ironside: Ordained of the Lord*, is available from the publisher.

THE WRITTEN MINISTRY OF
H. A. IRONSIDE

Expositions

Joshua
Ezra
Nehemiah
Esther
Psalms (1-41 only)
Proverbs
Song of Solomon
Isaiah
Jeremiah
Lamentations
Ezekiel
Daniel
The Minor Prophets
Matthew
Mark
Luke
John

Acts
Romans
1 & 2 Corinthians
Galatians
Ephesians
Philippians
Colossians
1 & 2 Thessalonians
1 & 2 Timothy
Titus
Philemon
Hebrews
James
1 & 2 Peter
1,2, & 3 John
Jude
Revelation

Doctrinal Works

Baptism
Death and Afterward
Eternal Security of the Believer
Holiness: The False and
   the True
The Holy Trinity

Letters to a Roman Catholic
   Priest
The Levitical Offerings
Not Wrath But Rapture
Wrongly Dividing the Word
   of Truth

Historical Works

The Four Hundred Silent Years
A Historical Sketch of the Brethren Movement

Other works by the author are brought back into print from time to time. All of this material is available from your local Christian bookstore or from the publisher.

LOIZEAUX

A Heritage of Ministry ...

Paul and Timothy Loizeaux began their printing and publishing activities in the farming community of Vinton, Iowa, in 1876. Their tools were rudimentary: a hand press, several fonts of loose type, ink, and a small supply of paper. There was certainly no dream of a thriving commercial enterprise. It was merely the means of supplying the literature needs for their own ministries, with the hope that the Lord would grant a wider circulation. It wasn't a business; it was a ministry.

Our Foundation Is the Word of God

We stand without embarrassment on the great fundamentals of the faith: the inspiration and authority of Scripture, the deity and spotless humanity of our Lord Jesus Christ, His atoning sacrifice and resurrection, the indwelling of the Holy Spirit, the unity of the church, the second coming of the Lord, and the eternal destinies of the saved and lost.

Our Mission Is to Help People Understand God's Word

We are not in the entertainment business. We only publish books and computer software we believe will be of genuine help to God's people, both through the faithful exposition of Scripture and practical application of its principles to contemporary need.

Faithfulness to the Word and consistency in what we publish have been hallmarks of Loizeaux through four generations. And that means when you see the name Loizeaux on the outside, you can trust what is on the inside. That is our promise to the Lord...and to you.

If Paul and Timothy were to visit us today they would still recognize the work they began in 1876. Because some very important things haven't changed at all...this is still a ministry.